Resistance and the Sermon in American Literature

NEW DIRECTIONS IN RELIGION AND LITERATURE

This series aims to showcase new work at the forefront of religion and literature through short studies written by leading and rising scholars in the field. Books will pursue a variety of theoretical approaches as they engage with writing from different religious and literary traditions. Collectively, the series will offer a timely critical intervention to the interdisciplinary crossover between religion and literature, speaking to wider contemporary interests and mapping out new directions for the field in the early twenty-first century.

Series editors: Emma Mason and Mark Knight

ALSO AVAILABLE IN THE SERIES

The New Atheist Novel, Arthur Bradley and Andrew Tate
Blake. Wordsworth. Religion, Jonathan Roberts
Do the Gods Wear Capes?, Ben Saunders
England's Secular Scripture, Jo Carruthers
Victorian Parables, Susan E. Colón
The Late Walter Benjamin, John Schad
Dante and the Sense of Transgression, William Franke
The Glyph and the Gramophone, Luke Ferretter
John Cage and Buddhist Ecopoetics, Peter Jaeger
Rewriting the Old Testament in Anglo-Saxon Verse, Samantha Zacher
Forgiveness in Victorian Literature, Richard Hughes Gibson
The Gospel according to the Novelist, Magdalena Mączyńska
Jewish Feeling, Richa Dwor
Beyond the Willing Suspension of Disbelief, Michael Tomko
The Gospel according to David Foster Wallace, Adam S. Miller
Pentecostal Modernism, Stephen Shapiro and Philip Barnard
The Bible in the American Short Story, Lesleigh Cushing Stahlberg and Peter S. Hawkins
Faith in Poetry, Michael D. Hurley
Jeanette Winterson and Religion, Emily McAvan
Religion and American Literature since the 1950s, Mark Eaton
Esoteric Islam in Modern French Thought, Ziad Elmarsafy

The Rhetoric of Conversion in English Puritan Writing, David Parry
Djuna Barnes and Theology, Zhao Ng
Food and Fasting in Victorian Religion and Literature, Lesa Scholl
The Economy of Religion in American Literature, Andrew Ball
Christian Heresy, James Joyce, and the Modernist Literary Imagination, Gregory Erikson
Marilynne Robinson's Worldly Gospel, Ryan S. Kemp and Jordon Rodgers
The English Modernist Novel as Political Theology, Charles Andrews

FORTHCOMING
Chaucer and the Invention of Biblical Narrative, Chad Schrock
Activism and the Literary Self in 20th and 21st Century Literature, Jeff Keuss
Weird Faith in 19th Century Literature, Mark Knight and Emma Mason

Resistance and the Sermon in American Literature

The Cultural Work of Literary Preaching from Emerson to Morrison

Matthew Smalley

BLOOMSBURY ACADEMIC
LONDON • NEW YORK • OXFORD • NEW DELHI • SYDNEY

BLOOMSBURY ACADEMIC
Bloomsbury Publishing Plc, 50 Bedford Square, London, WC1B 3DP, UK
Bloomsbury Publishing Inc, 1359 Broadway, New York, NY 10018, USA
Bloomsbury Publishing Ireland, 29 Earlsfort Terrace, Dublin 2, D02 AY28, Ireland

BLOOMSBURY, BLOOMSBURY ACADEMIC and the Diana logo are trademarks of
Bloomsbury Publishing Plc

First published in Great Britain 2024
This paperback edition published 2026

Copyright © Matthew Smalley, 2024

Matthew Smalley has asserted his right under the Copyright, Designs and Patents Act,
1988, to be identified as Author of this work.

For legal purposes the Acknowledgments on pp. x–xi constitute an extension of this
copyright page.

Cover design: Rebecca Heselton
Cover image © Petmal/iStock

All rights reserved. No part of this publication may be: i) reproduced or transmitted in
any form, electronic or mechanical, including photocopying, recording or by means of
any information storage or retrieval system without prior permission in writing from the
publishers; or ii) used or reproduced in any way for the training, development or operation
of artificial intelligence (AI) technologies, including generative AI technologies. The rights
holders expressly reserve this publication from the text and data mining exception as per
Article 4(3) of the Digital Single Market Directive (EU) 2019/790.

Bloomsbury Publishing Plc does not have any control over, or responsibility for, any
third-party websites referred to or in this book. All internet addresses given in this
book were correct at the time of going to press. The author and publisher regret any
inconvenience caused if addresses have changed or sites have ceased to exist,
but can accept no responsibility for any such changes.

A catalogue record for this book is available from the British Library.

Library of Congress Cataloging-in-Publication Data
Names: Smalley, Matthew, author.
Title: Resistance and the sermon in American literature : the cultural work of literary
preaching from Emerson to Morrison / Matthew Smalley, Fort Hays State University, USA.
Description: London ; New York : Bloomsbury Academic, 2024. |
Series: New directions in religion and literature; vol 32 |
Includes bibliographical references and index.
Identifiers: LCCN 2023046679 (print) | LCCN 2023046680 (ebook) |
ISBN 9781350400009 (hardback) | ISBN 9781350400252 (paperback) |
ISBN 9781350400252 (pdf) | ISBN 9781350400078 (ebook)
Subjects: LCSH: Religion in literature. | Sermons in literature. |
Preaching in literature. | American literature–19th century–History
and criticism. | American literature–20th century–History and criticism.
Classification: LCC PS217.R46 S63 2024 (print) | LCC PS217.R46 (ebook) |
DDC 810.90034–dc23/eng/20240108
LC record available at https://lccn.loc.gov/2023046679
LC ebook record available at https://lccn.loc.gov/2023046680

ISBN: HB: 978-1-3504-0000-9
PB: 978-1-3504-0025-2
ePDF: 978-1-3504-0005-4
eBook: 978-1-3504-0007-8

Series: New Directions in Religion and Literature

Typeset by Newgen KnowledgeWorks Pvt. Ltd., Chennai, India

For product safety related questions contact productsafety@bloomsbury.com.

To find out more about our authors and books visit www.bloomsbury.com
and sign up for our newsletters.

To Seeca,
with wonder

Contents

Acknowledgments	x
Introduction: The Cultural Work of Literary Preaching: Form, Affordance, and Resistance	1
1 "There Will Soon Be No More Priests": Surrogate Preachers in Emerson and Whitman	21
2 "But I Say Unto You": The Literary Pulpit Exchange in Nathaniel Hawthorne and Rebecca Harding Davis	59
3 Reprising *God's Trombones*: The Novel Sermons of William Faulkner and Zora Neale Hurston	103
4 Toni Morrison, the Anxieties of Literary Preaching, and the Circulated Sermon	149
Coda: "That's the Pulpit Speaking"	191
Works Cited	197
Index	211

Acknowledgments

Throughout the process of writing this book, I have been the beneficiary of tremendous resources, encouragement, and guidance. Many thanks are in order. First, I wish to thank the many authors and critics, living and dead, whom this project engages. One of the unique joys of academic labor involves finding oneself in the good company of far superior writers who are simultaneously complete strangers and intimate conversation partners. Writing can be a lonely task, but, as anyone who has ever felt the heady thrills of research will testify, it is not always one.

I wish also to thank the English Department at the University of Kansas for providing me with a dissertation-stage fellowship, an award that enabled me to devote my full attention to the completion of the first draft of this project. I cannot adequately express my gratitude to my mentor, Laura Mielke, who directed the dissertation out of which this book emerged. Laura's tireless support, authenticity, thoughtful and timely critique, and enthusiasm for my work propelled me onward when what Walt Whitman describes as "the dark patches" fell on me. Her brilliance is matched only by her compassion, and I am immeasurably grateful for her friendship. I am thankful for Laura Cope, Mark Knight, and Emma Mason of Bloomsbury Academic for their confidence in this project and for offering valuable feedback along the way. The subsections of the chapter treating Toni Morrison's literary preaching were previously published as articles in *MELUS* and *College Literature*, and I thank Oxford University Press and Johns Hopkins University Press for granting me the permission to include them in this monograph. Philip Barnard, Jim Carothers, Laura Dubek, Doreen Fowler, Randal Jelks, Jon Lamb, Stacie McCormick, Amani Morrison, Paul Outka, Misty Schieberle, Gary Totten, and Rhaisa Williams provided significant insights about the project and focused critique on various chapters. Certainly, no one has had better fortune with officemates than me. It is a roll of the dice, but I've won every time. Eric Hood, Chip Badley, and Jason Goodvin enriched me with their friendship, intelligence, and humor. Many other colleagues, including Marty Baldwin, Lexey Bartlett, Rob Byers, Cheryl Duffy, Doug Drabkin, Manamee Guha, Perry Harrison, Eric Leuschner, Aaron Long, Dan McClure, Catherine and Carl Miller, Gene Rice, Amy Richecky, and Brett Weaver proved to be valuable interlocuters throughout this process. The librarians at both the University of Kansas and Fort Hays State University enabled my research and helped me gain access to many of the works that appear in the Works Cited. I also wish to thank my students, at both the University of Kansas and Fort Hays State University, who made me look forward to coming to work each morning.

Finally, my family and friends have supported me throughout the course of this project. I especially thank Isaac Anderson, Jim Gum, Jordan and Erica Henry, Tim and Mimi Keel, George Linney, Sarah Lundy, Jessi Marcus, Wes Nash, Enuma Okoro, Dustin Pfeifer, and Grant Wood for their wise counsel and encouragement. My parents—Stephen and Amy Smalley—provided a household in which imagination, good books, and curiosity were far more important than cleanliness and chore charts, and they modeled for me a love of language and the pursuit of intellectual virtue. I also wish to thank Bonnie, Don, and Angie Green for their unflagging support. My siblings—Elizabeth, Ben, and Daniel—and their families have offered more encouragement than they know. Noah, Lena, and Robyn, my children, have provided no useful critique of my writing at all, only unconditional love and a seemingly boundless desire for play, laughter, and fun—what a gift. Above all others, I thank my wife and closest friend, Seeca Green Smalley, for her companionship, example, and love. I marvel at how she sees the world so clearly and tends to it so compassionately. I dedicate this project to her.

Introduction

The Cultural Work of Literary Preaching: Form, Affordance, and Resistance

Resistance and the Sermon in American Literature offers an analysis of US literature's engagement with the Protestant sermon from Emerson to Morrison. This book focuses on culturally and politically charged scenes of preaching in major works of American literature and privileges scenes in which an author's evocation of the sermon or identification with the figure of the preacher gestures in politically contradictory directions. I refer to these scenes as instances of *literary preaching* and contend that a focus on literary preaching uncovers crucial insights into an author's politics, sense of cultural authority, place in literary history, and, especially, imagination of the cultural significance of their literary works. More importantly, however, I argue that a study of major US authors' engagements with literary preaching discloses a significant, abiding, and undertheorized tradition in US literature.

Throughout this study, I treat literary preaching as a Janus-faced literary form and demonstrate that the cultural work of literary preaching inevitably involves two contradictory moves. The first move I refer to as prophetic unsettlement. This move is characterized by the use of literary preaching to unsettle established structures of thought, politics, or culture to generate a more egalitarian or humanitarian cultural ethos. It is a move marked by demands for sympathetic identification, justice and action, plurality, and radical democracy. In such scenes, which abound in US literature, the author mobilizes the literary sermon to *resist* dominant cultural formations, both religious and political. This is the first sense of "resistance" that I wish to highlight with the book's title. The second move works in an opposing direction and suggests another sense of "resistance." Throughout American literature, scenes of literary preaching consistently threaten to reify an ideology that narrowly locates moral authority in the figure of the preacher. Thus, these scenes *resist* the emergence of alternative, nonclerical modes of cultural authority. This dynamic presents a challenge for authors who aim to establish the moral authority of their works but rely on high-stakes adaptations of the preacher's voice to do so. The authors that I treat in *Resistance and the Sermon in American Literature* understand this dialectic tension and strain to devise narrative strategies through which they might engage in literary preaching while avoiding or mitigating the reification of clerical ideology or, relatedly, the uncomfortable association of their vocation with that of the preacher.

Throughout this book, I rest my claims about each author's engagement with literary preaching on close readings that highlight the author's historical, biographical, and literary contexts. Inflected by these contexts, each author's engagement with the sermon takes different shape, and the cultural work enacted by literary preaching differs in each author's oeuvre. When viewed together, however, these historically contextualized readings reveal surprisingly consistent patterns of engagement with literary preaching that transcend the particularities of time, region, and biography. By attending to various authors' strategies of engaging the sermon and the cultural and political significance of those engagements, I aim to reinvigorate our sense of the sermon's complex, persistent, and abiding influence on American literature and culture. Despite important work on this topic, we have only begun to understand the pervasiveness of this influence.

To analyze the sermon's multiple functions across this long literary-historical period, I approach literary preaching as a particularly conspicuous *form* in US literature. My model of forms derives from Caroline Levine's pathbreaking monograph *Forms: Whole, Rhythm, Hierarchy, Network* (2015). Levine approaches forms—which she defines broadly as "arrangement[s] of elements— an ordering, patterning, or shaping" (3)—in a "pluralizing way to include both social and aesthetic forms" and argues that "no single form dominates or organizes all of the others" (17). Crucially, Levine asserts that forms organize both literary texts and our social reality, and, more importantly, that "as different forms struggle to impose their order on our experience, aesthetic and political forms emerge as comparable patterns on a common plane" (16). By attending to the ways in which forms order our experience and collide with one another, Levine aims to break the fatalism that she believes emerges from the dominant mode of ideological criticism that posits the inexorable force of such deep forms as "capitalism, nationalism, and racism" (17). Levine rightly admits that such forms profoundly shape our political worlds, but she also argues that an "exclusive focus on ultimate causality has not necessarily benefited leftist politics" and distracts us "from thinking strategically about how best to deploy multiple forms for political ends" (17). In the texts that I examine, literary preaching frequently emerges as exactly such a form, an aesthetic form deployed for political or cultural ends and often in resistance to more established and seemingly potent social forms.

Treating literary preaching as a literary form enables us to work both within and beyond historical criticism. One of the key contributions of Levine's revision of our critical vocabulary is that it loosens the grip of new formalist understandings of aesthetic forms as anchored entirely to specific moments in cultural history. A guiding argument in this book is that we need to move beyond historical-cultural analysis to understand the significance of literary preaching in works of US literature. I am concerned with mapping the long tradition of literary preaching while simultaneously locating specific engagements with the form within their immediate cultural and historical contexts. Attention to form necessitates such a dual methodology because forms—again, understood as abstract organizations and patternings—are simultaneously "transhistorical, portable, and abstract" *and* "material, situated, and political" (Levine 11). While forms perform cultural and political work in specific contexts, they are also shockingly portable into new contexts. Levine explains:

> From the gender binary to rhyme and from prison cells to narrative prose, aesthetic and social forms outlive the specific conditions that gave birth to them: the scroll does not altogether disappear with the codex but in fact reemerges with surprising pervasiveness in the age of the Internet; the quest structure of ancient epic remains available to the contemporary novelist. None of these forms spring up anew in response to particular social facts but instead hang around, available for reuse. (12)

But why? Why do certain forms such as prison cells or quest tales "hang around" and seem especially inviting for reuse by subsequent designers? Levine does not answer this lurking question about the viability of certain forms, their relative likelihood for surviving the specific conditions of their emergence. Her discussion of the potentialities offered by various forms, however, suggests an answer. Drawing on design theory, she refers to a given form's latent potentialities as a form's *affordances* (6). I suggest that not all literary forms exhibit equal portability because some forms offer writers a constellation of desirable potentialities and productively troubling containments that ensure their survival beyond the historical moment that birthed them.

Something like an evolutionary principle—a survival of the fittest forms—seems to be at play here. Myriad examples of this sort of natural selection of literary forms exist. Contemporary poets draw on the sonnet much more frequently than the Puritan poetic form known as the "fourteener." Once immensely popular, the singsong fourteener affords memorization but perhaps little else. The sonnet, however, affords patient and complex meditation, an intricate and varied formal structure, and a connection to a rich literary heritage that becomes more impressive with each additional deployment of the form. Perhaps we will see the resurgence of the fourteener as a form in future generations. Because forms are abstract organizational principles, such a resurgence is certainly possible. We are wise to be on guard against the hubris of seeing our own moment as more settled and historically significant than it perhaps is. Who knows what forms will flourish in the generations ahead? But given our admittedly limited historical perspective, it seems safe to suggest that if it is not extinct, the fourteener is certainly not a thriving literary form.

The same cannot be said of literary preaching as a form in US literature. The form leaps off the pages of antebellum novels such as William Wells Brown's *Clotel* (1853) and Harriet Beecher Stowe's *Uncle Tom's Cabin* (1852), and it remains highly visible in such diverse contemporary novels as Cormac McCarthy's *Blood Meridian* (1985), Toni Morrison's *Beloved* (1987), David James Duncan's *The Brothers K* (1992), and Marilynne Robinson's *Gilead* (2004). It explodes as a moral force in realist works such as Drude Krog Janson's *A Saloonkeeper's Daughter* (1887), Mark Twain's "The War Prayer" (1916), and Charles M. Sheldon's best-selling *In His Steps* (1896). It galvanizes crucial moments in modernist fictions such as Zora Neale Hurston's *Jonah's Gourd Vine* (1934) and William Faulkner's *The Sound and the Fury* (1929). In the wake of such modernist deployments of the form, we see literary preaching recycled with powerful effect in James Baldwin's *Go Tell It on the Mountain* (1953), Ralph Ellison's *Invisible Man* (1952), and many of Flannery O'Connor's novels and short stories. From Elia Kazan's *On the Waterfront* (1954) to Quentin Tarantino's *Pulp Fiction* (1994) to P. T. Anderson's *There Will Be Blood* (2007), it organizes and structures the moral and cultural tensions highlighted by US films. This list merely scratches the surface of US cultural productions that deeply engage the sermon, and I suspect that readers who study US literature and culture have already begun adding their own titles to this short list. The literary sermon represents an especially portable, pervasive, and entrenched form in US literature and culture. It takes considerable effort not to see this pattern. Once one acknowledges it, the pattern appears with remarkable frequency.

Literary preaching involves two recurrent features in US literature: textualized sermons (e.g., the Father Mapple chapter of Herman Melville's *Moby-Dick* [1851] or Rev. John Pearson's sermon in Zora Neale Hurston's *Jonah's Gourd Vine*) and sustained narrative focus on the preacher, especially in moments where this narrative focus positions the figure of the preacher in the midst of crucial debates about contemporary crises (e.g., the narrator's comments about the failure of the social gospel preacher in Rebecca Harding Davis's *Life in the Iron-Mills* [1861], Hester Prynne's culturally loaded disputes with Arthur Dimmesdale in Nathaniel Hawthorne's *The Scarlet Letter* [1850], or Baby Suggs's discussion of God's justice and white violence in *Beloved*). In both types of scenes, literary preaching involves allusion to or commentary on Christian religious texts, moral exhortation, and the deployment of established sermonic tropes, a narrative pattern that Dawn Coleman helpfully refers to as the "sermonic voice" (17). The form emerges with special force as a response to deeply felt cultural crisis because it functions as a readymade form that affords moral authority. Consistently, US authors mobilize this literary form to voice eloquent and forceful dissent from their surrounding milieus and promote alternative imaginations of community, the self, religion, or politics.

For nineteenth-century US writers with designs on their audiences, literary preaching offered a unique narrative mode through which the artist could figure themselves as a compelling moral authority and the reading public as a vast body of potential converts. In the first half of the nineteenth century, writers were watching carefully, often from the pews, as dynamic preachers gathered tremendous audiences to themselves, delivered new styles of sermons, and, by doing so, reshaped American religion and politics. Literary preaching aims for revival, and it initially arises out of writers' responsiveness to contemporary demonstrations of sermonic power during and after the Second Great Awakening.[1] In their embrace of literary preaching, authors aim to perform "cultural work" in the classic sense laid out by Jane Tompkins: they intend to "redefine the social order," "win the belief and influence the behavior of the widest possible audience," and make "people think and act in a particular way" (xi). And they could see that the preacher in the pulpit represented an enviable nexus of moral authority, political power, and verbal artistry.

---

[1] For a classic analysis of how antebellum preaching shaped the style of writers of the "American Renaissance," see David S. Reynolds, *Beneath the American Renaissance: The Subversive Imagination in the Age of Emerson and Melville* (Oxford UP: 1988), 15–52. Like Reynolds, I am interested in the ways that novelists, poets, and essayists borrowed from contemporary preachers. However, I am especially interested in the political and cultural effects of this borrowing, the purposes to which authors put their literary sermons, while Reynolds's primary aim is to show the ways that innovations in literary style depended on popular modes of religious oratory.

If the prominence of the sermon in mid-nineteenth-century literature can be linked to the Second Great Awakening, why has the sermon persisted as such a summoning form for such a variety of US writers across such a long swath of cultural history? What have its effects been on US literary culture? What potentialities does it offer? What constraints does it contain? How do various authors engage and adapt this form? How has its presence shaped US literature? *Resistance and the Sermon in American Literature* itself serves as my extended answer to these questions, but I want to telegraph my responses in the remainder of this introduction. In answering these questions, I draw on Levine's discussion of a form's *affordances* to describe the multiple affordances of literary preaching. A focus on the affordances of literary preaching—the latent potentialities of the form—explains not only the form's attractive force at particular moments in US literary history but, more importantly, its remarkable portability across time. A discussion of literary preaching's affordances requires discussion of its constraints and limitations, and, paradoxically, the form's constraints contribute significantly to literary preaching's survival in contemporary cultural productions. To take up this examination, I wish to consider one of the most well-known examples of literary preaching in US literature—Herman Melville's chapter-length sermon in *Moby-Dick*, which offers an especially vivid example of the form and provides a useful entry point for an examination of literary preaching's affordances.

Before he joins the crew of the *Pequod*, Ishmael, who usually prides himself on thumbing his nose at genteel pieties, makes a surprisingly conservative decision. He decides to get right with God. To do so, he makes a visit to the Whalemen's Chapel in New Bedford and notes, a bit defensively, that he behaves exactly like almost all whalemen in making his pre-voyage visit to church: "Few are the moody fishermen, shortly bound for the Indian Ocean or Pacific, who fail to make a Sunday visit to the spot. I am sure that I did not" (Melville 43). When he enters the chapel, Father Mapple's stylized pulpit immediately arrests his attention. Though Father Mapple now serves as a chaplain, traces of his former profession as a sailor and harpooner saturate the scene. Towering high over the rest of the sanctuary, the pulpit can only be mounted by means of a nautical rope ladder (46). But most conspicuously, the pulpit itself is carved into the likeness of the prow of a ship. With his characteristic penchant for both overstatement and seeing metaphysical truths hinted at by material realities, Ishmael exclaims, "What could be more full of meaning?—for the pulpit is ever this earth's foremost part; all the rest comes in its rear; the pulpit leads the world ... Yes, the world's a ship on its passage out, and not a voyage complete; and the pulpit is its prow" (47).

Clearly, Ishmael overstates his point, and his celebration of the sermon seems to ignore its status as one among many forms. Indeed, at first glance, it is difficult to take Ishmael's comment seriously at all when one considers the world-steering power of the new articulations of industrial capitalism that Melville himself critiqued in "Bartleby the Scrivener" (1853), "The Paradise of Bachelors and the Tartarus of Maids" (1855), *The Confidence Man* (1857), and *Moby-Dick* itself. The exclamation seems equally wide of the mark when measured against the immense power of national politicians and statesmen, who, one year before the publication of *Moby-Dick*, passed the Fugitive Slave Law, the controversial bill that effectively extended the reach of slavery across the country. As his novella *Benito Cereno* (1855) makes perfectly clear, Melville—like Frederick Douglass—knew that the moral outrage of slavery represented a "slumbering volcano" that may explode at any moment (Wallace 110–11). Put simply, the pulpit hardly seems to be "the prow" of the real world driven by forms as potent as nationalism, expansionist ideology, racism, and militarized capitalism. In fact, as Melville learned during his voyages in the South Pacific, the pulpit often served as a functionary of precisely those deep forms. If we join Ishmael in his ever-evolving analogies, we might be tempted to respond, "Young Ishmael, if the pulpit is the world's prow, the market and its politicians are the wind and the sails." We would be justified in saying so.

Yet Ishmael's hyperbole expresses more than a germ of historical truth, and his emphasis on the power of religious rhetoric, specifically the Protestant sermon, sheds critical light on one of Melville's key narrative strategies in *Moby-Dick*. Predictably, the pulpit that awes Ishmael does not remain empty. Melville, through the character of Father Mapple, a character modeled on the popular nineteenth-century preacher Father Edward Taylor, inhabits the pulpit and delivers a sermon that culminates in a scathing critique of US legal institutions. In her perceptive reading of this scene, Toni Morrison argues that Melville uses this sermon to critique the Fugitive Slave Law and, specifically, his father-in-law, Judge Lemuel Shaw, a former Senator and the first US justice to enact the perverse law ("Unspeakable Things" 16–18). In the sermon's closing lines, Father Mapple contrasts the temporal laws of man against eternal truth and implores his congregation to pursue the latter. Here federal law and prophetic sermon collide, and Levine would call this a clash of forms in which, despite the potency of the dominant legal form, the outcome is not a foregone conclusion:

> Delight is to him whose strong arms yet support him, when the ship of this base treacherous world has gone down beneath him. Delight is to him, who gives no

quarter in the truth, and kills, burns, and destroys all sin though he pluck it out from under the robes of Senators and Judges. Delight,—top-gallant delight is to him, who acknowledges no law or lord, but the Lord his God, and is only a patriot to heaven. (54)

The passage's unmistakably political call suggests an irresolvable conflict of loyalties as Father Mapple preaches a message that bears a striking parallel to Thoreau's diatribe against the machinations of the state in "Resistance to Civil Government" (1849). The sermon places the auditors—both fictional and metafictional—in a moment of crisis. Will the congregants choose to be patriots of the nation or patriots to heaven? Significantly, Father Mapple covers his face as if in sorrow or shame after delivering these lines. His act of proleptic mourning seems to indicate that he fears which patriotism most of his congregants will choose. They will go down with the ship of "this base treacherous world" and, like the nation itself, "give quarter in the truth." Writing between 1850–1, it would have been hard for Melville to imagine otherwise.

This scene of preaching closes abruptly, but it reverberates throughout the novel. Indeed, its central images, call for loyalty to "the truth," and thinly veiled critique of American slavery provide crucial clues for a political reading of the novel's catastrophic conclusion, a conclusion that Michael Rogin shows Melville penned in the immediate wake of Judge Shaw's ruling in support of the Fugitive Slave Law (107). The entire crew of the *Pequod*, save Ishmael, drowns along with an American ship (of state) that has betrayed its initial mission. Melville draws attention to the fact that the last portion of the ship visible before it "sink[s] to hell" is an unmarked red flag (427). This odd detail, so curiously highlighted again and again throughout the final pages, echoes Father Mapple's warning about the fate of a nation that compromises on issues as morally serious as slavery. In the antebellum South, slave auctioneers gathered bidders to their slave sales by displaying blank red flags, and as Maurie Dee McInnis shows, the unmarked red flag became a crucial "pictorial detail" in abolitionist art of the mid-nineteenth century (85). Anticipating these visual artists, Melville places this symbolically loaded flag atop a doomed ship to highlight the replacement of a national flag for one associated with human trafficking. As Ishmael asked in the chapel, "What could be more full of meaning?" At the end of *Moby-Dick*, this red flag signals not only the crime of slavery but links this crime to a future national catastrophe; the *Pequod's* destruction anticipates the nation's fate. Thus, the political message dramatized in the catastrophic finale mirrors Father

Mapple's agenda-setting sermon, which also warns of the consequences of acquiescence to an immoral political form.

By analyzing Melville's foray into literary preaching, we can begin to consider literary preaching, more generally, as an especially summoning form in US literature. To some degree, we can account for this attraction to the sermon by considering Melville's historical context, a context Melville broadly shares with the authors who appear in the first two chapters of this book. In Melville's day, preachers effectively defined their role in US culture as arbiters of extralegal morality. Through the sermon, they spoke authoritatively of divine laws that superseded the transitory laws of man.[2] "Among the educated, predominately white congregations of the Northeast, the early nineteenth century saw a decisive shift in the conception of good preaching," writes Dawn Coleman, "from scholastic emphasis on explicating the Bible and expounding correct doctrine to a new focus on the sermon as a practical discourse that moved hearers to right belief and action" (30). To win over their audiences, preachers projected an air of "moral certitude" but mitigated the negative valences of this potentially authoritarian, moralistic demeanor with rhetorical performances designed to stir their auditors to action (Coleman 31). Melville's representation of Father Mapple clearly represents the conjunction of moral certitude with intense emotionalism. In tandem with the democratic religious movements that defined the Second Great Awakening, white antebellum preachers of the Northeast established the sermon as an authoritative mode of discourse that was accessible, practical, emotional, and operated on alternative terms than those enshrined by the orderings of the market and national politics. This construction of the sermon appealed strongly to the authors examined in this study, and we should understand the sermon's association with extralegal moral authority as one of the most significant affordances of literary preaching.

Yet Melville's high estimation of the sermon extends beyond his observation of white, Northeastern preachers. His attraction to the revolutionary political power of the sermon seems deeply shaped by his experience, however brief, with the African American church in New Bedford. Though Ishmael spends considerable time in Father Mapple's Chapel, modeled on Seaman's Bethel, we should note that it is the second church he visits in his wanderings. When he first

---

[2] In the *Oracle and the Curse: A Poetics of Justice from the Revolution to the Civil War* (Harvard UP: 2013), Caleb Smith describes a variety of antebellum orators' attempts to "suppresses the private self so that the commands of some transcendent, impersonal power could speak through them" (5–6). He refers to this tactic as the deployment of "self-abnegating modes of address" (xi). Smith treats a number of sermons in his analysis, and he focuses on the manner in which such speech-acts structured the contest between "human law and higher law in the juridical public sphere" (4).

arrives at New Bedford, Ishmael accidentally stumbles into an African American church where he encounters a preacher, "a black Angel of Doom ... beating a book in a pulpit" (24). Terrified, he retreats rapidly from the church. Ishmael's racist depiction of the scene suggests white panic in the presence of the powerful Black preacher, but it also unmistakably registers recognition of the political value of this aesthetic form as he describes the congregants as a "great Black Parliament" (24). Drawing on Melville's description of New Bedford's streets, Robert Wallace suggests that this church is a fictional representation of the Zion Methodist Church on Second Street, the church where Frederick Douglass preached during the time both he and Melville were in New Bedford (19). Wallace stops short of identifying Douglass as the fiery preacher who makes such a strong impression on Ishmael but suggests that the figure was modeled on either Douglass or one of his close associates. Moreover, "If Douglass was not the preacher in the pulpit, his face may have been among the hundred that turned around to peer at [Ishmael]" (20). Later in the novel, the *Pequod*'s African American cook, Fleece, delivers a trope-laden sermon that ends with a searing and thinly veiled indictment of America's greed and violence. Fleece's sermon reveals that when Melville ascended the pulpit he drew heavily on the rhetorical firepower of antebellum African American preaching. Many other scenes of preaching exist in *Moby-Dick* in which Melville—through Ishmael and Ahab—climbs into the pulpit and examines the sermon's persuasive power or moral force. We should realize that Ishmael's hyperbolic comment about the pulpit being the world's prow not only reflects Melville's tremendous responsiveness to the sermon in antebellum culture, but it also primes the reader for Melville's intense, but ambivalent, engagements with the form.

Melville's embrace of literary preaching in *Moby-Dick* evinces the rule rather than the exception in US literature. Though historical context alone cannot explain the endurance of literary preaching as a defining form in US literature, Melville's example demonstrates that historical context cannot be ignored. The sermon's importance in US history deserves to be acknowledged because it explains partially the form's endurance in US literature. Historically considered, the sermon wields significant authority in American culture from its colonial origins to the present. From Winthrop's "A Model of Christian Charity" to Puritan jeremiads to the "black-robed regiment" that promoted military opposition to Britain to William Apess's "An Indian's Looking-Glass for the White Man" to Jonathan Edwards's "Sinners in the Hands of an Angry God" to the Cane Ridge Revivals to the revolutionary preaching of Nat Turner to the abolitionist sermons of Henry Ward Beecher and Sojourner Truth to the Civil

Rights Movement, the preacher and the sermon have exerted striking influence on American politics and thought. This fact begins to explain why a wide variety of US authors identify the preacher as a figure against whom they imagine their own vocations and the sermon as a form against which they measure the cultural work of their essays, poetry, and novels.

In *Preaching and the Rise of the American Novel* (2015), a historicist study of preaching in mid-nineteenth-century US novels, Dawn Coleman argues persuasively that in the novels of this period we see authors attempt to establish the novel's authority through a variety of engagements with the preacher. She claims that "the cultural dominance of preaching in [the antebellum period] and novelists' desire to vindicate fiction against its still-powerful critics" account for the remarkable frequency of fictional preachers in American literature of the 1840s and 1850s (15). She also perceptively notes that some writers saw analogues between their "market-defiant art and the cultural stance of the period's ministers, who claimed to declare unpopular truths regardless of their reception" (15). On the other hand, because many clergy failed to voice unpopular truths, especially about slavery and the exploitation of the urban poor, novelists saw them as a target for ridicule and censure (Coleman 15). Coleman acknowledges that US literature in other periods engages the sermon but argues that the mid-nineteenth century represents an especially intense engagement with literary preaching and that this engagement leads to the rise of the moral authority of the novel.

My debt to Coleman's work is ample, especially as I understand my study as a response to Coleman's call for ongoing analysis of how preaching "radiated out of the church to shape the country's poems, songs, political oratory, fiction, films and other cultural expressions in ways we have barely begun to recognize" (3). However, I disagree with her claim about the unique density of engagements with the minister and the sermon in the literature of the 1840s to 1850s. American literature's intense engagement with preaching extends far beyond the antebellum period, and this intense engagement cannot always be neatly traced to specific historical or biographical factors such as those that Coleman so helpfully identifies in her study. *Resistance and the Sermon in American Literature* intervenes in this discussion to argue that in the antebellum moment we see no unique succession or coup of the literary over and against the preacher, but the first stage of a protracted struggle, a vexed identification, between the writer and the preacher occasioned by writers' frequent reliance on literary preaching to perform cultural work. If one reads across major works of American literature, this engagement with the preacher and the sermon begins to look like a national obsession, something like a neurotic tic writ large. If one were to substitute each preacher in US literature or film with a practitioner of any other highly visible profession, we would immediately be convinced of an enduring cultural obsession with that vocation.[3]

To account for the conspicuous persistence of literary preaching as a form in US literature, I want to discuss four of the form's affordances besides its primary affordance of extralegal moral authority. Highlighting these four additional affordances allows us to move beyond historical-cultural criticism while at the same time acknowledging that any intellectually honest account of the persistence of literary preaching must involve such analysis. The four affordances that I discuss are (1) a performative sensuality, or a music-like ability to communicate beyond words; (2) a granting of access to a culturally valued literary heritage; (3) its potential to reify the cultural authority of the preacher; and (4) its potential to encourage identifications between the author and the preacher. These final two affordances seem like latent potentialities that would limit literary preaching's portability across historical periods. But, as I argue below, these potentially constraining affordances paradoxically contribute to the form's endurance.

First, each of the authors discussed in *Resistance and the Sermon in American Literature*, in varying degrees, identifies literary preaching as a form that affords a sensual and quasi-musical mode of address. Literary preaching, thus, holds out the possibility of breaking through the cold medium of print. Unlike potentially inert text, the impassioned human voice unites speaker and auditor in an intensely sensual circuit that enables the transcendence of both individuated subjectivities and the inadequacies of mere words. Literary preaching, thus, not only appears as a morally authoritative form but also as a uniquely sensual form that appeals to authors who strain against the limitations of symbolic language and the medium of print as they engage their readers. The sermon, as these authors modify it into their narratives, becomes performative language that seizes on and can be seized on by the body, language that (even when represented in textual form) *sounds*, *moves*, and *touches*. Literature tends toward orature in these performative narrative moments and gains semiotic force. Moral authority joins oral artistry

---

[3] Imagine, for example, if we substituted a physician or an extended scene of medical diagnosis for each preacher or scene of preaching that appears in the major works of US literature during the period covered in this study. Would we not instantly suspect that an obsessive concern with bodily health gripped the nation and deeply inflected its cultural productions? Moreover, would we not ask what it meant for authors to attempt to establish their fiction or poetry in the shadow of medical practice? Too often we fail to see one of the most striking features of US literature because, like the purloined letter, it hides in plain sight.

in the sermon, and the latter affordance is often as compelling as the former for it enables a mode of suasion that transcends mere argumentation. For example, in 1919, when James Weldon Johnson witnesses a masterful folk preacher, he cannot help but become envious of the preacher's ability to

> br[ing] into play the full gamut of his wonderful voice, a voice—what shall I say?—not of an organ or a trumpet, but rather of a trombone, the instrument possessing above all others the power to express the wide and varied range of emotions encompassed by the human voice—and with greater amplitude. He intoned, he moaned, he pleaded—he blared, he crashed, he thundered. I sat fascinated; and more, I was, perhaps against my will, deeply moved; the emotional effect upon me was irresistible. (*God's Trombones* 8–9)

Johnson's discussion of this scene of preaching—an encounter that launches *God's Trombones*—records that the preacher's voice breaks through the reified orderings of the everyday. He describes the sermon's ability to transform a banal moment into one "alive and quivering" (8). After the preacher began to intone his sermon, the individual auditors, including Johnson, become united as though an "electric current" ran through them (8). In *God's Trombones*, Johnson rewrites seven African American folk sermons in verse form to try to represent this moaning, pleading, crashing, and thundering voice that so irresistibly affects listeners. While Johnson's embrace of literary preaching as a musical, sensual, and unifying form that shatters the limitations of mere words appears striking, what is much more striking is the way similar representations of the sermon recur throughout US literature.

A case in point: I do not treat Hawthorne's primary scene of literary preaching in *The Scarlet Letter* (1851) in the subsequent chapters, but Hawthorne's representation of Arthur Dimmesdale's Election Day sermon at the conclusion of the novel evinces a sense of the sermon's semiotic force that closely resembles Johnson's analysis of the folk preacher nearly seventy years later. Like Johnson, Hawthorne does not focus on the preacher's words, but on the timbre and aural texture of his sermon. Indeed, Hawthorne characterizes Dimmesdale's actual words as a hindrance to the sermon's primary meaning; they are a "grosser medium" that would block "the spiritual sense" (*Scarlet* 154). The reader listens along with Hester who cannot enter the church but hears the whole sermon "in the shape of an indistinct, but varied, murmur and flow of the minister's very peculiar voice" (154). Here, Hawthorne's evocation of the sermon shuttles between the musical and the baldly erotic. Though in the fictive world of the novel Dimmesdale is a seventeenth-century Puritan, he preaches like an early nineteenth-century revivalist. The sermon appears less as the discourse of a moral authority than as an artistic event in which the highly emotional preacher seduces the entire audience. Crucially, Dimmesdale's voice ushers his parishioners into a heightened state of sensibility where they communicate with the preacher and each other beyond the need for words:

> This vocal organ was in itself a rich endowment; insomuch that a listener, comprehending nothing of the language in which the preacher spoke, might still have been swayed to and fro by the mere tone and cadence. Like all other music, it breathed passion and pathos, and emotions high or tender, in a tongue native with the human heart, wherever educated ... [The voice] touched a sensibility in every bosom! At times this deep strain of pathos was all that could be heard, and scarcely heard, sighing amid a desolate silence. But even when the minister's voice grew high and commanding,—when it gushed irrepressibly upward,—when it assumed its utmost breadth and power, so overfilling the church as to burst its way through the solid walls, and diffuse itself into the open air,—still, if the auditor listened intently, and for the purpose, he could detect the same cry of pain. (154)

The musical and sexual imagery that suffuse this scene combine to suggest that the sermon, understood as an emotional and performative oral form, opens an alternative modality of communication that prioritizes the desires of the body and circulates beyond the realm of words. Throughout the course of the sermon, this parallel channel of communication connects all the auditors and remains democratically available, a quivering source of new identity formation. Individual subjectivity and conventional logic collapse before the power of Dimmesdale's sermon, which speaks not in any specific human language but in a "tongue native to the human heart" (154). At the conclusion of this sermon, the auditors appear "released from the high spell that had transported them into the region of another's mind" and "return[ed] into themselves, with their awe and wonder still heavy on them" (157). From Hawthorne's era to James Weldon Johnson's to our own, the sermon's ability to conjure this primary language, a language that resides buried within our linguistic systems, beckons authors who, as Faulkner once put it, sense that "words dont ever fit even what they are trying to say at" (*As I Lay* 171). How might we begin to theorize this persistent desire to invoke a "tongue native to the human heart," an alternative to symbolic language that revels in the sound, timbre, and rhythm of speech and song?

Julia Kristeva's account of the semiotic provides a useful, if perhaps surprising, model for thinking about the frequent evocation of the sermon in US literature.

It does so because Kristeva stresses the presence of a repressed—but potentially liberatory—modality within the signifying system that is language. Megan Becker-Leckrone, a Kristevan commentator, describes the semiotic as "a kind of language before language" that is "closely associated with the mother" (162). Kristeva's understanding of the subject's acquisition of language depends on "the distinction between two distinct linguistic forces—'two modalities ... within the same signifying process that constitutes language'—the semiotic and the symbolic" (Becker-Leckrone 162). For Kristeva, the semiotic is associated with primary drives and denotes a pre-Oedipal, nonverbal signifying system. This primary modality of signification relies on a "provisional articulation that is essentially mobile and constituted of movements and their ephemeral stases ... Neither model nor copy, it is anterior to and underlies figuration and therefore also specularization, and only admits analogy with vocal or kinetic rhythm" (qtd. in Moi 160). With the subject's fall into language, or the symbolic, the semiotic "*chora* will be more or less successfully repressed and can be perceived only as a pulsational *pressure* on symbolic language" (Moi 161; unless otherwise specified all emphases are in the original). Yet this repression necessarily fails. When this pulsational pressure becomes strong enough, when the repressed semiotic returns in waves of sound or rhythm, it proffers resources for political transformation because it "tap[s] into a well of as yet unordered language processes and unarticulated sounds to generate new possibilities for thought and society" (Rivkin and Ryan 454).[4] In their highly performative forays into literary preaching, US authors aim to invoke not only a language of authority but a "language before language," a uniquely sonic form, that rejects cultural givens and attempts to draw the reader, albeit momentarily, into a creative realm beyond the control of the symbolic.

An additional affordance of literary preaching is the access it grants the writer to a fecund and contentious literary heritage. This form flourishes in American literature far beyond "the golden age of preaching" (i.e., the mid-nineteenth century) because as authors attempt to insert themselves in American literary history they often do so by engaging and adapting the works of other writers. In the wake of the explosion of highly charged scenes of preaching in antebellum novels and poetry, subsequent writers not only

---

[4] In *Maternal Body and Voice in Toni Morrison, Bobbie Ann Mason, and Lee Smith* (U of Missouri P: 2002), Paula Gallant Eckard usefully corrects the tendency among some critics to simply lionize the semiotic *chora* without considering how, in Kristeva's writings, it also represents danger and chaos: "A life-infusing, creative force, the semiotic chora is also a deeply disturbing and troubling realm" (26).

respond to their own immediate historical, cultural, or biographical contexts but also to their literary predecessors. They often do so through rewriting their predecessors' literary sermons and preachers. Who is Faulkner's Rev. Whitfield in *As I Lay Dying* if not a twentieth-century Southern version of Hawthorne's Dimmesdale? Can we begin to understand the literary significance of Morrison's representation of Baby Suggs and her sermon without seeing her, at least partially, as a revision of Harriet Beecher Stowe's sentimental preachers in *Uncle Tom's Cabin* (Duvall 126)? Is not David James Duncan's climactic scene of literary preaching in *The Brothers K* unimaginable without Twain's "The War Prayer"? Is not Twain's "The War Prayer," in turn, unimaginable without Hawthorne's counter-sermon in "The Gentle Boy"? In the mid-nineteenth century, novelists and poets responded to their culture and established literary preaching as a powerful form in American letters. In this literary-historical moment, literary preaching became part of the DNA of US literature. Subsequent scenes of literary preaching allow postbellum authors to establish themselves as inheritors of and participants in this literary heritage. This affordance not only explains the puzzling persistence of literary preaching in US literature but also the remarkable frequency with which scenes of literary preaching appear in writers' initial works. In these early works, authors often attempt to write themselves into an established literary tradition, and they do so by displaying their facility with one of its favored forms.

The first three affordances of literary preaching that I identify—moral authority, performative sensuality, and access to a literary heritage—work in a more-or-less uniform manner. These intensely attractive affordances enable authors to perform specific cultural work and establish a commanding authorial identity. The final two affordances of literary preaching that I now discuss reveal the unavoidable and often repulsive affordances of the form. These last two affordances—the reification of clerical ideology and the identification of the author with the preacher—generate significant cultural tensions and authorial anxiety. For a long period of US literary history, authors have attempted to mitigate the effects of these final affordances, and the strategies they use to do so fuel their works in ways that have remained unacknowledged.

The first of these undesirable affordances of literary preaching is the reification of clerical ideology. With the phrase clerical ideology, I want to denote a way of seeing, knowing, and behaving that construes the preacher as the singular paradigm of moral authority in US culture. Paradoxically, the preacherly voice that calls auditors to new considerations of justice or reexaminations of the meanings of democracy often does so effectively because they speak in an established mode of hierarchical authority. Alternative modes or idioms of literary authority have been difficult to establish in US literature, precisely because the frequent inclusion of literary preaching sustains an ideology in which the sermon or religious address is vested with enormous symbolic power. No straightforward cultural coup occurs in the aftermath of the explosion of literary preaching in the antebellum period. Instead, these engagements promote a massive reification of clerical ideology. Thus, this affordance contributes significantly to the portability of the form across historical periods.

Consider again Father Mapple's sermon and Melville's engagement with literary preaching in *Moby-Dick*. Does Melville's coded antislavery message outweigh the manner in which this scene of literary preaching seems to centralize authority in the figure of the preacher? Has Melville's ascent to the pulpit not, in fact, strengthened the preacher's authority and weakened any bid for a more egalitarian ethos? What are the stakes of such a reification of clerical ideology for the authority of literature or the artist themselves? These questions about the moral authority of literature vis-à-vis preaching haunt authors. Henry David Thoreau speaks for generations as he writes bitterly about the "almost despotic" power of preachers (qtd. in Kevorkian 13). This affordance suggests the intensity of that despotism. Melville clearly understood this problematic affordance of literary preaching, and *Moby-Dick* reveals that it troubled him deeply. He highlights this dilemma—literary preaching's contradictory affordances of moral authority and reification of clerical ideology—in the novel's subsequent scene of literary preaching. The next preacher to appear in *Moby-Dick* is none other than Captain Ahab, who turns the multipurpose quarterdeck into his church and shows that he too knows how to preach (and deliver the sacraments!). Ahab's impassioned sermon converts the entire crew, save Starbuck, to his will. Commenting on this scene of mass conversion, Ann Douglas observes, "Ahab is probably the greatest orator, the finest preacher in American literature" (306). Powerful preaching, it would appear, is a tool that can both liberate and subjugate.

Finally, literary preaching affords a complex identification of the author with the figure of the preacher, an identification with serious consequences for the construction of vocational identity. Throughout this study, I argue that authors often aim to construct their vocational identities through their complex engagements with literary preaching. In order to clarify the way engagements with literary preaching participate in this complex construction of authorial identity, I want to suggest a parallel between this construction of vocational identity and a larger construction of national identity that Philip Deloria describes in *Playing Indian* (1998). In his magisterial study, Deloria argues that from the colonial period through the present Euro-Americans construct national identity through invoking variously attractive and repellent images of Native Americans and thus "setting up a 'have-the-cake-and-eat-it-too' dialectic of simultaneous desire and repulsion" (3).[5]

While US writers from the mid-nineteenth century until now participate in this larger project of developing a national identity, they also participate in a parallel project of establishing a vocational identity. This latter attempt proved to be as fraught as the first. What sort of cultural figure was a writer, especially a US writer of fiction and poetry? In order to address this vocational identity crisis, authors often resorted to a mode of identity construction that bears considerable similarity to the dialectic that Deloria describes so effectively. Instead of invoking the variously attractive and repulsive Native other, these authors invoked the variously respected and scorned figure of the preacher. Preachers served US writers as oppositional figures because their power in US culture often seemed deeply opposed to the desires of writers to establish themselves in positions of moral authority.[6] Additionally, in American literature preachers often appear as figures who provide theological defense for injustice along the lines of race, class, and gender. The texts I examine in *Resistance and the Sermon in American Literature* pulse with a desire to supplant the preacher and define the author as a unique figure of moral authority, a sort of surrogate preacher who refuses to buttress dominant ideology. At the same time, the preacher also serves as a figure of intense desire due primarily to their verbal artistry, extralegal authority, and, at times, fearlessness commitment to proclaiming unpopular and countercultural truths. When we examine engagements with literary preaching, we can see writers anxiously negotiating this interstitial space between repulsion and desire. Yet because this dialect refuses to resolve, because the preacher remains both desirable and repulsive, this affordance contributes significantly to

---

[5] Deloria observes that on the one hand "savage Indians served Americans as oppositional figures against whom one might image a civilized national Self" (3). This constructed image of the Savage Indian functions as an imaginary other against whom Euro-Americans define themselves as civilized. Yet this process of constructing a national identity in relation to the native other becomes infinitely more complex than this simple relation suggests because Deloria also shows that Euro-Americans simultaneously idealized Native American identity as emblematic of uniquely American freedom: "Coded as freedom, however, wild Indianness proved equally attractive, setting up a 'have-the-cake-and-eat-it-too' dialectic of simultaneous desire and repulsion" (3). Americans have sought to answer a national identity crisis through negotiating, often ambiguously, the tension inherent in this dialectic. What Deloria so convincingly displays is the manner in which the Native American other—more an imaginary construct than any flesh-and-blood human—functions simultaneously as a figure of desire and repulsion.

[6] For a useful analysis of writers casting the figure of the preacher as an oppositional figure, see Martin Kevorkian, *Writing Beyond Prophecy: Emerson, Hawthorne, and Melville after the American Renaissance* (Louisiana State UP: 2013).

the portability of the form. When authors take up the form of literary preaching, they take up an unresolved dialectic.

Taken together, these five affordances—extralegal moral authority, sensual performativity, access to literary heritage, reification of clerical ideology, and a vocational dialectic—disclose literary preaching's contradictory nature. When we examine the cultural work of literary preaching from a long historical perspective, we see not only the potency of this form for addressing specific crises but also an enduring pattern of both enablement and entrapment that US authors often perceive as a nettlesome paradox. Attending to the seemingly obsessive recurrence of the sermon in these texts allows us to hear a previously untold story of US literature tethered to a form that it often desires to overthrow yet, paradoxically, continues to embrace. *Resistance and the Sermon in American Literature* begins to tell this story. We may have good reason to be skeptical of Ishmael's claims about preaching's world-steering power. But from Melville's era to our own, US writers seem to insist that we should not entirely ignore preaching or its contradictory potentialities as a literary form. They certainly have not.

1

"There Will Soon Be No More Priests": Surrogate Preachers in Emerson and Whitman

On a balmy summer evening in 1838, Ralph Waldo Emerson addressed an intimate group of friends, family, and professors that had gathered to celebrate Harvard Divinity School's graduating class. Of the seven men who graduated that summer, only six were in attendance. In his controversial Divinity School Address, which he later described to Thomas Carlyle as "a kind of sermon," Emerson publicly acknowledges his doubt that the church's shortcomings could be easily corrected (*Correspondence* 174). "I confess," Emerson admits, "all attempts to project and establish a Cultus with new rites and forms, seem to me vain. Faith makes us, and not we it, and faith makes its own forms" ("Address" 92). Rather than attempt to establish new rites and forms to rehabilitate American religious culture, Emerson challenges the graduates to "let the breath of new life be breathed by you through the forms already existing" (92). In particular, he celebrates "the institution of preaching,—the speech of man to men,—essentially the most flexible of all organs, of all forms" (93). In Emerson's analysis, preaching, a flexible and privileged form, affords the expression of "the very truth, as your life and conscience teach it" (93). The proclamation of such truth, Emerson suggests, emboldens humanity with "new hope and new revelation" (93). At the address's conclusion, Emerson provocatively imagines preaching being freed from the traditional confines of the pulpit and breaking out "in lecture-rooms, in houses, in fields" (93). Yet even as he brought his controversial "kind of sermon" to a close, Emerson was far from done reimagining the form. In the years ahead—under Emerson's considerable sway—preaching would also break out in US literary productions and establish itself as one of American literature's most potent and problematic forms.

This chapter unfolds in two interlocking sections. It opens by tracing the development of Emerson's reimagination of preaching. Unlike the other authors examined in this study, Emerson does not write poetry or novels that evoke the sermon. And though his essays and lectures incessantly allude to scripture and pulse with the sermonic voice, I focus here on Emerson's foundational efforts to adapt the sermon to new literary and cultural contexts. Emerson's journals and essays make clear the evolution of his understanding of the imbrications of preaching, poetry, and language that eventually led him, in 1844, to call for the poet to replace the preacher in the American cultural imaginary. When Walt Whitman heard Emerson's revolutionary call, he responded powerfully. In the chapter's second section, I examine Whitman's embrace of literary preaching as he penned *Leaves of Grass*, his "evangel-poem of comrades" (*LG* 1860: 11). Yet, as Whitman clearly understood, his literary preaching afforded the reification of clerical authority and, thus, resisted his intensely democratic project. Whitman frequently attempted to ameliorate the hierarchal dilemma created by his embrace of the poet-as-preacher, and the frequency of his attempts to address this problem suggests that Whitman regarded this as an abiding tension in *Leaves of Grass*. Emerson's and Whitman's attempts to replace the preacher with the author—more particularly, the poet—helped inaugurate an intricate and protracted struggle for cultural authority and clarified the key maneuvers through which subsequent writers' engagements with literary preaching would evolve.

Emerson and the Poet as Surrogate Preacher

On September 11, 1832, Emerson submitted his letter of resignation to Boston's Second Church. His break with formal Christianity had been brewing since at least 1829, and the controversy over the celebration of the Lord's Supper was a symptom of a more comprehensive dissatisfaction with Protestantism and its rituals (Richardson 125). After leaving the ministry, Emerson would devote himself to promoting what, in a journal entry on April 7, 1840, he referred to as the "one doctrine" that united all his lectures, "the infinitude of the private man" (*JMN* 7: 342). This doctrine of Self-Reliance, so central to Emerson's expansive vision, defies any easy definition because it blurs distinctions between a variety of discourses. The keynote of Emerson's thought "interweaves disparate strands of religious, philosophical, aesthetic, and political thought" including radical Protestantism's insistence on the communion of the individual believer with God, international romanticism's celebration of the creative imagination, Goethe's "cosmopolitan" sense of a "plastic" self, and republican-democratic political theory's assertion of all people's essential equality (Buell, *Emerson*: 60–3). Lawrence Buell helpfully describes Emerson's multivalent message as, above all, a "personal life practice" that provides a "corrective therapy" for conformists (63). This practice involved jettisoning secondhand faiths and cultural orthodoxies—especially those associated with institutional religions, the political status quo, and deference to European tradition—and committing one's allegiance to the promptings the soul. Emerson practiced what he would later preach, turned away from the faith of his fathers, and resigned from his post as the minister of Boston's Second Church to develop and promote this new, far-reaching doctrine.

Emerson's resignation from the pulpit, however, was hardly definitive. After he resigned, Emerson remained a supply preacher until 1839. Between his famous "The Lord's Supper" sermon, delivered September 9, 1832, and his final sermon on January 20, 1839, he preached on 183 Sundays, often delivering both the morning and evening sermons.[1] Though he no longer occupied the pulpit of the Second Church of Boston, his journal entries from these formative years reveal that the sermon remained central in his thought as he struggled to harness the form's power while simultaneously liberating it from traditional religious contexts.

Emerson's journal entries from the winter of 1834–5 reveal a particularly intense reflection on the sermon. Ideas that receive extended analysis in both the Divinity School Address and "The Poet," the central essays for tracing Emerson's eventual celebration of literary preaching, appear in these entries in embryonic form. In an entry from Sunday, December 28, 1834, Emerson reveals his abiding interest in preaching by venting his disgust at contemporary pulpit oratory. "If I were called upon to charge a young minister," Emerson writes, "I would say Beware of Tradition: Tradition which embarrasses life and falsifies all teaching. The sermons that I hear are all dead of that ail. The preacher is betrayed by his ear" (*Journals* 3: 420). As he often does in his journals, Emerson rapidly shifts focus in these aphoristic lines, shuttling attention from the problem of the preacher's teaching to the prior and more insidious problem of the preacher's reception of other voices. As the final sentence suggests, the tradition that threatens the preacher is, curiously, not a theological abstraction or article of faith but rather an inherited storehouse of shopworn religious idioms that strip him of

---

[1] In *The Complete Sermons of Ralph Waldo Emerson*, v. 4 (U of Missouri P: 1993), Wesley T. Mott provides a table that documents the dates and locations of Emerson's sermons during this period, see 6–19.

oratorical power. The witty provocation, "The preacher is betrayed by his ear," both telegraphs Emerson's diagnoses *and* models the linguistic inventiveness he counsels. With the line, he cleverly adapts the Biblical accusation, "Thy speech betrayeth thee" (The Holy Bible, Mt. 26:73), which is leveraged at the apostle Peter when he denies knowing Jesus, and, instead, suggests that the preacher's original act of self-betrayal depends on passive reception.

In Emerson's formulation, the occupation of the preacher's consciousness by a traditional religious vocabulary sets a trap that the preacher cannot easily avoid. Emerson's absorption of Romantic aesthetic theory informs his conception of this problem. The moral-aesthetic error of disclaiming one's original creative power leads inexorably to the religious errors that Emerson believes haunt the culture. For Emerson, these types of error are two sides of the same coin. The aesthetic error ensures the religious error. The religious error propagates an ideology that makes avoiding what Emerson might describe as "aesthetic sins" highly unlikely. Emerson discusses the mechanics of this self-betrayal with remarkable sympathy: "[The preacher] begins to inveigh against some real evil, and falls unconsciously into formulas of speech which have been said and sung in the church some ages and have lost all life. They never had any but when freshly and with special conviction applied" (*Journals* 3: 420). The unconscious "fall" into moribund "formulas of speech" blocks the preacher's best efforts to address "real evil." This "fall" recapitulates the fall from an Edenic state of grace but with a difference. Both self-destructive acts lead to the loss of life and original energy. But, in this entry, Emerson rewrites damnation not as a dramatic instant but as the forfeiture of one's own office through quotidian, imperceptible acts of self-betrayal. The preacher unconsciously falls into a discourse that forecloses his ability to perform the sine qua non of his profession—to speak with power. At the end of his lengthy journal entry on December 28, 1834, Emerson observes, "I am prolix on this instance, yet the fault is obvious to a discerning ear in almost every sentence of the prayers and sermons that are ordinarily heard in the church" (421).

Despite the entry's reproachful tone, Emerson closes it with a brief celebration of an exception that proves the rule and reveals the seeds of his emerging vision of literary preaching. He notes that this nearly ubiquitous error does *not* appear in the sermons of Father Edward Taylor, "that living Methodist, the Poet of the church" (421). Here, Emerson's loaded use of the word "poet" measures his positive regard for Taylor's heady style and responsiveness to the promptings of intuition. Saundra Morris observes that, like other Romantics, Emerson "valued poetry above every genre of writing," but astutely adds that Emerson operated with an expansive definition of the poet: "By *poet*, Emerson does not mean exclusively a writer of verse, but instead one whose energy is simultaneously iconoclastic and affirmative, devoted to justice, enthusiastically generative, and intuitive rather than cognitive" (75). Morris's analysis helps explain the odd fact that Emerson referred to Taylor as one of "the two great poets of America" (Richardson 96). If traditional preaching is synonymous with a performance of stale idioms, perhaps the antidote to culture's ills depends on preachers like Taylor, artists who offer sermons so characterized by verbal inventiveness and responsiveness to intuition that they could rightly be called, in Emerson's terms, "poetry."

Emerson's December 28, 1834, journal entry, the first of Emerson's several entries that reference Edward Taylor, illuminates Emerson's developing thought about the imbrications of ministerial authority, eloquence, and poetics. Taylor was a "shouting Methodist" and the pastor of Seaman's Bethel in Boston's North End. Theologically, Emerson's attraction to the evangelical Taylor seems unlikely. His imaginative preaching, however, attracted numerous literary figures of the mid-nineteenth century, including Charles Dickens, Harriet Martineau, Jenny Lind, Herman Melville, and Walt Whitman (Coleman 141; Reynolds, *Beneath*: 25). As I discuss below, Taylor's preaching influenced Whitman's poetics, and Taylor also served as the model for Melville's Father Mapple. Some literary figures expressed concern that attention would negatively affect Father Taylor, but Emerson insisted that Taylor remained impervious to the threats such celebrity might present. Taylor's elite visitors "never made him," Emerson boasted, "and such as they cannot unmake him" (*Journals* 3: 431). After his father's death, Edward Emerson found among his papers a manuscript entitled "Improvisation – Rev. Edward Taylor," portions of which appear to have been incorporated into both "The Poet" and "Eloquence" ("Father Taylor" 177). The manuscript's title highlights what Emerson regards as most significant about Taylor's preaching—the improvisational, almost fragmentary, quality of his sermons. With his meditations on Taylor, Emerson explores the authority of a performance artist whose power depends on a bold embrace of an evanescent aesthetic.

Emerson's attempt to draw broader implications regarding cultural authority from Father Taylor's sermonic practice comes into clear focus in a journal entry from January 6, 1835. Emerson composes the adulatory entry on a Tuesday, two days after hearing Taylor preach. Significantly, he notes that he decided to go hear Taylor preach *during* a church service one week earlier, presumably the church service that led to the critical entry on December 28, 1834. I wish to draw attention to two key features of this entry. First, and most predictably, Emerson focuses his entry on Taylor's powerful use of language. He describes Taylor as occupying "the opposite pole, say rather in another Zone" from an unnamed preacher whose "method and manner had much the style of a problem of geometry" (*Journals* 3: 430). Taylor eschews conventional language in his pulpit performance for he is "guided by instincts diviner than rules" (431). With obvious enthusiasm, Emerson quotes Taylor's prayer that "every deck ... be stamped by the hallowed feet of godly captains" and his description of the sailors as God's "servants of the brine" (431). Emerson remarks that "this poet of the sailor" spoke in order to "fus[e] all the rude hearts of his auditory with the heat of his own love, and mak[e] the abstractions of philosophers accessible and effectual to them also" (431). Emerson's entry clearly marks Taylor as a figure of vocational emulation, a religious orator and performance artist of the highest order.

Emerson's journal entry on Taylor, however, does more than simply praise his use of language. Emerson also attempts to define the economy through which Taylor's preaching affects his auditors. After comparing Taylor to Demosthenes, Shakespeare, and Robert Burns, Emerson, fantasizing about the possibilities of his own eloquence, writes

> his whole discourse is a string of audacious felicities harmonized by a spirit of joyful love. Everybody is cheered and exalted by him. He is a living man and explains at once what Whitefield and Fox and Father Moody were to their audiences, by the total infusion of his own soul into his assembly, and consequent absolute dominion over them. How puny, how cowardly, other preachers look by the side of this preaching! He shows us what a man can do. (431–2)

Taylor's eloquence, Emerson senses, dissolves the psychological boundaries that separate the audience members from the speaker and each other. Twice Emerson uses some variant of the word "fusion" to describe the result of Taylor's genre-bending oration. Yet Emerson's description of this fusion remains profoundly— and paradoxically—hierarchical. Harmonious fusion and hierarchical dominion impossibly coexist in the sermonic circuit. In one breath, he argues that Taylor's preaching exalts and joins together all who hear him. In the next breath, however, he notes that the sermon results in Taylor's "absolute dominion" over his auditors (432). Perhaps surprisingly, Emerson celebrates the process whereby Taylor's externalization of power returns to him as massively reified authority. In fact, the dynamic Emerson describes in this passage establishes Taylor as a heroic figure who provides a living example to all would-be artists and public speakers, including Emerson himself, of what "a man can do" (432).

In his next two journal entries, Emerson considers historical analogues to Taylor's preaching. As he meditates on Taylor, he attempts to theorize the relationship between the form and content of efforts to reform culture through language. In a passage that contains the seeds of both his address to the Divinity School and his oft-cited conclusion to "The Poet," Emerson describes the new teacher he seeks:

> The Teacher that I look for and await shall enunciate with more precision and universality, with piercing poetic insight those beautiful yet severe compensations that give to moral nature an aspect of mathematical science. He will not occupy himself in laboriously reanimating a historical religion, but in bringing men to God by showing them that he is, not was, and speaks, not spoke. (434)[2]

The final sentence suggests that eloquence dramatizes the truth of the new formation that will replace historical religion. By virtue of their eloquence, the new teacher reveals that the divine still speaks, that the universal soul remains accessible in mid-nineteenth century America. Form confirms content and confers authority.

These concentrated journal entries record a problem that galvanized Emerson's thought in the years ahead: how the sermon, at its poetic best, might be translated into an alternative cultural form that evades the stultifying dogmatism associated with traditional religious practice. Emerson adapted his journaling practice in the mid-1830s to welcome and record ideas and insights in their most incipient forms (Richardson 201). For this reason, Emerson's journals during this era offer many fleeting notations and observations. The ideas recorded in the winter of 1834–5 about preaching, eloquence, and poetry, however, were hardly fleeting. When Harvard's graduating divinity students, a group of seven, invited Emerson to speak at their graduation, Emerson returned to his journals to prepare his remarks. He found a storehouse of material. It was an address that he had, in many respects, been drafting for years.

The heavy signposting Emerson employs in the Divinity School Address underscores his principle doctrinal critiques of Unitarianism, but it does so at the risk of obscuring his significant concerns with issues of language, creativity, and power. In the address, Emerson flags two crucial "defects" of what he refers to throughout the address as "historical Christianity." "Historical Christianity" functions as Emerson's shorthand for denominations adhering to a revealed

---

[2] This line gets cannibalized in the future. In the Divinity School Address, the second sentence appears, after getting dressed up in a bit of King James English, as, "It is the office of a true teacher to show us that God is, not was; that He speaketh, not spake" (90). In "The Poet," the first formulation gets rewritten as "I look in vain for the Poet whom I describe … Time and nature yield us many gifts, but not yet the timely man, the new religion, the reconciler, whom all things await" (204).

religion that understood miracles as proofs of Jesus's divinity and ascribed a personality to the divine (Robinson, *Apostle*: 125). First, Emerson argues that historical Christianity "dwells, with noxious exaggeration about the *person of Jesus*" rather than embracing "the doctrine of the soul" ("Address" 83). By "doctrine of the soul," Emerson means the idea that individuals could, without the aid of external tradition, perceive spiritual truth through intuition and a proper reading of the natural world. The divine spirit that flows through the universe, including individual humans, Emerson suggested, remained available to all, continually providing revelation, moral guidance, and creative energy. Historical Christianity's second defect follows naturally from the first. Historical Christianity misunderstands Jesus's apprehension of what, Emerson argues, is true for all humans—the divinity and "greatness of man" (83), and, as a result, "the Moral Nature, that Law of laws whose revelations introduce greatness—yea, God himself—into the open soul, is not explored as the fountain of the established teaching in society" (85).

Though Emerson outlines his doctrinal disagreements with historical Christianity, he also gives voice to his longstanding grievance with Christianity's formalized idioms and forms of public expression. Emerson insists that an inescapable calcification of language contributes to a veneration of the person of Jesus that is both narrow and deleterious: "The manner in which his name is surrounded with expressions, which were once sallies of admiration and love, but are now petrified into official titles, kills all generous sympathy and liking" (84). Here, Emerson articulates, in an alternative form, his conviction, expressed in "Self-Reliance," that "power ceases in the instant of repose; it resides in the moment of transition from a past to a new state, in the shooting of the gulf, in the darting to an aim" (105). Emerson contrasts the original expressions he refers to as "sallies of admiration" with "petrified" utterances that kill "all generous sympathy" ("Address" 84). Crucially, however, the very "petrified … official titles" evolve out of what were, for a sacred moment, piercing religious utterances. The "sally"—"a sprightly or audacious utterance or literary composition" ("Sally," n.1)—is a "petrified title" in the making. For further evidence, Emerson appeals to what he takes to be the common experience of his auditors: "All who hear me, feel that the language that describes Christ to Europe and America is not the style of friendship and enthusiasm to a good and noble heart, but is appropriated and formal,—paints a demigod, as the Orientals or the Greeks would describe Osiris or Apollo" ("Address" 84). The passage underscores a moribund religious vocabulary as the catalyzing agent in this process. Indeed, the tragic history of Christianity that Emerson offers is a history of soul-denying aesthetic cowardice coupled with formalized language.

Emerson's remedy to this debased cultural situation logically follows his diagnosis: preachers must make a bold return to inspired poetic utterance. Such preaching would reveal the creative presence of what Emerson variously refers to as the soul, spirit, or reason. Emerson suggests that the graduates should take Jesus as their model for preaching. Throughout the address, Emerson describes Jesus's most religiously significant utterances as poetry, as aphoristic sermons. Both Jesus's own and subsequent generations received his words from his "poet's lips," Emerson asserts, and rapidly converted them into dogma: "The idioms of his language and the figures of his rhetoric have usurped the place of his truth; and churches are not built on his principles, but on his tropes" (83). Predictably, Emerson extends this discussion of usurpation to diagnose the waning power of the Unitarian pulpit. The pulpit, Emerson argues, is often "usurped by a formalist" (86). Thus, when Emerson charges each of the graduates to speak as "a newborn bard of the Holy Ghost" (91), he imagines this as a return to proper religious oratory, a reversal of a longstanding coup. Here, the preacher-as-poet replaces the preacher-as-formalist, and in so doing reclaims the proper mode of declamation and offers "new hope and new revelation" (93). Emerson remains coy about the precise nature of the "new hope and new revelation" he imagines these graduates offering, and it is not merely better preaching but a more wholesale revision of American culture that he has in mind. Emerson is not considering an improved institution. He is not imagining an institution at all. He imagines a life practice that is genuinely "new" and will reshape every area of human conduct. And, crucially, the novelty of Emerson's vision depends every bit as much on his celebration of humanity's latent aesthetic power as it does on his theological claims about the soul, the divine, or Jesus's most important message.[3]

This reading of the Divinity School Address helps clarify the meaning of the strange celebration of "the institution of preaching" with which it concludes. Emerson's celebration of bardic preaching has the dual function of embracing

---

[3] Emerson understood his vision to be both "new" and ancient. His reading of religious texts and biographies confirmed his sense that he was teaching an aesthetic-religious doctrine that was attested throughout human history but often hidden beneath the accretions of institutionalized religion. Emerson frequently uses the word "God" interchangeably with "soul," "spirit," and "reason" throughout many of his essays, at times capitalizing these nouns, aiming to shift the meanings of the word "God" away from its associations in monotheistic faiths. In the Divinity School Address, for example, Emerson takes specific aim at historical religions, especially Christianity, that consider the divine as a transcendent personality. "Emerson's god," Buell writes, "is an immanent god, an indwelling property of human personhood and physical nature, not located in some otherworldly realm" (*Emerson* 162). For an especially useful analysis of Emerson's complex and evolving religious sensibility that emphasizes his interest in Indian scriptures, see Lawrence Buell, *Emerson* (The Belknap Press of Harvard UP: 2003), 158–98.

the longstanding authority associated with the pulpit in American culture *and* refiguring that authority as the authority of the poet to generate new insights—religious, political, and philosophical. No longer the cold, petrified language of the formalist, the sermon, as Emerson reimagines it, becomes "the most flexible of all organs" (93). The formalized speech becomes a sally. The sermon becomes a poem. And though Emerson remains interested in the spatial dimension of this authority—how the pulpit, as a particular symbolic space, gathers to itself a willing audience (87)—he also imagines the possibility of the preacher-as-poet leaving the pulpit and circulating through "lecture-rooms," "houses," and "fields" (93). The Divinity School Address registers a crucial moment in which Emerson attempts to transpose the authority of the sermon into a broader model of literary influence.

In his 1844 essay "The Poet," Emerson extends this discussion and argues for the recognition of the poet as the proper replacement for the preacher. The poet, Emerson avers, should be the new cultural authority from whom individuals and society expect liberation and guidance. In the Divinity School Address Emerson argues for the preacher-as-poet, the sermon-as-poem. In "The Poet" he shifts his emphasis to call for the poet-as-preacher, the poem-as-sermon. In the essay, Emerson enunciates the nature and purpose of poetry along the lines of Romantic expressionism. More important, however, Emerson establishes and demarcates a privileged cultural space for the poet. In this regard, the essay is more generative than descriptive. It concerns, centrally, questions of authority. In his affirmation of the poet as a figure of cultural authority, Emerson writes his own high regard for the genre of poetry—exemplified by his penchant for frequently citing "a certain poet" in his own essays—on a national scale. "He is the true and only doctor," Emerson asserts, "he knows and tells; he is the only teller of news" ("The Poet" 190). Society, Emerson claims, waits for new poets to contribute their insights to the commonwealth: "The poet has a new thought; he has a whole new experience to unfold; he will tell us how it was with him, and all men will be the richer in his fortune. For the experience of each new age requires a new confession, and the world seems always waiting for its poet" (190–1).

Throughout the essay, Emerson oscillates between a capacious and a genre-specific definition of the poet, but his tendency is to privilege the latter. As I noted earlier, Emerson often uses the word "poet" in an expansive manner to describe the orator, artist, or writer who prizes Reason over Understanding, fresh insight over stale formula. In "The Poet," however, the American bard that Emerson seeks, in fact, writes verse. Emerson identifies Homer, Milton, and Dante as key models because they fully embraced the material and historical circumstances of their cultures. After arguing that "the barbarism and materialism of the times" are a "carnival of the gods," Emerson writes that America "will not wait long for meters" (204). The poet Emerson calls for in this essay represents an evolution of the preacher that he celebrates in the Divinity School Address because the poet offers a "new religion" and "new confession" (204, 191).

The poet rightly serves as the culture's moral authority for two reasons. The first reason may be called the spiritual therapy of poetry. Reprising themes he develops throughout *Nature* (1836), Emerson argues that the poet functions as a healer: "For as it is dislocation and detachment from the life of God that makes things ugly, the poet, who re-attaches things to nature and the Whole,—reattaching even artificial things, and violation of nature, to nature, by a deeper insight,—disposes very easily of the most disagreeable facts" ("The Poet" 195). The poet retains and nourishes an attachment to Spirit and honors their own Reason. Thus, they, like a modern preacher, can provide others with a healing word, a clarifying vision, and a summons to reclaim the divinity or Spirit that comprises humanity's essential nature.[4] Additionally, poetic genius enables the reclamation of not only persons but also nonhuman things. As Branka Arsić notes, Emerson's ideal poet "perceives the truth in what others discard as forgettable … and picks up what was thrown away … [he] saves things from desertion" (80). The poet's unique ability to turn "the world to glass" and reveal "all things in their right series and procession" ("The Poet" 196) makes them the key figure for spiritual renewal, and Emerson refers to the poets as "liberating gods" who fill their audience with "emancipation and exhilaration" (200). In these lines, Emerson rewrites Plato's allegory of the cave to suggest that after undergoing the spiritual therapy offered by the poet, all who hear their messages can emerge "out of a cave or cellar into the open air" and see the world and their place in it rightly (200).

---

[4] For a more developed account of Emerson's vision of poetry as spiritually restorative, see David M. Robinson, "Poetry, Poetic Perception, and Emerson," in *Shaping Belief: Culture, Politics, and Religion in Nineteenth-Century Writing* (Liverpool UP: 2008) and Branka Arsić, *On Leaving: A Reading in Emerson* (Harvard UP: 2010), 80–1. Robinson offers a particularly useful discussion of the restorative effects of poetry in Emerson's *Nature*:

> In this moment of mystical transport [the 'transparent eye-ball' scene] Emerson offers witness to his experience of a profound merger with the infinite, providing a tangible point of reference for the later proclamations of the Orphic Poet. What the poet enunciates as a lost estate and an aspiration for the future, Emerson's earlier persona has in fact already achieved, though briefly, in the 'transparent eye-ball' experience. The Orphic Poet reanimates this possibility, making it clear that it is through the work of poetry and imaginative expression that 'the redemption of the soul' must be pursued." (96)

The second reason the poet occupies the key position of moral authority in Emerson's thought relates to the first and dovetails with his sense of the poet as a surrogate preacher. The poet's ability to offer alternative perceptions of the world enables the poet to perform significant cultural and political work. Put differently, Emerson imagines the poet as a figure whose words, like modern sermons, liberate societies as well as individuals. The poet disrupts settled habits of seeing. This prophetic unsettlement creates space for progressive reforms and enables resistance to modes of oppression that have been naturalized through custom and precedent. David M. Robinson observes that

> Emerson's deepening involvement in reform politics and antislavery work in the 1840s and 1850s seems at first divorced from his engagement with poetry, poetry translation and poetic theory during the same period, as if he is being drawn in two quite opposite directions. But these apparently disparate commitments were for Emerson actually complementary activities, pragmatic responses to the ethical challenges of modern society. The activist, like the poet, convinced others to see beyond the apparent and resist in the name of principle the pressures of immediacy and expediency. Such resistance entailed deeper thinking and a longer view of social progress. ("Poetry" 109)

Robinson's invaluable assessment compels us to see connections between the fact that 1844 marked the publication of "The Poet" and Emerson's impassioned—and long overdue—"An Address . . . on . . . the Emancipation of the Negroes in the West British Indies."

If Robinson's discussion of the complementary nature of poetry and activism in Emerson's vision is accurate, as I believe it is, Emerson's litany of poetic topoi at the end of "The Poet" appears potentially politically explosive. In an oft-quoted passage, Emerson calls for a poet daring enough to address America's times and circumstances. In particular Emerson notes, "Our logrolling, our stumps and their politics, our fisheries, our Negroes and Indians, our boasts and our repudiations, the wrath of rogues and the pusillanimity of honest men, the northern trade, the southern planting, the western clearing, Oregon and Texas, are yet unsung" ("The Poet" 204). These topics are not mere fodder for the aesthetic idealist. These notations of loosely joined pairs of "stumps and their politics," "Negroes and Indians," "the wrath of rogues and the pusillanimity of honest men," and "Oregon and Texas" all suggest the poet's imaginative engagement with the sociopolitical problems and ethical failures of mid-nineteenth century America. Ostensibly, the poet will address these issues in a new manner and with moral clarity. By doing so, they will break the imaginative gridlock that haunts contemporary American society.

In the Divinity School Address, Emerson refers to the office of ordained ministry as "the first in the world" (86). But by the publication of "The Poet," he changes tack and identifies "the birth of a poet" as "the principal event in chronology" (191). It is the poet, not the preacher, whom Emerson identifies as the long-awaited teacher of the masses: "Man, never so often deceived, still watches for the arrival of a brother who can hold him steady to a truth until he has made it his own" (191). Emerson's "The Poet" presses for what we might refer to as authorial surrogation, the replacement of the preacher with the poet. Emerson's hypostatization of the poet-as-preacher parallels to his own transition from preacher to public intellectual. It also responds to what he saw among the audiences for his lyceum lectures—people generally disaffected with Protestant religious traditions and interested in belles-lettres (D. Robinson, *Apostle*: 72). In "The Poet," Emerson attempts to summon a literary figure who might replace the preacher while retaining the desirable affordances of literary preaching— the moral authority necessary for prophetic unsettlement and the semiotic force of the sermon. When Whitman heard Emerson's summons, he was more than ready to respond.

"The Priest Departs, the Divine Literatus Comes": The Literary Preaching of Walt Whitman

View'd, to-day, from a point of view sufficiently over-arching, the problem of humanity all over the civilized world is social and religious, and is to be finally met and treated by literature. The priest departs, the divine literatus comes.
Walt Whitman, *Democratic Vistas*, 1871

I too, following many, and followed by many, inau-
    gurate a Religion—I too go to the wars,
It may be I am destined to utter the loudest cries
    thereof, the conqueror's shouts,
They may rise from me yet, and soar above every
    thing.
Walt Whitman, *Leaves of Grass*, 1860

No major literary figure in the antebellum period more fully embraced Emerson's claim that the poet would function as the surrogate preacher than

Walt Whitman. Almost as soon as he begins the Preface to the 1855 edition of *Leaves of Grass*, Whitman activates the sermonic voice, issuing commandments, encouraging regular readings of his new religious text, and promising conversion. And in the opening line of "Song of Myself," he boldly assumes the office of the minister and announces a new Eucharist in which he "celebrate[s]" himself, a common American, and encourages his followers to do the same (*LG* 1855: 13). In an oft-quoted *Atlantic Monthly* article published in 1902, Whitman describes his reception of Emerson by saying, "I was simmering, simmering, simmering; Emerson brought me to a boil" (Trowbridge 166). This fact has led to a deeply entrenched narrative that traces Emerson's influence on Whitman to the key lines at the end of "The Poet" wherein Emerson calls for a poet who will view antebellum America with a "tyrannous eye," see "in the barbarism and materialism of the times, another carnival of the same gods whose picture he so much admires in Homer," and write a national epic incorporating the nation's "incomparable materials" (204). This theory of reception links Whitman and Emerson primarily through their shared investments in literary nationalism. But this narrative only tells a partial story of Emerson's influence on Whitman. It is accurate but incomplete.

When Emerson sowed his vision of the poet-as-preacher, he found fertile soil in Whitman. Whitman's unpublished manuscripts, historical sketches, and journals suggest that Whitman's "simmering" should be understood, at least partially, as a longing to possess something like the power that antebellum preachers wielded as they reshaped American culture through their oratory. Whitman thrilled at the idea of aligning himself with Emerson, via their shared appreciation of the sermon, and fulfilling his call for "the timely man, the new religion, the reconciler, whom all things await" ("The Poet" 204). The first edition of *Leaves of Grass* not only celebrated the discovery of new subjects for a national literature—the possibilities of democracy, the ample geography of the United States, and America en masse—but also announced an ecumenical, anti-institutional, and anticlerical structure of belief that Whitman understood as the fitting religious framework for a modern, democratic nation (Kuebrich, "Religion": 197). Casting himself as one of the peripatetic "newborn bard[s]" for whom Emerson called, Whitman set out to convert America and to breathe new life into its intertwined social, aesthetic, and religious imagination (Emerson, "Address": 91).

From his earliest years as a newspaper reporter, Whitman longed for an American religious culture appropriate for the nation and sensed that American Protestantism was at odds with the nation's democratic ideals.

Protestant churches' largely uncritical embrace of capitalism, pursuit of ever-more elaborate properties, and willingness to uphold class-based distinctions troubled him deeply (D. Reynolds, *Whitman's America*: 237–8). In unpublished manuscripts, Whitman excoriated America's religious culture and bemoaned the spiritual malaise it spawned: "I say that to-day the mummery of the churches in which none believes but all agree to countenance, with secret sarcasm and denial in their hearts, is what stands most in the way of a real athletic and fit religion for these States" (*NUPM* 6: 2061). Yet as the sentence's final words indicate, Whitman does not limit his task to criticizing what he saw as feudalistic, antidemocratic religious forms. He also embraces the task of promoting a "real athletic and fit" religion. The bizarre adjectives defamiliarize the noun, making what initially seems conventional suddenly curious. The arresting phrase indicates Whitman's desire to inaugurate a religious ethos that prizes both body and soul, absorbs emerging scientific insights, and "fits" America's unique political circumstances. To promote this vision and unite a country rife with division, Whitman wrote a sprawling poem and self-published it, believing wholeheartedly that, if it was read properly, it could save America and affirm democracy.

Whitman's oddly messianic expectations for *Leaves of Grass* become significantly more intelligible if we identify it as a textual production with intentional affinities to the nineteenth-century sermon. At first glance, Whitman's ambition to write poetry that would unite a nation on the verge of civil war seems embarrassingly naïve. As John Marsh humorously puts it, "If you think about it for any period of time at all, Whitman's argument seems absurd. The spectacle of American democracy, then and now, is appalling, and the cure for this spectacle is … poetry? Why not juggling? Or baking? Or line dancing? At least Americans like those things" (202). If, however, Whitman's poetic imagination draws on contemporary religious culture and the populist sermonic form, his sense that his poetry could profoundly impact culture seems much more comprehensible. When Whitman suggests that the cure for what Marsh refers to as "the spectacle of American democracy" lies in poetry, we might note that for Whitman, following Emerson's directive, only a razor thin line separated poetry from preaching. Whitman had no models for a national poet whose lines could knit together a diverse body of people, but there were numerous historical and contemporary models of preachers who, through the intellectual and physical power of their iconoclastic oratory, transformed the lives of their auditors and summoned new social bodies. Using his "new sermons," as he referred to his poems at the beginning of his career, Whitman aimed at precisely such a mass conversion (*NUPM* 1: 314).

Whitman understood that his audience fervently embraced public oratory, especially preaching, and especially when the preacher delivered theatrical, earthy, and colloquial sermons. His optimism depended on both his absorption of Emerson's hypostatization of the poet as a surrogate preacher and on his observation of preaching's power in US culture. The confluence of these two forces led to Whitman's frequent embrace of a preacherly persona. Accordingly, he laced his lines with the rhythms of the impassioned human voice and the diction of the King James Bible. This reliance on literary preaching gave rise to a productive struggle in his work. Despite Whitman's iconoclastic lines, democratically progressive ethos, and opposition to traditional religion, the poet's direct engagement with literary preaching suggests a surprisingly conservative cultural affiliation. While the lines are striking in both topic and meter, the sermonic form affords the concretization of a clerical and hierarchical ideology, an indelible trace of a power formation that Whitman seeks to subvert. Troublingly, prophetic unsettlement exists alongside a reification of religious authority. And, though Whitman discerns this situation, he struggles to solve the problem. What does it mean to preach democratically? Can today's prophet avoid becoming tomorrow's pedagogue? Can the "conqueror's shouts" avoid drowning out other American voices? These questions were crucial to the long foreground of *Leaves of Grass* and remained with Whitman through its nine iterations.

Ecstasy in the Pews: The Formation of a Preacherly Persona

Whitman's sense of the sermon's power derives from multiple sources, and he spoke honestly when, in section 33 of "Song of Myself," he described himself as "looking seriously at the camp-meeting" (*LG* 1855: 37).[5] In his writing about antebellum preaching and preachers, Whitman reveals his fascination with

---

[5] I have chosen to highlight three cultural scenes of preaching that were especially important to Whitman's embrace of a preacherly persona throughout the many revisions of *Leaves of Grass*, but other historical preachers and events influenced Whitman's vocational imagination. The most important is Henry Ward Beecher, the most famous preacher in New England at the time *Leaves* was first published. Beecher is an important figure in David Reynolds's cultural biography of Walt Whitman, *Walt Whitman's America: A Cultural Biography* (Vintage: 1995), 38–40. Additionally, in *Whitman's Ecstatic Union: Conversion and Ideology in* Leaves of Grass (Routledge: 2005), Michael Sowder discusses Charles Grandison Finney in his treatment of historical preachers who seem to have shaped Whitman's poetics, 33–5.

preachers' ability to elicit psychological and physiological responses from their auditors. He celebrates preachers' ability to generate a semiotic circuit that unites auditors with orators, breaks through the reified orderings of symbolic language, and catalyzes the transcendence of individuated subjectivities. Through observing scenes of preaching, Whitman began to sense that the sermon afforded more than a morally authoritative idiom: it was also a sensual form that stimulated and satisfied bodily desire. It would be difficult to overstate the attractiveness of this affordance for an author who famously complained, "I was chilled with the cold types, cylinder, wet paper between us [...] I pass so poorly with paper and types, I must pass with the contact of bodies and souls" (*LG* 1860: 143). Literary preaching presented itself as a form that approximated the transformative sensory contact that he witnessed from the pews. In Whitman's own words, Emerson's call for the poet to replace the preacher "brought [him] to a boil." Whitman's significant encounters with pulpit oratory represent an insufficiently theorized reason he was "simmering" and make clear that he remained deeply responsive to preachers as he wrote and rewrote his "evangel-poem of comrades" (*LG* 1860: 11).

The revivals that swept through New York after the 1837 economic crisis contributed to Whitman's awareness of religious oratory's attractive and transformative power. In the historical sketches later collected as *Brooklyniana*, Whitman describes how these revivals united different social classes and reorganized the auditors' affections. He describes a Methodist church on Sands Street as "very crowded, every Sunday—and every night during the week" because "that was the time of 'Revivals'" (*UPP* 2: 293). Energetic language, surprising metaphor, and democratic appeal characterized the preaching of antebellum Methodist revivalists. Whitman marvels that though many "roughs" attended the events for amusement, they found themselves being moved by the preachers. "Many who came to scoff were irresistibly drawn up to the altar," Whitman writes, "and spent the night in tears and mental wrestling" (293). Not only were these auditors "irresistibly drawn" by the preachers but the sermons also led to emotional displays (i.e., "tears") and productive intellectual crisis (i.e., "mental wrestling"). How is it, Whitman wonders, that the preacher's voice overwhelms emotional resistance and produces bodily responses that testify to the stirrings of the soul? Whitman notes that some auditors' reactions proved to be "an ebullition of the moment," but in other cases "the arrows of prayer and pleading sometimes took effect" (293). Whitman sees something attractive in these events—a surprising reversal of power. The confident "roughs," among whom Whitman sits, plan to hurl insults at the preachers, and, instead, find themselves wounded by "arrows of pleading and prayer" (293). Crucially, the sermon effects change among those who do not believe they need to be changed, among those who refuse to acknowledge their spiritual hunger. Whitman could not ignore this summoning power and sought to channel it in his poetry. Indeed, he opens one of his sermonic poems, section 41 of "Song of Myself," offering to bring "help for the sick" and "for strong upright men I bring yet more needed help" (*LG* 1855: 45). For an overconfident nation that remained ignorant of its need for conversion, literary preaching suggested itself as precisely the form fit for Whitman's purpose.

The 1837 revivals amplified Whitman's already deep-seated awe of religious orators, which developed, in part, out of his childhood experience of meeting the radical Quaker preacher Elias Hicks. Whitman's admiration for Hicks remains interesting because Hicks's place in Whitman's imagination seems disproportionate to his actual encounter with Hicks. Whitman's sole encounter with Hicks occurred when, at the age of ten, he watched Hicks, then eighty-one-years-old, address a crowd at Morrison's Hotel in Brooklyn (D. Reynolds, *Whitman's America*: 37). Whitman recalls the evening in a biographical portrait published in *November Boughs* and celebrates Hicks's ministry as an itinerant preacher. Hicks's travels, Whitman notes, took him "not only through Long Island, but some of them away into the Middle or Southern States, or north into Canada, or the then far West—extending thousands of miles … and never receiving a dollar of money for 'salary' or preaching—Elias, through good bodily health and strength, continue[d] till quite the age of eighty" (*PW* 2: 636). Hicks's peripatetic ministry involved a sweeping and generous interaction with the American continent, and Whitman clearly saw Hick's wide-ranging ministry as an analogue to his own, as he embraced a project that would demand the construction of a persona who was "a southerner soon as a Northerner" and "at home on the hills of Vermont or in the woods of Maine or the Texan ranch" (*LG* 1855: 23).

Aside from the sermon's opening line, the first clause of the Westminster Catechism, Whitman cannot recall the content of Hicks's sermon. But whatever it was, it paled in significance to the psychological and physiological experiences the sermon engendered among the crowd. Whitman's recollection registers both a personal response to Hicks and a precocious curiosity about mass psychology. Though he recalls being impressed by Hicks's physical appearance, the young Whitman also has one eye on the audience: "I can almost see him and the whole scene now" (*PW* 2: 637). In his shocking description of the event, he describes the delivery of the sermon as a proto-sexual encounter. Whitman characterizes

Hicks's oratory as organic, unstudied, and "penetrating": "A pleading, tender, nearly agonizing conviction, and magnetic stream of natural eloquence, before which all minds and natures, all emotions, high or low, gentle or simple, yielded entirely without exception, was its cause, method, and effect" (637–8). Whitman remembers the sermon's powerful, emotional impact and, significantly, how that impact registered somatically. "Many," he recalls, "very many were in tears" (638).

As Whitman matured, Hicks remained a figure through whom he imagined his poetic vocation. The centerpiece of Hicks's radical message—the authoritative priority of the "the divine light within"—resonates strongly with the religious content of Whitman's own literary preaching. In 1827, Hicks's theology led to a schism within Quakerism, in large part because Hicks expressed willingness to dismiss any creed or institutional structure in favor of following "the light within" (D. Reynolds, *Whitman's America*: 37).[6] Hick's preaching career, Whitman wrote, centered on an injunction to "follow the inward, Deity-planted law of the emotional soul" (*PW* 2: 639). Hicks's valuation of the individual's spiritual capacity led naturally to an oppositional stance against any hierarchical or creedal institution. Whitman found in this Quaker principle a religious notion that championed mystical, life-giving religious experiences while also upholding a powerfully democratic ethos. This religious principle, Whitman realized, did not naturalize hierarchies—it shattered them.

Finally, Whitman's interest in religious oratory also made him responsive to the aforementioned Father Taylor. Father Edward Taylor's preaching impressed Whitman, who visited Taylor's church in 1859–60, even more than it did Emerson. Though Whitman had already published the first two versions of *Leaves of Grass* by the time he encountered Taylor, his reflections on Taylor's preaching underscore the awe with which he regarded the sermon, his ongoing sense of authorial identification with a powerful preacher, and the authoritarian threats he understood as inextricable from the sermonic form.

In an era in which public oratory flourished, Whitman identifies Taylor as the "one essentially perfect orator" (*PW* 2: 549). Whitman's recollections of Taylor were published in 1887 in *The Century Magazine* under the title "Father Taylor (and Oratory)" and later reprinted in Whitman's 1888 *November Boughs*. According to Whitman, Taylor alone "satisfied those depths of the emotional

---

[6] Ironically, if predictably, Hicks's theological radicalism led to a schism within Quakerism. Yet Hicks's response to his detractors—a response formed by his theological commitments—embodies precisely the democratic virtues Whitman admires. When Hicks's supporters attempt to "bluff off some violent orthodox person" who critiqued Hicks's positions, he quieted the crowd and, as "the tears roll'd in streams down his cheeks," said, "Let the Friend speak; Let the Friend speak!" (*PW* 2: 645).

nature that in most cases go through life quite untouch'd, unfed—who held every hearer by spells which no conventionalist, high or low—nor pride or composure, nor resistance of intellect—could stand for ten minutes" (549). Taylor's oratory thrills Whitman, and the article reveals Whitman's struggles to explain the physicality of Taylor's oratory and its impact on all auditors, including Whitman himself. Emerson—who famously referred to his body as the "not me" in "Self-Reliance"—admired Taylor primarily for his "audacious felicities" and his ability to make "the abstractions of philosophers accessible" to sailors who lacked formal education (*Journals* 3: 431). Whitman, by contrast, underscores the sensual pulsations of Taylor's sermons. In the observation that Taylor's sermons proved irresistible to all auditors, Whitman confesses his inability to remain a detached observer from the event. Yet Whitman's confession does not suggest any shame. Instead, it registers both Whitman's pride at his psychological and physiological receptivity to Taylor's impassioned voice and his inability to offer a satisfactory explanation for the overwhelming effect of Taylor's preaching.

Whitman's article begins in a journalistic mode and then quickly shifts toward a meditation on Taylor's power as an orator. He recalls the variety of social classes that gather in the chapel, their varied physical appearance, the chapel's unique architecture, and Taylor's diminutive stature. As soon as Taylor begins preaching, however, Whitman's stance shifts from that of objective journalist to enraptured congregant: "Soon as he open'd his mouth I ceas'd to pay any attention to the church or audience … a far more potent charm entirely swayed me" (*PW* 2: 550). In a description that seems to refer not only to Taylor but also himself, Whitman describes Taylor's diction as "colloquial in a severe sense" and "lean'd to Biblical and oriental forms" (550). He writes that listening to Taylor preach gave him a sense of the power associated with "words-of-mouth talk" such as that attributed to Socrates and Epictetus (550). More importantly, Whitman describes Taylor's oratorical power as "grip" (550). For Whitman this use of "grip" is not a shallow idiom. Rather, "grip" indicates the undeniably physical quality of Taylor's oratory—the way the sermon impacts the auditor's entire sensorium.

After praising Taylor's sermons, Whitman describes the effect of Taylor's prayers and, in so doing, attempts to account for the summoning, sublime power of his oratory. He admits to feeling the "deepest impression" during Taylor's prayers and notes that they "invariably affected me to tears" (550). "Never, on similar or any other occasions," Whitman recalls, "have I heard such … probing to the very depths of that latent conscience and remorse which probably lie somewhere in the background of every life, every soul" (551). Whitman seems especially interested in the ineffable quality that he says allows Taylor's words to disappear. The "mere words" of Taylor's rhetoric, according to Whitman, "seem'd altogether to disappear, and the *live feeling* advanced upon you and seiz'd you with a power before unknown" (551). His arguments were "brief and simple" (550) but were communicated in such a way that they "sen[t] to the winds all the books, and formulas, and polish'd speaking, and rules of oratory" (551). Whitman observes that his reaction was typical of Taylor's auditors: "Everybody felt this marvelous and awful influence" (551).

Whitman's closing description of Taylor's influence as "awful" gestures in two directions. First, and most obviously, it gestures toward the *awe-inspiring* capacity of Taylor's influence. To render this phrase differently, Whitman might have simply written, "All who heard him were in awe of his sermon" or "he awed all who heard him." But Whitman's multivalent phrase, his description of Taylor's influence as "awful," also gestures toward a more threatening, gothic aspect of Taylor's virtuosic preaching. In this sense, there is something *terrible* or *menacing* about Taylor's ability to summon and affect such a diverse congregation with seemingly irresistible power. Whitman's encounters with Taylor struck him as awful in both senses of the word and registered as a poignant reminder of the paradox of literary preaching that, as Whitman knew all too well by 1859, animated his own attempts to wield the sermon.

Whitman's Literary Preaching: "I Will Write the Evangel-Poem of Comrades, and of Love"

Whitman's famous sermonic exhortation about how to approach the genre-bending *Leaves of Grass*—and how readers should anticipate being remade by reading it—introduces the complexity of Whitman's literary preaching and the theme of his subsequent literary sermons. Whitman offers the literary sermon in a paragraph that anticipates objections to *Leaves* based on its flouting of conventional poetic forms. He begins by stating that, in poetics, "who troubles himself about his ornaments or fluency is lost" (*LG* 1855: v). To instruct his readers how to encounter the poetry rightly, Whitman figuratively enters the pulpit and offers jolting instructions:

> This is what you shall do: Love the earth and sun and the animals, despise riches, give alms to everyone that asks, stand up for the stupid and crazy, devote your income and labor to others, hate tyrants, argue not concerning God,

have patience and indulgence toward the people, take off your hat to nothing known or unknown or to any man or number of men, go freely with powerful uneducated persons and with the young and with the mothers of families, read these leaves in the open air every season of every year of your life, reexamine all you have been told at school or church or in any book, dismiss whatever insults your own soul, and your very flesh shall be a great poem and have the richest fluency not only in its words but in the silent lines of its lips and face and between the eyelashes of your eyes and in every motion and joint of your body. (*LG* 1855: v–vi)

As far as prefatory instructions go, Whitman's sermon sets the bar *quite* high for his readers. I quote this well-known passage at length because the series of commands and the subsequent rewards that Whitman promises enables us to discern his embrace of a heterodox preacherly persona. A moral call for virtuous behavior, the cadences and idioms of the sermon, and a nearly totalizing reification of something like theological authority commingle in these familiar lines. The first ten commands (from "love the earth" to "go freely with powerful uneducated persons") encourage the rejection of identarian forms of attachment and compel the reader to see afresh the relation of the human to the other-than-human natural order, the place of wealth in one's life, and the restrictions that hierarchies and religious disputes place on broader human solidarity. And what emerges, initially, seems more like a revised decalogue than a discussion for how to read a poem.

The literary sermon turns abruptly, however, when Whitman outlines a program for approaching the poem itself and hints that *Leaves* offers an alternative, modern religious vision. A focus on religious innovation links the next three commands. Whitman counsels his reader to, first, "read these leaves in the open air every season of your life," second, "reexamine all you have been told at school or church or in any book," and third, "dismiss whatever insults your own soul" (*LG* 1855: vi). The first command—which suggests both Transcendentalism's celebration of nature's regenerative power and Methodism's "open-air" revivals—anticipates the second. Whitman imagines that the practice of open-air readings and rereadings of his poem will generate a reappraisal of all knowledge previously gained through ecclesial authority, school, or text. The third command seems to be a logical extension of this reexamination, and it stacks the deck in favor of Whitman's own religious text that celebrates the individual's soul.

The payoff for following these thirteen instructions reveals the project's ambition. In Whitman's first of many engagements with literary preaching in *Leaves of Grass*, he closes by promising the readers a conversion experience that redefines human ontology—"and your very flesh shall be a great poem" (11). The phrase both summons and frustrates. It defies precise explication even as it seems to carry Whitman's central aim. Whitman seems to promise what Paul Outka refers to as a "democratically available reverse Incarnation via reading and praxis" (413) or, alternatively, Whitman may be prophesying the incarnation of the poem itself. Either the readers' fleshly bodies become word (i.e., "poem") or the poem appropriates the readers' flesh in the act of being read. But, as Outka rightly notes, interpretations such as these may tempt us to miss Whitman's critical point, which is less about a definitive teleology or a stable anthropology and more about seeing "human identity and agency as constitutively and inseparably part of larger material systems that dynamically entwine a variety of human, non-human, and inorganic agents" (412). Whitman suggests that the human, rightly understood, is a dynamic, porous, and God-like entity—a potent, evolving nexus of matter, soul, and language.[7] Like a "great poem" or a celebrated work of art, human bodies, after being remade by his work, will command reverence and communicate powerfully with a wide variety of strangers. Whitman sees this modern anthropology, which centers on a reimagination of the body, as a source of previously unrecognized power, generosity, and potential. And with his sermonic poem, he aims to convert his readers to this new imagination of what it means to be human and to tease out the personal and social implications suggested by this anthropology.

Though reading involves the reader's physical manipulation of the poem, Whitman's Preface inverts this relation and imagines that his poem, through the activity of being read, touches, heals, and converts the reader. In one of the many sermonic passages in "Song of Myself," Whitman, who often made little distinction between his book and his body, announces, "I make holy whatever I touch or am touched from" (*LG* 1855: 29). In this line, which helps make sense of the conversion experience promised in the Preface, the speaker redefines holiness not as a spiritual achievement based on proper observance of religious laws but as something ironically akin to highly contagious disease. The odd notion that the poet heals what he is "touched from" alludes to the

---

[7] Christian theology seems to shape the union of flesh and poem that Whitman imagines in this passage because the doctrine of the incarnation affirms a hypostatic union of God and humanity. William C. Placher's *A History of Christian Theology* (Westminster John Knox Press: 1983) offers an especially useful discussion of the Christological debates of the fourth and fifth centuries, see 80–5. Placher's analysis allows us to see how central the bending and creation of the technical language of philosophical classification became in addressing these fundamental issues in early Christology. Whitman's 1855 Preface attempts a similar bending of language, a provocative, paradoxical, and intentional misapplication of terms that produces a novel entity who, in their dynamic nature, is perfectly fit for participation in democracy in its highest forms.

biblical narrative of the hemorrhaging woman who was cured when she violated ritual proscriptions against physical contact and secretly touched the hem of Jesus's garment (Mk 5:24-34). The irony of this scriptural account depends on its reversal of culturally embedded notions of contagion and purity. According to religious ritual, the diseased woman should remain away from the healthy and holy members of her culture, but the gospel narrative reverses this notion and suggests, as Whitman does centuries later, that contact, not boundary, creates holiness and community. One does not achieve the sort of holiness Whitman values through setting oneself apart; one catches it through touch. Whitman imagines the exchange between his reader and the text they hold in their hands as a visceral experience that will catalyze a pleasurable remaking of both individual and social bodies.

Through this sustained, healing contact with *Leaves*, Whitman's imagined reader becomes converted to a new religious sensibility and attains new power. In a predictably strange phrase, Whitman refers to this conversion as the reader's attainment of a new "fluency not only in [the flesh's] words but in the silent lines of its lips and face and between the lashes of your eyes and in every motion and joint of your body" (*LG* 1855: vi). What can it mean for the human body to become "fluent"? To untangle Whitman's phrase, we should note that newly attained fluency with language enables exchanges previously unimaginable. In Whitman's America, the ability to interact and engage with a diverse citizenry constitutes a fundamental democratic virtue. Yet Whitman believed that these interactions might involve more than spoken or written language. Thus, the new "fluency" that Whitman proffers the reader centers on the body and celebrates it as a previously untapped site of communication and exchange. Throughout *Leaves*, Whitman highlights the similarity of humanity's sensory responses to various stimuli and sees in these responses potential for newly realized unions. W. C. Harris rightly points out that Whitman celebrates material contact as a "non-differentiated language": "Without words, the implication runs, communication is immediate; discourse, transparent" (82). Crucially, the conversion proffered here does not debase the body at the expense of the soul or language. Instead, the remade body will be regarded as fluent, able to communicate, in the "silent lines of its lips and face" (*LG* 1855: vi). The obedient reader will possess a new vision "between the lashes of [their] eyes" and new mobility in "every motion and joint of [their] body" (vi). A new being emerges from this exchange with the text. This entity, however, is not simply a more informed version of an essentially stable human subject, for the category of the human itself becomes delightfully problematized and, eventually, apotheosized in Whitman's sermonic poem.

Whitman slips into and out of the sermonic voice throughout *Leaves*. He embraces literary preaching's interlocking affordances of moral authority and performative sensuality to encourage beliefs appropriate for democratic citizens and to move his readers to properly see themselves and the universe. In the linked sections 31 and 32 of "Song of Myself," Whitman delivers an extended literary sermon that significantly advances his interrelated visions of human subjectivity and an "athletic and fit" religion. Whitman activates literary preaching, predictably, after he dismisses traditional sermons. In section 30, the poet claims, "Logic and sermons never convince, / The damp of the night drives deeper into my soul" (*LG* 1855: 33). The poet links "sermons" (the discourse of religious traditionalists) and "logic" (the discourse of secular lecturers) as two modes of traditional rhetorical authority that not only fail to convince the speaker but exacerbate his spiritual anxiety. Here, as in American literature more broadly, this denouncement of a conventional sermon paves the way for an alternative literary sermon.[8]

The speaker's opening phrase in section 31, "I believe," imitates the liturgical performance of creedal recitation and, appearing as it does after the refutation of unconvincing "logic and sermons," suggests the proclamation of an alternative structure of belief.[9] The poet's religious confession, rendered in the pleasurable cadences of a skilled orator, turns attention away from traditional theological topoi toward a contemplation of humanity's relationship to nonhuman nature:

> I believe a leaf of grass is no less than the journeywork of the stars,
> And the pismire is equally perfect, and a grain of sand, and the egg of the wren,
> And the tree-toad is a chef-d'oeuvre for the highest,
> And the running blackberry would adorn the parlors of heaven,
> And the narrowest hinge in my hand puts to scorn all machinery,
> And the cow crunching with depressed head surpasses any statue,
> And a mouse is miracle enough to stagger sextillions of infidels. (*LG* 1855: 34)

The literary sermon's first line—"I believe a leaf of grass is no less than the journeywork of the stars"—playfully collapses the distinction between earth and the heavens, suggesting that the divine is not wholly a transcendent creative force (*LG* 1855: 34). The leaf of grass, the poet-preacher instructs his auditors,

---

[8] Like Emerson, Whitman responds to a conventional sermon's failure with a new, poetic sermon of his own. The former, it seems, prepares the way for the latter by providing an easy target. In Emerson's journals, this pattern appears when Emerson moves from the uninspiring conventional preacher to the richness of Father Taylor's preaching.

[9] This is not the only time Whitman ironically imitates the Nicene Creed. W. C. Harris offers an insightful reading of section 5 of "Song of Myself" as another creedal poem in *E Pluribus Unum: Nineteenth-Century American Literature and the Constitutional Paradox* (U of Iowa P: 2005), 80–3.

is atomically consubstantial with the stars and derives from them. The first line of section 31 echoes one of the key claims of section 1 and expands it: just as Whitman acknowledges that "every atom belonging to me as good belongs to you" (*LG* 1855: 13), he now insists that every atom belonging to the earth "as good belongs to" the heavens.

The poem's first stanza, which is threaded with theological language, continues the argument of the opening line and proceeds by treating minute or overlooked entities as previously unacknowledged miracles, products of eons of evolution and each imbued with its share of the divine soul.[10] Like the leaf of grass, these small entities, both animate and inanimate, are "the journeywork of the stars" and bespeak the universe's ongoing generative power. Whitman cannot help being convinced by them. Initially, the speaker offers an ant, a grain of sand, and a bird's egg as examples of "perfection"; he notes that "a running blackberry" would be a fitting decoration for "the parlors of heaven"; he argues that the intricacy of the joints of the wrist "puts to scorn all machinery"; and he describes a mouse as "miracle enough to stagger sextillions of infidels" (*LG* 1855: 34). This seems to be an unlikely opening for a sermonic poem that will ultimately end with the speaker's boast about humanity's divine potential, but this discovery of a universe which continually recycles and reformulates all matter funds Whitman's mystical vision of human subjectivity. The poem insists on a redescription of the universe as an intimate and fluid network in which apparent alterity masks a more fundamental shared consubstantiality. Indeed, the poem demands that the reader begin to sense, to *feel*, their perception of all alterity as a misperception of the deeper truth that all entities in the universe cohere through a highly democratic exchange of atoms.[11] For Whitman, a

---

[10] Whitman's syncretic religious vision incorporated numerous strands of established religious thought and emerging mid-century spiritual movements: Transcendentalism, Unitarianism, Swedenborgianism, Spiritualism, Harmonialism, and Quakerism. Like traditional theists and more radical religious thinkers of his era, Whitman believed in the reality of an immortal soul. However, Whitman believed that soul infused all matter and, thus, fused the material world—including humans, pismires, and blackberry vines—with the divine. This pervasive divine immanence was not, Whitman believed, stagnant but rather "a dynamic spiritual force which impels the evolution of nature, the advancement of history, and the development of human beings" (Kuebrich, "The Soul": 677). For this reason, Whitman understood the longings and capacities of the body as "spiritual," not simply "physiological," and essential for the soul's progressive development. More broadly, Whitman sensed that the most overlooked material "miracle" was the human creature, the "acme of things accomplished" (*LG* 1855: 50): "None," he argued, "has begun to think how divine he himself is" (*LG* 1860: 12). For analysis of Whitman's responsiveness to mid-century religious culture and his religious vision, see David Kuebrich, *Minor Prophecy: Walt Whitman's New American Religion* (Indiana UP: 1990); M. Jimmie Killingsworth, *The Cambridge Introduction to Walt Whitman* (Cambridge UP: 2007), 30–4; and David Reynolds, *Whitman's America*, 251–78.

[11] Whitman's notations of a universe sustained and organized by an ongoing atomic exchange evince his absorption of the scientific theories of his day (Aspiz 216–27 and Reynolds, *Whitman's America*: 239–51). In particular, the German chemist Justus Liebig and the Scottish biologist Robert

modern understanding of this relation—an atomist-evolutionary account of the mutual interpenetration of all matter—carries tremendous religious and political significance. Whitman understood nineteenth-century scientific discourse, with its emphasis on the universe's constant exchange of atoms and progressive evolution, as confirming his belief in a "'governing principle' of evolution," a "possibly divine … evolutionary 'urge'" (Aspiz 219). Yet, crucially, the poet-preacher does not instruct his readers to venerate this immanent creative force.

Instead, in the lines that follow, Whitman deploys literary preaching to proclaim humanity as the proper object of religious veneration. It is not the governing "urge" that guides the creation of grass out of stardust but the apex of the creative process's result—the divine human—that the preacher extols. For Whitman, this was not idolatry, but the proper, modern fulfillment of humanity's religious impulse. Humans, Whitman believed, existed as a stunning result of a divinely guided evolutionary process and, simultaneously, as beings permeated by a divine soul that continually sought further development. The human, an entity far more wondrous than one initially intuits, thus, "marks a particular phase in the ascent of divine immanence" (Kuebrich, "The Soul": 669). At multiple points in *Leaves*, Whitman asserts that humanity's impulse for communion with an entity greater than the self can only be met through rightly seeing the human subject and, by extension, the human community. For Whitman, this humanistic devotion was a sacred task, the fulfillment of all previous religious formations. "What do you suppose I have intimated to you in a hundred ways," Whitman asks his reader in "Law of Creations," "but that man or woman is as good as God? / And that there is no God any more divine than Yourself" (*LG* 1860: 186). Similarly, in an unpublished notebook entry that he tellingly titles "A Spinal Thought," Whitman describes the aim of his sermonic poems as collapsing the human-divine hierarchy and proclaiming the ascension of "the com[mon] divine man" (*NUPM* 6: 2097). Whitman writes, "The whole scene shifts.—The relative positions change.—Man comes forward, inherent, superb,—the soul, the judge, the common average man advances,—ascends to place.—God disappears" (2097).

Chambers respectively furnished Whitman with the two key scientific ideas that inform this poem: a continual exchange of atoms through the process of decomposition and regrowth and a theory of progressive evolutionary process, beginning with astral nebulae and culminating in humanity. Whitman absorbs these strands of nineteenth-century scientific discourse and deploys them as part of a religiously and politically significant description of the universe's structuring principles. Modern cosmology revises religious belief and informs the political imagination. The poet's sermon attempts to identify these basic principles in order that men and women might bring their political and religious lives into alignment with them.

Section 31's second stanza advances these arguments as the poet-preacher describes the human as the miraculous culmination of an evolutionary process. The human subject the speaker celebrates is a humanity radically refigured by a new reverence for the body. The flesh is now seen as bearing signs of and capacities for dramatic exchange between the self and the world. The speaker celebrates the human, but not the human *qua* liberal subject, not the human *qua* subject of God. In a surreal and theatrical image, the speaker turns his attention from overlooked nonhuman organisms to his own body and, filled with wonder, exclaims, "I find I ... am stucco'd with quadrupeds and birds all over" (34). In this line—as well as in the poet-preacher's thrill at discovering that he "incorporate[s] gneiss and coal and long-threaded moss and fruits and grains and esculent roots"—Whitman redefines the human body as a remarkable result of a dynamic, material, and ongoing evolutionary processes. Here the poet-preacher comes to understand himself, to adjust Emerson, as part and parcel of this ongoing evolutionary urge, separate neither from the natural world nor from the divine life that infuses it.

In the final stanza of section 31, the poet-preacher drives home these findings through a densely layered play with the word "vain." Nine of the ten lines of the stanza begin with the phrase "in vain" and follow the phrase with descriptions of animals, plants, or geological formations attempting to "stand leagues off" from the speaker. Punning on "vain/vein," Whitman indicates that any attempt to create distance between the human and the nonhuman, by either party, will fail because the human and the nonhuman remain intimately connected through an active evolutionary process that involves the ongoing exchange of atoms. Though anthropocentric vanity may tempt humans to deny their connections to plant, animal, and mineral, this denial is "in vain" for, as Ed Folsom nicely puts it, "the teeming [evolutionary] past is literally in our veins, part of our very blood" ("Foreword").

Whitman's anaphoristic deployment of the phrase "in vain" underscores the poem's engagement with literary preaching. The phrase performs an inversion of the well-known refrain of Ecclesiastes. In Whitman's era, biblical critics typically attributed the book of Hebrew wisdom literature to Solomon, the Son of David. According to the scriptural narratives, God offers Solomon anything he desires, and Solomon requests that God grant him unparalleled wisdom (II Chron. 1:1-13 and I Kgs 3:4-14). After referring to himself as "the Preacher, the Son of David, the King of Jerusalem," (Eccl. 1:1) he offers numerous catalogues of "all that is done under the sun" and describes human pursuit as "vanity and vexation of spirit" (Eccl. 1:12-13). The Hebrew word *hebel*, translated in the King James

Version as "vanity," appears thirty-eight times in the short book. In Ecclesiastes, the repetition of the word vanity contributes to the author's pessimistic view of independent human endeavor. In large part, the author's assessment of human striving appears to be conditioned by the fact that the cycles of the earth frustrate human progress and belie the meaninglessness of human activity: "The sun also ariseth, and the sun goeth down, and hasteneth to the place where he arose ... and there is no new thing under the sun" (Eccl. 1:5, 9b). Aside from the author's poetic style, it would be difficult to imagine a preacher whose vision more starkly opposes that of Whitman, who joyously proclaimed, "You shall possess the good of the earth and the sun .... there are millions of suns left" (*LG* 1855: 14). For Whitman, a proper vision of human subjectivity and the cosmos leads to a rejection of biblical wisdom literature because the ongoing cycles of the cosmos do not confirm the futility of human endeavor. They tilt toward infinite progress, growth, and new knowledge.

Building on these insights, section 32 elaborates the nature of modern human subjectivity and culminates with a full-throated celebration of humanity's God-like potential. First, however, Whitman—still awed by his material connections to plant, animal, and mineral—turns his attention toward animal life and draws his audience's attention to animals' admirable behavior:

> They do not sweat and whine about their condition,
> They do not lie awake in the dark and weep for their sins,
> They do not make me sick discussing their duty to God,
> Not one is dissatisfied .... not one is demented with the mania of owning things,
> Not one kneels to another nor to his kind that lived thousands of years ago,
> Not one is respectable or industrious over the whole earth. (*LG* 1855: 34)

Here, Whitman's method of preaching recalls Jesus's practice of urging his followers to draw spiritual lessons from nonhuman organisms, such as ravens and lilies (Lk. 12:22-31). Casting himself as a modern prophet, Whitman critiques a culturally dominant form of Protestantism that prioritizes "weep[ing] for [one's] sins" and "discussing [humanity's] duty to God" while all the while remaining possessed by dissatisfaction, false respectability, and "the mania of owning things" (*LG* 1855: 34). Whitman believes that animals teach humans to be wary of religious traditions that inculcate shame and operate through a feudalistic imagination of duty to one's lord. Likewise, they also teach humans the dangers of worshipping money. Yet though the poet affirms humans' connection to nonhuman animals and admits that they "bring me tokens of myself," he also knows humanity cannot long for an earlier state of being. Humans have "distanced what is behind [them] for good reasons" (34).

At section 32's conclusion, Whitman describes the human as "moving forward then and now and forever, / Gathering and showing more always and with velocity" (34). The modern human subject, at last, arrives on the scene as "infinite and omnigenous"—with all the freedom and potentiality such an ontological status entails (35). Whitman describes himself as *infinite* because he participates in both the eternal progression of the divine soul and in the eternal exchange of atoms. He describes himself as *omnigenous* because he realizes that his body participates in the evolutionary process and contains atoms that were other entities (55). In these apotheosizing lines, Whitman makes good on his prefatory promise to deliver a message that counters every cultural narrative that "insults [the] soul" (*LG* 1855: vi) and anticipates his boast in "Song at Sunset" at being "this incredible God that I am! / To have gone forth among other Gods, these men and women I love" (*LG* 1891: 375). The literary sermon offered in sections 31 and 32 gives rise to an imagination of a divine human subject that remains inextricably entwined with other human and nonhuman creatures, and, for this reason, transgressive of the narrow limits of liberal subjectivity. This capacity for exchange with both human and nonhuman others that the poet discovers enables him to imagine human subjectivity as simultaneously permeable *and* powerful. Or, more accurately, he discerns humanity's permeability as the index of its potency.

In this new faith, the poet discerns grounds for hope in America's democratic project. Whitman believed his nation's democratic project required a fusion of two seemingly oppositional traits. First, democracy requires heroic individuals such as those championed by Emerson. Cornell West aptly describes Emerson's model of the heroic self as "one who has appropriated God-like power and might and has acquired the confidence to use this power and might for the 'conversion of the world'" (13). Whitman embraced this belief and saw justification for this appropriation in the theory of progressive evolution that culminated in the "infinite and omnigenous" human subject who was permeated with divine soul.

Yet the poet-preacher tethers this trait to a second trait that qualifies and productively troubles the meaning of the first. The divine common man or woman was also—as sections 31 and 32 make clear—hardwired for connection. The body—by virtue of its history, composition, and suffusion by divine soul—needed to move toward and commune with the world. Following the literary sermon that spans sections 31 and 32, section 33 opens with the ecstatic language of religious confirmation: "My Soul! *Now* I know it is true what I guessed at; /

What I guessed at when I loafed on the grass" (*LG* 1855: 35; emphasis added). At this precise moment, after a literary sermon expounding the mystical oneness of all things and humanity's divinity, the poet confirms his earlier sense that "the spirit of God is the eldest brother of my own, / And that all the men ever born are also my brothers .... and the women my sisters and lovers, / And that a kelson of the creation is love" (16). And in the subsequent stanza, the poet images an ascension, a figure of his apotheosis. In a joyous image of apotheosis only Whitman would dare, he, a bit comically, imagines ascending into the air in a hot-air balloon: "My ties and ballasts leave me .... I travel .... I sail [...] I am afoot with my vision" (35). The poet's following journey reveals the results of practicing this new religious vision. The speaker's God-like ascension does not isolate him in the heavens, beyond the reach of other humans. Rather it enables a level of democratic exchange, empathetic identification, and engagement with the natural world previously unimaginable.

By *far* the longest section of "Song of Myself," the following lines provide an expansive catalogue in which the speaker, surreally traversing the nation, testifies to the alternately joyous and painful blurring of the self and the other (37). A God-like democratic citizen who knows himself to be literally connected to others and the land itself, he identifies fully with the pleasure and suffering of other Americans, claiming "all these I feel or am" (39) and "I take part .... I see and hear the whole" (40). This, the poet-preacher suggests, is what it means to have one's "very flesh" attain the "richest fluency" (vi). This is what it feels like to be an adherent of a "real athletic and fit religion of these States" (*NUPM* 6: 2061). This is a suitable structure of belief that confidently celebrates the glories of the body and the soul, reveres the self and others, and dovetails with democracy's highest ideals.

"I Teach Straying from Me, yet Who Can Stray from Me?": Whitman and the Ideological Threat of the Sermonic Voice

To promote his sacred vision of democracy, Whitman wrote and rewrote a sermonic poem designed "to drop in the earth the germs of a greater Religion" (*LG* 1860: 13). The besetting paradox of Whitman's literary preaching is that he sought to inspire his readers so that his own magnetic preaching would be superfluous. The poet's success depends, in large part, on his ability to liberate the reader from religious narratives of human subjectivity that underwrite hierarchies. Whitman telegraphs this aspect of his poem in the agenda-setting

Preface to the 1855 *Leaves*: "There will soon be no more priests ... every man shall be his own priest" (xi). The primary targets in Whitman's cultural effort were traditional religions that suggested a feudalistic relationship between God and humanity, posited a transcendent deity, and maintained cultural dominance by consolidating power in the hands of specialized clergy. At the same time, however, Whitman's effort to liberate Americans from any religious formation that "insults [the individual's] soul" demanded that he attempt to rein in the power of the forceful speaker of the poems themselves. Addressing Whitman's awareness of this dilemma, Vivian Pollack notes the poet's eagerness "to reveal his weakness" and to inculcate a "fear [of] cultural distillations, such as *Leaves of Grass*, especially those claiming to be natural or good for our health" (250). If, as he claims in the Preface to the 1855 edition, Whitman sought to be absorbed by his country, he also sought to control that absorption.

Whitman sensed the ideological threat embedded in the literary form he found so productive, and he recognized that literary preaching transmits and perpetuates a hierarchical power structure by consolidating authority in a religious orator. The power Whitman appropriates through his forays into literary preaching both thrills and troubles him. "I know perfectly well my own egotism," the poet admits, "And know my omnivorous words, and cannot say any less" (*LG* 1855: 47). Yet the poet follows this confession with a statement of his democratic intent: "And [I] would fetch you whoever you are flush with myself" (47). The subjunctive mood ("would") reveals an anxiety, however, that his "omnivorous words" might devour others. He fears the inauguration of a new religious formation in which power becomes centralized in yet another holy man declaiming religious truths.

Whitman's concerns about this problem derive not only from his keen sense that literary forms themselves function as vehicles for the transmission of ideology but also from observations of the dynamics of American populist religion. He observed that American crowds lionized promoters of new, democratic religious doctrines and readily submitted their will to them, casting out traditional clergy only to install demagogues.[12] Indeed, Whitman's own account of his response to Father Taylor proved to him how easily a magnetic speaker could overwhelm an auditor, subjecting them, often pleasurably, to a "power previously unknown" (*PW* 2: 551). For this reason, Whitman attempts,

---

[12] For a classic study of this tension in American religion, see Nathan O. Hatch, *The Democratization of American Christianity* (Yale UP: 1989), 3–16.

at times successfully and at times unsuccessfully, to redistribute authority by withholding closure and directing attention away from himself.

For example, in section 44, on the heels of yet another sermonic discussion of how Whitman's poem offers "the greatest of faiths and the least of faiths" (*LG* 1855: 48), the poet-preacher begins by directing the imagined audience to join him in something like a benediction. "It is time to explain myself," he announces, "let us stand up" (49). The explanation that follows, however, withholds resolution. Or, more accurately, the speaker offers deferred resolution as the only resolution appropriate for this democratic sermon that takes seriously a scientific account of the universe. "What is known I strip away," the speaker says, "I launch all men and women forward with me into the unknown" (49). Though the poem promotes a modern, religious, and politically useful redescription of human subjectivity, the speaker refuses to proclaim a telos for his vision. Instead, he asks his readers to ponder the fact that "we have thus far exhausted trillions of winters and summers" and that "there are trillions ahead, and trillions ahead of them" (49). Yet amid this incalculable expanse of time, the enduring atomic matter that composes us, as individuals, has traveled and cohered, for this precious moment, into our physical embodiment. "What have I to do with lamentation?" Whitman asks laughingly. He imagines the various journeys the matter that he now *is* has taken and, knowing that what is true of him is true of each human, he says, "Immense have been the preparations for me, / Faithful and friendly the arms that have helped me" (50). As the reader stands with Whitman, the poet-preacher seems to explain himself by saying only "All forces have been steadily employed to complete and delight me, / Now I stand on this spot with my soul" (50). And here, too, the reader stands, with Whitman, on the precipice of an unknown future—the "acme of things accomplished" and, because humans are composed atoms that will eventually become other entities, an "encloser of things to be" (50). But what those things may be or, more importantly, where precisely the democratic project is headed, Whitman refuses to say and suggests he cannot because America's future depends on the efforts of future Americans—not the bardic preacher. The benediction ends abruptly, and the promised explanation remains inchoate. With this self-effacing tactic, which reappears throughout *Leaves*, Whitman hopes to mitigate the likelihood of his own sermonic rhetoric becoming a barrier to the elevation and development of "the com[mon] divine man" (*NUPM* 6: 2097).

A similar rhetorical tactic appears in section 47 as the poet explicitly directs his audience to embrace self-reliance and resist dependence on him. But in this section this speaker's rhetoric generates anxiety that cannot be easily assuaged.

In the opening lines, the poet claims, "He most honors my style who learns under it to destroy the teacher" (*LG* 1855: 52). The line's contradiction reveals the self-canceling speaker's paradox; it is a paradox, in this instance, figured as an impossibly attained object of desire. The section reveals a submerged sorrow about the dynamic of reception the sermonic voice constructs. The poet writes, "The boy I love, the same becomes a man not through derived power but in his own right" (53). The conditions upon which the boy becomes the object of the speaker's love are clear: he eschews "derived power" and matures through the exercise of his own will. So far, so good. Yet just a few lines later, the speaker laments the foreclosure of these conditions being met: "I teach straying from me, yet who can stray from me? / I follow you whoever you are from the present hour; / My words itch at your ears till you understand them" (53). Part brag and part lament, these are lethal sentences. They kill the beloved by preempting the conditions upon which they might come into existence and register the speaker's distrust of his own self-effacing tactics. Despite his attempts to free his readers from external religious authorities, Whitman openly doubts that his audience can escape the *awful* power of his sermons. The lines confirm Whitman's abiding concern about the project of authorial surrogation and, relatedly, about literary preaching as a form appropriate to the larger cultural work of *Leaves of Grass*.

Finally, we see literary preaching's affordance of a reification of a hierarchical ideology dramatized in Whitman's most famous sermonic poem concerning world religions—section 41 of "Song of Myself." The iconoclastic poem frustrates the poet's self-canceling attempt and indicates the ideological threat inherent in the project of replacing the preacher with the poet. The poem begins with Whitman boldly evoking the sermon, taking aim at the founders of other religions (the "old cautious hucksters"), and suggesting the superiority of the modern religious formation he preaches:

> Magnifying and applying come I,
> Outbidding at the start the old cautious hucksters,
> The most they offer for mankind and eternity less than a spirt of my own seminal wet,
> Taking myself the exact dimensions of Jehovah and laying them away,
> Lithographing Kronos and Zeus his son, and Hercules his grandson,
> Buying drafts of Osiris and Isis and Belus and Brahma and Adonai,
> In my portfolio placing Manito loose, and Allah on a leaf, and the crucifix engraved,
> With Odin, and the hideous-faced Mexitli, and all idols and images,

> Honestly taking them all for what they are worth, and not a cent more,
> Admitting they were alive and did the work of their day,
> Admitting they bore mites as for unfledged birds who have now to rise and fly and sing for themselves.
> Accepting the rough deific sketches to fill out better in myself.... bestowing them freely on each man and woman I see,
> Discovering as much or more in a framer framing a house,
> Putting higher claims for him there with his rolled-up sleeves, driving the mallet and chisel; (*LG* 1855: 45–6)

Whitman opens by striking a defiant tone and taking a commanding position. He crudely insults other religious prophets and their offerings, and, as he puts it elsewhere, seems to "go to the wars" to "inaugurate a religion" (*LG* 1860: 11). Though he promises to measure "honestly" all other religions for "what they are worth, and not a cent more," the lines reveal that he believes that they are no longer worth much at all—not compared to the image of the divine, democratic human he offers (*LG* 1855: 45). The poet-preacher boasts that he will incorporate these antiquated deities into the pages of his modern religious text through a variety of print-making practices such as "lithographing," "buying drafts," and "engrav[ing]" (45). Just as each individual human depends on but ultimately "distance[s] what is behind" them "for good reasons" (34), Whitman nods to the past, acknowledges that these religions "were alive and did the work of their day" (45), notes them in his poetry, and presses toward the future.

This poem opens with Whitman establishing himself as a brash religious speaker, yet after swiftly "outbidding" these religious rivals, the preacher-poet attempts to elevate his would-be disciples. Here, Whitman attempts to limit literary preaching's tendency to advance a clerical ideology that locates authority in the individual preacher. The speaker returns to the image of the ascendant commoner, saying that all previous religions "bore mites as for unfledged birds who have now to rise and fly and sing for themselves" (46). To enable men and women to embrace their inherent divinity, he redirects the religious impulse away from gods and demigods toward common, contemporary humans. Crucially, the speaker does so, first, by noting that he sees more divinity in "a framer framing a house" than he does in any of the traditional gods (46). Here, Jesus, the Galilean carpenter, gives way to a New York carpenter "with his rolled-up sleeves, driving the mallet and chisel" (46). This key scene, however, dramatizes the paradoxical character of literary preaching because the poet's description of the framer clearly recalls the iconic frontispiece of the 1855 edition, the so-called "carpenter portrait," including the detail of the rolled sleeve that appears above Whitman's right wrist. At this critical juncture, when the poet leverages the sermon to celebrate the divinity of the commoner, the remark boomerangs back to Whitman himself, divinizing the confident preacher of *Leaves of Grass*.

Rather than enacting a democratic fusion of the poet-preacher with the masses, the scene uncomfortably suggests the reinstallment of Walt Whitman as a new religious leader and blocks the rise of a nonclerical mode of authority. Whitman lists other "divine commoners" after the New York carpenter, but the authorial persona emerges as the firstborn of the new creation, the modern Christ. Though Whitman actively courted a "messianic aura," he often sought to avoid installing himself as an elevated religious leader and reinscribing yet another hierarchy (Herrero-Brasas 10). Whitman sensed this threat, wrote beautiful poetry attempting to circumvent it, but worried about the moments when the ideological function of his literary preaching seemed beyond his own containment. Indeed, in 1860, after two previous editions of *Leaves* in which he sought, with varying degrees of success, to mitigate the repellant affordances of his literary preaching, he cautioned his readers against establishing societies or schools associated with his works: "I charge that there be no theory or school founded out of me, / I charge you to leave all free, as I have left all free" (*LG* 1860: 226). Subsequent generations of readers confirmed that this was no delusion of grandeur on Whitman's part and was, in fact, a perceptive concern for a poet who so frequently relied on literary preaching and styled himself as a religious visionary.

In *Walt Whitman's Mystical Ethics of Comradeship* (2010), Juan A. Herrero-Brasas focuses on a cadre of readers who, in 1894, established The Walt Whitman Fellowship, "a cult" that sought to distribute Whitman's poetry and identified him as a modern prophet (7). Whitmanite cults flourished for only a short period of time and were virtually nonexistent by the mid-1920s. But they confirm Whitman's alarm regarding literary preaching's deleterious effects in a culture that, despite its democratic rhetoric, retained a hankering for feudalism and sought out new "kings" of all sorts (Edmundson xii). These early Whitmanites wrote biographies and essays devoted to *Leaves of Grass*'s religious vision, and they should be understood as the literary works of an alternative "missionary organization" that frequently placed Whitman "among the *universal prophets—to be precise ... above* them" (Herrero-Brasas 14). Will Hayes's 1921 biography, *Walt Whitman, the Prophet of the New Era*, exemplifies the missionary spirit that mobilized this group. As Herrero-Brasas suggests, a sample of Hayes's chapter titles alone telegraph his alarming reading of Whitman—"I. The Christ of our Age," "II. The Carpenter of Brooklyn," "IV A Prophet in His Own Country," and "V. The City of Friends: Whitman's 'Kingdom of God'" (17). Nothing about the Whitmanites' impulse to elevate Whitman would have surprised the author of the Divinity School Address. At one memorial gathering the group designated Whitman "the most divine of men" (Kuebrich, *Minor Prophecy*: 1). The cringe-inducing superlative would have embarrassed and saddened Whitman, but it becomes readily understandable when we trace the inevitable ideological function of his literary preaching.

In this foundational scene of literary preaching represented by Emerson and Whitman, we do not see the accomplished replacement of the preacher with the poet, even though both authors understood authorial surrogation as one of their central ambitions. Indeed, to the extent that the authority of the poet depends on recognizable sermonic idioms or the stylization of the author as the modern preacher, literary authority remains parasitic, dependent on a more powerful host for its force. Whitman understood traditional religious formations to be passing away, memorably describing "bat-eyed and materialistic priests" as "a stale cadaver" that blocked the passage to America's progress (*LG* 1856: 232). But his heavy reliance on literary preaching affirmed and solidified the preacher's centrality in American literature and culture. The literary preaching of *Leaves*, thus, drew strength from *and* strengthened American culture's expectation that the language of authority should sound sermonic. Throughout his career, Whitman struggled against literary preaching's tendency to reify clerical ideology, even as he continuously sought to leverage the potent form to promote a new, democratic faith. In the mid-nineteenth century, Emerson and Whitman were not alone in their attempt to harness the power of the sermon for literary ends. In Chapter 2, I turn to a different—at times concurrent—scene of literary preaching and examine another pair of nineteenth-century US authors who sought to engage the form through alternative strategies.

2

"But I Say Unto You": The Literary Pulpit Exchange in Nathaniel Hawthorne and Rebecca Harding Davis

Instead of merely empowering the American author to engage their surrounding culture in an authoritative manner, literary preaching simultaneously blocked the rise of a nonclerical mode of cultural authority. This double bind generated ambivalence for antebellum American writers who longed to embrace a form that threatened to marginalize the moral authority of the literary itself. If authorial surrogation—the attempt to replace the preacher with the poet—generated as many problems as it solved, what other options were available to antebellum authors? How might American authors employ a form that provided so many attractive affordances but do so in a manner that mitigated the extent to which employing that form reified the prevailing clerical ideology? In his classic study *Literary Transcendentalism* (1973), Lawrence Buell notes that major authors of the antebellum period "saw themselves in competition," above all, with religious conventionalism and, at the same time, "among their most important literary models [were] the Bible, hymnody, John Bunyan, and the sermon" (103). To address this paradox and confront literary preaching's troublesome affordances, Nathaniel Hawthorne found a richly suggestive resource in a religious practice that flourished in the nineteenth century—the pulpit exchange.

Innovative preaching, populist appeals, and emotional excess characterized the Second Great Awakening; however, the movement also underscored religious oratory's undeniably disruptive power. Across a variety of denominations, highly educated religious leaders praised and feared revivalists' pyrotechnic preaching. They did so for good reason. As E. Brooks Holifield shows, the first preachers of the Second Great Awakening targeted both the sins of the unredeemed and, in a proto-Jacksonian move, the "erudition of a clerical elite" (291). According to Abner Jones, one of the key figures of the Second Great Awakening's early stages, academic theology perverted early Christianity by generating extra-biblical or nonessential sectarian distinctions. Jones and his associates called Americans to repent not only of their individual sins but also for their membership in established denominations rife with extra-biblical human error, including denominationally specific "creeds and confessions" (Holifield 291). Predictably, then, one of the immediate results of the Second Great Awakening was denominational schism. Indeed, the result of "The Great Revival" at Cane Ridge in 1801—the first major revival of the Second Great Awakening—was the fracturing of the Presbyterian Kentucky Synod. When the Kentucky Synod charged the revival's organizer, the Presbyterian minister Barton Stone, with heresy for rejecting Calvinist doctrine, Stone simply left the denomination. And when he did, he took his numerous followers with him.[1] The shocked synod realized belatedly that Stone's remarkable vocational assets—his populist appeal and oratorical skill—threatened to enervate the very denomination that ordained him.

In the second decade of the Second Great Awakening, as revivalism moved from the frontier into urban centers, New England clergymen attempted to harness the moment's revivalist fervor without risking their own institutional authority. Threatened by the currents of revivalism, these established ministers sought to embrace the power of new styles of sermons and, simultaneously, contain the threat that skilled revivalists presented. One of the key strategies that church leaders employed to accomplish this task came to be known as the pulpit exchange, an arrangement in which skilled preachers would be invited to another church for a limited speaking engagement. Preachers involved in these exchanges circulated through a prearranged ecclesiastical network and delivered energetic sermons that strengthened denominational ties. The pulpit exchange endured as an important and contentious Protestant practice throughout the nineteenth century, and the willingness to engage in pulpit exchanges indicated shared respect and theological agreement.[2]

---

[1] For more on the relationship between the Second Great Awakening and denominational schism and Barton Stone, in particular, see E. Brooks Holifield, *Theology in America: Christian Thought from the Age of the Puritans to the Civil War* (Yale UP: 2003), 292 and Barry Hankins *The Second Great Awakening and the Transcendentalists* (Greenwood Press: 2004), 11–13.

[2] By the same logic, the refusal to engage in pulpit exchanges also signaled a significant theological rift. For instance, in 1840, the refusal of Unitarian ministers to exchange pulpits with the radical Theodore Parker marked "a genuine belief that what Parker was preaching could no longer be considered Christianity" (Packer 498). Parker, a Unitarian minister who embraced Transcendentalism, decided not to follow Emerson's lead by resigning his pulpit and attempted to rehabilitate Unitarianism from within. In 1840, he increasingly pressed Unitarians to embrace Transcendentalist principles and a variety of social reforms, and they reacted strongly. As Barbara Packer puts it, "By the end of the year he had already started to suffer from the polite freezing out that was Boston's only form of excommunication: his colleagues in the ministry began refusing to exchange pulpits with him" (419).

"But I Say Unto You" 61

The pulpit exchange adapted the Methodist practice of circuit riding to an urban context and served a similar institutional function. Though circuit riding emerged as a way of addressing an inadequate supply of preachers, it also served conservative organizational ends that tend to be downplayed in US religious history. The intense travel schedule associated with circuit riding prevented any single preacher from exerting an outsized pastoral influence that could threaten the larger authority of the denomination itself (Hankins 13). Circuit riding encouraged intense denominational affiliation and limited the opportunity for the emergence of personality cults. Pulpit exchanges functioned in a similar manner: they enabled congregations to hear "new ideas from fresh voices and ... to be stirred to repentance and rededication" (Hankins 15). At the same time, the pulpit exchange, which William McLoughlin aptly describes as "a conservative form of revivalism," ensured established clergymen that these new, energizing voices would not threaten to usurp their congregations (111). They were temporary guest preachers, not rival authorities.[3]

This chapter describes a strategy of literary preaching that I will refer to as the *literary pulpit exchange*, an approach to the form that draws variously on the radical energies and conservative impulses that defined the historical pulpit exchange. I begin by focusing on the literary preaching of Nathaniel Hawthorne, an author uniquely haunted by the specter of clerical authority. After examining Hawthorne's strategy of negotiating the form's affordances, I turn to the literary preaching of one of Hawthorne's protégées, Rebecca Harding Davis. The literary pulpit exchange both differs from and bears marked similarity to the historical pulpit exchange. To analyze the contours of this inventive approach to literary preaching, I wish to distinguish between how the literary pulpit exchange operates in the immediate scenes featuring the literary sermons and within the broader arc of the fiction's emplotment.

First, within the isolated scenes of literary preaching, the literary pulpit exchange underscores the destabilizing power of upstart preachers who subvert established authority structures through their brilliant, iconoclastic preaching. The texts I examine include instances of literary preaching in which a "visiting preacher,"

---

[3] No clergyman in New England manipulated pulpit exchanges more successfully than Lyman Beecher, the minister of the First Congregational Church of Litchfield, Connecticut. In 1814 Billy Hibbard, a Methodist revivalist and self-proclaimed healer, converted over three hundred people in Beecher's hometown of Litchfield, Connecticut. Hibbard's missionary raid into Congregationalist territory motivated Beecher's initiation of a series of pulpit exchanges that offered the energy and renewal of revivalism without the schismatic threat. Between 1818 and 1828, Beecher effectively enlisted and supervised the most skilled Congregationalist preachers he could find to combat the incursions of revivalists. For more on Beecher's conservative use of the pulpit exchange, see McLoughlin, *Revivals, Awakenings, and Reforms: An Essay on Religion and Social Change in America, 1607-1977* (U of Chicago P: 1978), 111.

often an uninvited intruder, occupies an establish minster's pulpit, addresses the startled congregation, and delivers a politically charged sermon. At one level, then, this "sharing" of pulpits and congregations mirrors the historical pulpit exchange. These literary pulpit exchanges differ from the historical pulpit exchange, however, because hostility between the visitor and the host, not cooperation, marks the literary pulpit exchange. Within the world of the fiction, the literary pulpit exchange is a usurpation, not an agreement between two affiliated ministers who seek to shore up their threatened authority. Like the revivalists who made bold declarations against established religious authorities and sought to convert their rivals' congregations, the fiery preachers imaged in these literary pulpit exchanges take aim at repressive theological or cultural formations. Above all, these literary pulpit exchanges disclose their authors' attraction to the form's primary affordances of extralegal moral authority and verbal artistry. Consistently, these fictional visiting preachers function as authorial doubles, figures set on unsettling the staid conventionalism of religious or cultural orthodoxy.

Within the broader arc of the narrative, however, something subtler and more significant happens in the literary pulpit exchange because the affirmation of the sermonic voice that these scenes construct is subsequently mitigated through attempts at the reclamation of narrative control. When placed within a more comprehensive perspective of the fiction's emplotment, these isolated scenes involving renegade preachers and their sermons, in fact, draw deeply on the conservative energies of the historical pulpit exchange. The controlling author temporarily diminishes the established authorial voice, allows the potent voice of the visiting preacher to temporarily take center stage in the narrative's diegesis, and then, crucially, attempts to recoup authorial control. In this sense, literary pulpit exchanges bear striking similarity to historical pulpit exchanges because they aim to shore up threatened authority. We should understand such literary pulpit exchanges as attempts to embrace the voice of the preacher—even the most radical or oppositional preachers—while also keeping the preacher in their place. Thus, the literary pulpit exchange involves two oppositional moves: the embrace of radical literary preaching and the subsequent containment of literary preaching's repellant affordances through recuperative narrative developments. Using these literary pulpit exchanges, the controlling author aims to transform the voice of a potential rival into the voice of an accomplice.

While Hawthorne enjoyed writing fiction that allowed him to play the unlicensed preacher and deliver literary sermons against the cultural formations he detested, he was concerned about overidentifying with the preacher and positioning his work in relation to a cultural figure of seemingly despotic power.

For this reason, his engagements with literary preaching tend to be sudden, violent, and episodic, and he follows these engagements with awkward attempts to banish his preachers and reassert authorial control. Yet because Hawthorne consistently places his remarkable scenes of literary preaching at narrative junctures where the fiction's moral or cultural questions hang in the balance, these scenes resist Hawthorne's subsequent efforts to bracket the preacherly voice.

After addressing Hawthorne's literary pulpit exchanges, I examine the literary preaching of Rebecca Harding Davis, a writer who identified Hawthorne as one of her most important literary mentors. In *Life in the Iron-Mills* (1861), Davis embraces literary preaching in order to correct her culture's failure to attend adequately to the brutalization of the laboring class. In contrast to Hawthorne, Davis's embrace of literary preaching produced little vocational anxiety, and she remained unconcerned about the form's ideological function. Indeed, she seems to have understood literary preaching as her means of gaining something like a pulpit in US culture, an authoritative religious space largely unavailable to her because of her gender. The publication history of Davis's novella, however, vividly dramatizes how literary preaching was perceived as a threat to the construction of autonomous literary authority in the mid-nineteenth century. In a manner that recalls Hawthorne's attempts to bracket the effects of his own literary sermons, James T. Fields's editing of Davis's initial manuscript enacts a dramatic attempt to regulate the sermonic voice and, thereby, constrain the undesirable affordances of the novella's key scene of literary preaching. By examining Hawthorne's and Davis's literary preaching, we gain a fresh perspective on each author's works and, more important, insight into their engagement with one of US literature's most enduring and nettlesome narrative forms.

Hawthorne, the Shadows, and Moralizing in a Post-Theological Mode

> I have not yet concluded what profession I should have. The being a minister is of course out of the question ... What do you think of my becoming an author, and relying for support upon my pen?
>
> Nathaniel Hawthorne, Letter from Bowdoin College to His Mother, March 13, 1821[4]

---

[4] From Julian Hawthorne, *Nathaniel Hawthorne and His Wife: A Biography*, vol. 1 (Houghton Mifflin: 1884), 107–8.

The Scarlet Letter (1850) opens with "a throng of bearded men, in sad-colored garments, and gray, steeple-crowned hats" gathering to publicly shame Hester Prynne (Hawthorne 36). If the reader has been paying attention, however, this opening constitutes the second appearance of these shadowy figures. In the novel's prefatory chapter, "The Custom-House," these same "stern and black-browed Puritans" gather to shame Nathaniel Hawthorne for the profession he has chosen: "'What is he?' murmurs one gray shadow of my forefathers to another. 'A writer of story-books! What kind of a business in life,—what mode of glorifying God, or being serviceable to mankind in his day and generation,—may that be? Why, the degenerate fellow might as well have been a fiddler!'" (12). As the mocking ghosts swirl around him, Hawthorne responds in a manner both subtle and revealing: "And yet, let them scorn me as they will, strong traits of their nature have intertwined themselves with mine" (12). Hawthorne's wry reply—a sort of schoolyard riposte—suggests that Puritans mock themselves when they mock their heir. The success of his retort, however, depends on Hawthorne's admission of an internal haunting. The ghosts not only swirl around him; they swirl within him—eradicable aspects of his personality.

The shade of his Puritan ancestor William Hathorne, a man he describes as "a soldier, a legislator, a judge … a ruler in the Church," especially troubles Hawthorne. As he probes the nature of this haunting, seeking to trace the source of his anxiety, he suggests that the trait that links him with his ancestors might be called "a moral quality" (11). Commenting on this passage, Martin Kevorkian points out that Hawthorne identifies that he and his forefathers have a shared interest in promoting morality and realizes that he "has found a way of expressing it that [his ancestors] would not recognize" (12). Like his most famous ancestor, Hawthorne wants to inflect his culture's moral vision, and, thus, his ancestor's status as a "legislator," "judge," and "ruler" seems especially resonant with Hawthorne's aim of examining, in a post-theological literary mode, what he later refers to as "the truth of the human heart" (Hawthorne, *House*: 3).

Hawthorne's phrase "the truth of the human heart" may strike contemporary readers as ill-defined, but by defining the types of moral truths he aims to tell in this manner, Hawthorne orients his work toward addressing humans' emotional and psychological needs. This redirection of energy away from abstract or transcendental truths toward the immanent needs and desires of human "hearts" motivates Hawthorne's literary preaching. He engages the form, above all, for the purpose of reining in the intensities of American religion and pointing out the dangers of unchecked devotion to ideals. Clearly this emphasis had both historical and contemporary resonances in Hawthorne's culture. Nothing,

Hawthorne suggests, poses as much danger to human flourishing as intensely held theological beliefs or the single-minded pursuit of abstract notions of truth. Devotion to such ideals, Hawthorne believes, enables the devotee to disregard the desires or perspectives of others, often at tremendous human cost.

To voice his dissent from this antihumanist devotion to idealism, which he observed in multiple eras and professions in US culture, Hawthorne longs for something like clerical authority but knows better than to try to outpreach the preacher. The iconic figure of the holy man speaking, Hawthorne understood, was no "stale cadaver," no rapidly fading authority figure (Whitman, *LG* 1856: 232). Hawthorne believed that writing fiction at this cultural moment demanded an awareness that the author labored in the shadow of the pulpit. For Hawthorne, recognition of the enduring cultural power of the preacher necessitated the development of the literary pulpit exchange. These intense episodic engagements provided Hawthorne with a manner of addressing the preacher without engaging in direct and extended confrontation. Instead, through a series of razor-sharp literary pulpit exchanges that occur in his oeuvre, Hawthorne embraces and then seeks to contain literary preaching.

In his literary pulpit exchanges, Hawthorne consistently constructs female characters who attempt to usurp the pulpit. He does so for several reasons. First, as I will demonstrate, a charged and violent event in New England's early history involving a female Quaker preacher captivated Hawthorne's imagination. Second, Hawthorne's method of deploying these incisive pulpit exchanges emphasizes the gender exclusions inherent in Protestant models of authority and questions the validity of patriarchal structures that seem to abet a dangerous fixation on abstract ideals. In Hawthorne's fiction, the female preacher becomes a figure through whom he expresses his own convictions about the human costs of idealism. These women preachers rarely succeed in Hawthorne's narratives, but their resistance to patriarchal-clerical authority highlights its abuses and exposes its dangers. Finally, and perhaps most importantly, women often play the role of uninvited preacher in Hawthorne's literary pulpit exchanges to enable his ensuing attempts to contain the undesirable affordances of literary preaching through the assertion of domestic ideology.

Hawthorne's Literary Pulpit Exchanges

In 1832, Hawthorne published "The Gentle Boy" in the gift book *The Token*. "The Gentle Boy" centers on Puritan violence toward Quakers during the seventeenth century and represents one of Hawthorne's earliest excavations of American mythology. The story focuses primarily on the religious development of Tobias Pearson, a man who grows disillusioned with Puritan culture, rejects it, and converts to Quakerism. This conversion, however, does not satisfy Pearson, and he begins to sense that the Quakers' theological vision threatens human flourishing in a manner that mirrors the antinatural bent of Puritan idealism. Though Pearson's conversion provides the story's central plot, it is through a volatile scene of literary preaching that Hawthorne most clearly denounces the dangers he associates with the persistent cultural authority of the pulpit and quests for purity, both historical and contemporary.

In constructing the story's explosive scene of literary preaching, Hawthorne drew deeply on the historical narrative of Margaret Brewster. On July 8, 1677, Margaret Brewster and four other Quakers burst into a Puritan meetinghouse during a sermon. Brewster's head was uncovered and her hair was down. Dressed in sackcloth and ashes, Brewster warned the Puritans that God would judge them for enforcing legislation that compelled Puritan authorities to disband all Quaker meetings (Besse 259–65 and Bouldin 64). In his diary entry on July 8, 1677, Samuel Sewall recalls the event: "In Sermon time there came a female Quaker, in Canvas Frock, her hair disheveled and loose like a Periwigg, her face as black as ink, led by two other Quakers and two others followed" (43). According to Sewall, this interruption "occasioned the greatest and most amazing uproar I ever saw" (43). Though it is not clear what Brewster said when she entered the church, she offered an eloquent and sermonic defense during her trial. The governor began by describing her appearance as "like the Devil incarnate," but Brewster countered by saying that she entered the church in response to God's command that she preach to "the bloody town of Boston" (Besse 262). She identified her performance as comparable to Biblical prophecy and then claimed "the Desire of my Soul, is that it may be with this Town as it was with Nineveh of old, for when the Lord sent his Prophet Jonah to cry against Nineveh, it is said, They put on Sackcloth, and covered their Heads with Ashes, and repented, and the Lord withdrew his judgment for forty years" (Besse 264). Brewster then accepted her sentence, as she put it, "As chearfully [sic] as Daniel went to the Lion's Den, for the God of Daniel is with me" (Besse 264). Governor Richard Bellingham, a target of Hawthorne's criticism in *The Scarlet Letter*, condemned Brewster to be tied to a cart and whipped. She was the last Quaker woman to receive such punishment from Puritan authorities (Larson 375). A marginalized prophet whose preaching incites terror and disorder, Brewster became the muse through whom

Hawthorne explored literary preaching's power to indict idealistic quests that disregard human suffering.

As Hawthorne directed his study of New England history toward his writing, mining it for source material and its revelations about national culture, he meditated especially on the suffering of innocent people caught in the crossfire of ideological wars.[5] One of these suffering innocents became the titular character of "The Gentle Boy," Ilbrahim. Ilbrahim, a Quaker child, becomes an orphan when Puritans hang his father for heresy and banish his mother, Catharine, to the wilderness "to perish there by hunger or wild beasts" (11). Pearson and his wife adopt the boy after Tobias finds Ilbrahim weeping beneath the tree on which his father was hanged. The Pearson's actions do not sit well with the Puritan leaders, who already doubt the intensity of Tobias's faith. These tensions are all in play as the Pearsons and their adopted son walk down their accustomed path to attend a Puritan church service.

Hawthorne emphasizes the moment's potential for violence through the substitution of war drums for the gathering church bell: "As the parish was then, and during many subsequent years, unprovided with a bell, the signal for the commencement of religious exercises was the beat of a drum; in connexion with which peculiarity it may be mentioned, that an apartment of the meetinghouse served the purposes of a powder-magazine and armory" (13). In his perceptive study of "The Gentle Boy," Colacurcio rightly identifies this substitution as one of Hawthorne's "sharp ironies" that indicates "the rigorously anti-natural bent of Puritan piety" (175). The "marital call to the place of holy and quiet thoughts" (Hawthorne, "Gentle": 13), however, does more than ironically comment on the Puritan community. The juxtaposition underscores the imbrications of religious oratory and physical violence. The congregation gathers in a meetinghouse that doubles as an armory because, like the powder-magazine and armory, the Puritan preacher equips the congregants for their battle against ideological rivals. Indeed, Hawthorne's use of martial imagery throughout this scene identifies religious oratory as the taproot of violence. Moreover, the beating of the drums signals the approaching conflict at the story's center, a conflict that occurs when an unexpected visiting preacher challenges Puritan ideology.

---

[5] Hawthorne's study of New England history highlighted the human costs of religious zeal. Over time, he began to discern an analogy between the highly polarized theological climate of seventeenth-century New England and the increasingly tense political and theological climate of nineteenth-century New England. For an invaluable study of Hawthorne's sense of analogy between seventeenth- and eighteenth-century New England and the United States in the nineteenth century, see Larry J. Reynolds, *Devils and Rebels: The Making of Hawthorne's Damned Politics* (U of Michigan P: 2008).

The meetinghouse scene centers on the pulpit and begins with a sermon in which the Puritan preacher praises the congregants for their participation in anti-Quaker violence. Unlike the Jeremiads that since Sacvan Bercovitch scholars typically associate with Puritan sermons, this sermon celebrates the community's righteousness. The preacher defines Quakerism as a religion "in which error predominated, and prejudice distorted the aspect of what was true" (15). Quakers' alleged theological errors justify Puritan violence against Quakers, and the sermon becomes a call to arms. The preacher figures this contest not as a dispute between rival sects but as a larger metaphysical battle between orthodoxy and heresy. Thus the preacher warns against "calling in question the just severity, which God-fearing magistrates had at length been compelled to exercise" and highlights "the danger of pity" in relation to persecuting the sect (15). Evidently angered by Ilbrahim's presence, the preacher "observed that such was [the Quakers'] devilish obstinacy in error, that even the little children, the sucking babes, were hardened and desperate heretics" (15). Heresy, in this formulation, arises not from a failed human practice of reasoning or hermeneutics but from an external, diabolical menace that possesses Quaker communities. As such, heresy cannot be corrected except through the extermination of heretics.

As the preacher draws his sermon to a close, the narrator shifts from discussing content to form and notes that the sermon includes "frequent specimens of a dull man's efforts to be witty—little ripples fretting the surface of a stagnant pool" (15). Unimaginative, violent, and authoritarian, the Puritan preacher's sermon represents the most dangerous aspects of religious oratory.

Like many subsequent US authors who would turn to literary preaching, Hawthorne uses the Puritan's sermon to set the stage for the entrance of a rival preacher. Consistently, Hawthorne's emplotment of the literary sermon involves the substitution of a failed preacher with a preacher bent on prophetic unsettlement. As the congregation begins singing a hymn, a muffled woman who "had hitherto sat motionless in the front rank of the audience, now arose, and with slow, stately, and unwavering step, ascended the pulpit stairs" (15–16). The woman, Hawthorne later reveals, is Ilbrahim's mother, Catharine. With the substitution of the word "rank" for the more conventional "row" or "pew," the narrative again connotes military activity and connects the Puritan sermon's rhetorical violence to its enactment in militaristic Puritan policy. Here, however, this woman "breaks rank," usurps the pulpit, and removes the muffler covering her face. She thus performs the first action of a literary pulpit exchange—an aggressive takeover of an established preacher's pulpit and the delivery of an oppositional sermon to a curious audience.

Hawthorne's initial characterization of this antagonistic preacher draws on both the previously discussed historical account of Margaret Brewster and classical literary sources. Beneath the veil, Catharine, like Brewster, reveals a symbolically loaded costume and visage: "A shapeless robe of sackcloth was girded about her waist with a knotted cord; her raven hair fell down upon her shoulders, and its blackness was defiled by pale streaks of ashes, which she had strewn upon her head" (16). Even before she speaks, the sackcloth and ashes identify Catharine as a prophetic figure. Like the biblical prophets Joel, Daniel, Isaiah, and Jonah, Catharine dons this symbolically loaded ensemble to urge her auditors to repent. To the already spectacular image the historical record offered him, Hawthorne adds an allusion to the classical tradition of Medusa. The wild-haired Catharine freezes the congregants with her eyes: "This figure stood gazing earnestly on the audience, and there was no sound, nor any movement, except a faint shuddering which every man observed in his neighbour, but was scarcely conscious of in himself" (16). Like the formerly beautiful Medusa, Catharine's appearance results from prior trauma at the hands of patriarchal authorities: "Her eyebrows, dark and strongly defined, added to the deathly whiteness of a countenance which, emaciated with want, and wild with enthusiasm and strange sorrows, retained no trace of earlier beauty" (16). In these ways, before she even begins to speak, Catharine strikes an oppositional, accusatory tone.

Catharine's counter-sermon begins by imaginatively playing on Puritan anxieties regarding witchcraft. As the audience listens, she conjures an image of confused Puritan leadership taking counsel and discussing how they should respond to the Quaker presence. She then shifts to a decidedly gothic scene calculated to terrify the congregants:

> And lo! the devil entereth into the council-chamber, like a lame man of low stature and gravely apparelled, with a dark and twisted countenance, and a bright, downcast eye. And he standeth up among the rulers; yea, he goeth to and fro, whispering to each; and every man lends his ear, for his word is "slay, slay!" (17)

Catharine's haunting narrative not only plays on extant Puritan anxieties, but it also seeks to force the congregants into a critical review of the sermon that preceded hers. Was the Puritan preacher's message, which cautioned the congregants against pity or attempts to convert the Quakers, the word of God or the word of the Devil?

As Catharine pivots from this opening into her central message, she employs the characteristic rhetorical figure of US literary preaching: antithesis. In an allusion to the Sermon on the Mount, Catharine preaches "But I say unto ye, Woe to them that slay! Woe to them that shed the blood of the saints! Woe to them that have slain the husband, and cast forth the child, the tender infant, to wander homeless, and hungry, and cold till he die; and, have saved the mother alive, in the cruelty of their tender mercies!" (17). Catharine's biographically inflected testimony identifies the family as the primary casualty of zealous theological idealism. In particular, she identifies the vulnerability of the mother–child relationship in a climate shaped by theological extremism. This assessment mirrors Hawthorne's own. As Larry Reynolds has shown, for Hawthorne, the familial order functioned as a canary in a gold mine; a breakdown in familial order, among both victims and perpetrators, indicated deleterious social conditions (15). Indeed, Catharine's warning to the Puritans that their "children's children shall revile the ashes of the fathers!" (17) anticipates Hawthorne's shame over his Puritan ancestors' religiously motivated violence.

Catharine concludes her short sermon by stealing a page from the revivalists' playbook and demanding that the congregants imagine their eternal fate if they proceed with their current policy. "Woe, woe, woe," she cries, "at the judgement, when all the persecuted and all the slain in this bloody land, and the father, the mother, and the child, shall await them in a day that they cannot escape!" (17). She knows she preaches to an inhospitable crowd but hopes her message, which has invited them to imagine both the prehistory of their policy and its eternal effects, has begun to sow doubt among the rank-and-file Puritans. She closes her counter-sermon with an appeal to any congregants "whose hearts are moving with a power that [they] know not" to "arise" and "wash [their] hands of this innocent blood" (17). Thus, her closing appeal echoes the initial call to repentance she communicates through her rhetorically loaded costume.

In "The Gentle Boy," Catharine's "unearthly eloquence" simultaneously attracts and repels Hawthorne; it is at once parallel to his art and a threat to it. More violently than any other character in his oeuvre except Matthew Maule in *The House of the Seven Gables*, Catharine denounces the inhumanity of Puritan policy and the theological extremism that horrified Hawthorne. Moreover, Catharine's eloquence, in contrast to the Puritan preacher's tedious oratorical style, strongly suggests Hawthorne's own romantic aesthetic. Catharine's sermon gives

> evidence of an imagination hopelessly entangled with her reason; it was a vague and incomprehensible rhapsody, which, however, seemed to spread its own atmosphere round the hearer's soul ... beautiful but shadowy images would

sometimes be seen, like bright things moving in a turbid river; or a strong and singularly-shaped idea leapt forth, and seized at once on the understanding or the heart. (16)

In this description of Catharine's oratorical style, the entanglement of reason and imagination and the emphasis on the aesthetic beauty and didactic power of "shadowy images" anticipates Hawthorne's later description of his own literary art. In "The Custom House," Hawthorne compares the Romance to the combined effect of moonlight and firelight on a familiar scene. The moonlight, he writes, invests the familiar with "a quality of strangeness and remoteness" and creates a "neutral territory, somewhere between the real world and fairy-land, where the Actual and Imaginary may meet, and each imbue itself with the nature of the other" (29). After the moonlight casts shadows and smears the boundary between the real and the imaginary, the "dim coal-fire" casts a "warmer light" that "mingles itself with the cold spirituality of the moonbeams, and communicates, as it were, a heart and sensibilities of human tenderness to the forms which fancy summons up" (29). Reading Catharine's sermon as a romancer's curse aimed at "seiz[ing] at once on the understanding or the heart" allows us to see her as Hawthorne's thinly disguised authorial double, a double that simultaneously attracts and repels him ("Gentle" 16).

In a more general sense, Hawthorne also seems to have been attracted to Quaker women's principled resistance to Puritan patriarchy and to have seen in it an analogue to his own animosity toward his Puritan forefathers. Alison Easton notes that in "The Gentle Boy," "Quakerism is not only an image of civil disturbance; it is also the means of suggesting a complex femininity, apparently conventional in its stress on pacifism and the promptings of the 'heart' that can make the men 'tender' or 'gentle,' and yet giving strikingly eloquent, angry public voice to anti-patriarchal dissent and 'mighty passion'" (85). As political historian James Morone notes, the Quaker celebration of women preachers posed a clear threat to the Puritan sense of "godly order" (69). Indeed, as Morone's study indicates, Margaret Brewster's trial highlighted the disregard for the gendered authority structures that Puritans saw as crucial for social stability (69). When the magistrates asked Brewster if her husband consented to her decision to invade the Boston church, she responded that God's voice had commanded her to preach to the Puritans and her husband "durst not withstand it" (69). In "The Gentle Boy," Hawthorne fictionalizes this exchange by depicting how the Puritans reaction focuses, primarily, on a violation of gender protocols. After Catharine completes her sermon, the Puritan preacher highlights her offenses by first shouting, "Get you down, *woman*, from the holy place you profane" (Hawthorne, "Gentle": 17; emphasis added). Catharine, like Brewster, appeals to "the voice" and accepts whatever punishment the temporal authorities might dispense (18). In Hawthorne's fictional retelling of Brewster's trial—a retelling that involves a queer identification between Hawthorne and a radical Quaker woman—we see him drawing on the anti-patriarchal elements of Quaker worship to respond to the shadowy fathers whose censure he constantly felt, even as he acknowledged that he shared their interest in legislating morality.

Yet Catharine's prophetic voice, which contains Hawthorne's own, must be contained. Her sermon expresses eloquently Hawthorne's central moral insight in the tale: the pursuit of cultural purity always guarantees violence and that the family is one of the first casualties of such quests. But this evocation of the sermon troubles him for several reasons. First, the sermon's violent imagery and rhetorical force suggest the frightening possibility of merely replacing one antihuman religious construct with another, a moral disaster realized later in the novel when a fanatical Quaker congratulates himself for abandoning his dying daughter because he believes the inner voice prompted him to do so (31). If Puritan clergy represented one form of antinatural and transcendent authority, the Quaker's fanatical devotion to the inner divine light seemed to represent another potentially threatening form.

More importantly, the sermon also troubles Hawthorne because Catharine's sermon's distillation of his theme resists his authority as a literary author and the moral authority of nontheological discourse more broadly. Having used this fictional preacher to perform an act of prophetic unsettlement and verbal artistry, Hawthorne reasserts narrative control, bracketing Catharine's powerful voice to reestablish the priority of his own. Just as Catharine expresses Hawthorne's critique of Puritanism, the Puritan preacher's command that this female preacher remove herself from a place of authority gives voice to Hawthorne's anxiety to reestablish the moral authority of the literary author by containing the story's explosive scene of literary preaching. In this sense, Hawthorne's literary pulpit exchange mirrors the conservative dynamics of the historical pulpit exchange. Hawthorne "invites" the character of the Quaker preacher into the narrative to provide a jolt of revival energy. He follows her sermon, however, with a series of narrative gestures designed to banish her preacherly voice and, thereby, strengthen his own project and establish a distinct vocational identity. These recuperative gestures make clear Hawthorne's discomfort with the identification between author and preacher afforded by literary preaching. His urge to free himself of this simultaneously attractive and repulsive identification accounts for the awkward rapidity with which the narrative focus returns to Tobias Pearson's spiritual journey as Catharine silently leaves the church alone and returns to her wilderness exile.

Catharine's peaceful and sudden exit from the church, a bizarre event within the story's diegesis, evinces Hawthorne's attempt to limit the preacher's voice within his fiction. To contain Catharine's voice and enable her improbable escape, Hawthorne dramatically alters his characterization of her (and the Puritans) and converts this radical Quaker preacher into a concerned mother whose love for her child and religious piety fit comfortably within nineteenth-century domestic ideology. Hawthorne's recourse to this ideological reframing of Catharine would be impossible if it were not for her gender. After she finishes her sermon, the heretofore bloodthirsty Puritans allow her to leave the church because they are temporarily moved by watching her interact with Ilbrahim. As she embraces her son,

> her long, raven hair, discoloured with the ashes of her mourning, fell down about him like a veil. A low and interrupted moan was the voice of her heart's anguish, and it did not fail to move the sympathies of many who mistook their involuntary virtue for a sin. Sobs were audible in the female section of the house, and every man who was a father drew his hand across his eyes. (19)

The Puritans' effusion of sentiment and goodwill makes little sense given the way the community identifies the persecution of Quakers as a sign of proper worship and has committed multiple acts of aggression against Quaker families. Where, we might reasonably ask, was such "involuntary virtue" when they hanged Ilbrahim's father or exiled his mother to the wilderness? Here, Hawthorne makes a telling departure from Brewster's story. Catharine's marginal status—a result of both her gender and nondominant religion—allows the character to be exiled from the narrative, contained by Hawthorne's evocation of domestic ideology. She is a figure ideally suited for convenient embrace *and* rejection, a symbolically loaded other who Hawthorne creates in order to construct his complex identity as an author who has accepted, albeit on highly original terms, the task of purveying moral influence.

"The Gentle Boy" demonstrates Hawthorne's responsiveness to both the impassioned oratorical style that typified the unlettered preachers of the Second Great Awakening and the historical pulpit exchange. The results of Hawthorne's inventive engagement with these cultural phenomena are mixed. Though Hawthorne attempts to reestablish narrative control after engineering the story's intense scene of literary preaching, Catharine's sermon nevertheless hangs over the narrative, the tale's most incisive, imaginative, and eloquent critique of precisely the antinatural religious formations that the story decries. The preacher may be easily dispelled from the world of the fiction, but the literary sermon continues to reverberate precisely because it distills Hawthorne's central lesson and communicates it powerfully. Through writing "The Gentle Boy," Hawthorne began to sense that despite his attempt to limit literary preaching's undesirable affordances, the literary sermon, once invited into a text, continues to haunt it. He returned to this problem, the literary pulpit exchange, and figure of the prophetic but vulnerable woman preacher in his 1852 novel *The Blithedale Romance*.

In many ways, *The Blithedale Romance* revisits the key theme of "The Gentle Boy": the humanitarian costs of organizing either individual lives or communities around devotion to transcendent ideals. Hawthorne sets his fiction in a utopian community modeled on George Ripley's Brook Farm, a socialist community based on Charles Fourier's social theories. Despite his distance from Ripley's ideals, Hawthorne helped found the community in 1841. His motivation for doing so was largely economic (Wineapple 147). Philip Gura nicely sums up *Blithedale*'s central question when he writes that by setting the novel in a would-be utopian community "Hawthorne confronted the reasons why such utopian experiments were established on this side of the Atlantic—that for all its rhetoric of equality, the United States was not yet a true democracy" (*Truth's* 192). Gura's comment also indicates the way *Blithedale* explores the fantasy of a return to origins, the way in which it examines the possibility of, as Hester Prynne puts it in *The Scarlet Letter*, beginning "all anew" (127). As Hawthorne examines these moral conundrums, he returns to the pulpit exchange, and, as before, he does so through the figure of the woman preacher.

To analyze how Hawthorne mobilizes literary preaching in *Blithedale*, one must note that throughout the novel the most intense debates about ideals, justice, and America's future occur in the shadow of a geological formation that Miles Coverdale, the unreliable first-person narrator, refers to as "Eliot's pulpit," the alleged site of Puritan missionary John Eliot's sermons to Native Americans. Improbable as it seems, Hawthorne drew on local legend as he created this key setting. According to regional tradition, Eliot preached from the large boulder, commonly referred to as "Pulpit Rock," that marked the northern border of the farmland that George Ripley purchased for his Brook Farm experiment (Gura, *American Transcendentalism*: 155). The role of this natural setting in the novel and its association with Eliot remains inadequately theorized. Lauren Berlant astutely draws an analogy between Eliot's pulpit in *Blithedale* and the scaffold in *The Scarlet Letter*. Both sites, they argue, are places of "sexual, juridical, and theological confrontation" (Berlant 351). I concur and would add *historical* to Berlant's list of adjectives because at Eliot's pulpit these confrontations occur in the shadow of Hawthorne's ideal intellectual.

For Hawthorne, John Eliot functioned as a model intellectual, an admirable seventeenth-century figure against whom he measures the characters in this novel set in the nineteenth century. According to Larry Reynolds, Hawthorne celebrates Eliot in *The Whole History of Grandfather's Chair* (1841), Hawthorne's collection of children's stories, to critique contemporary Indian removal policies (37). Hawthorne admired Eliot as a uniquely humanitarian figure and as someone content to be at odds with the prevailing norms of his surrounding culture. Certainly, as Reynolds points out, from our contemporary perspective, Eliot's missionary actions, including his fourteen-year effort to translate the Bible into the Massachusetts language, participate in larger forces of colonialism and cultural imperialism. Hawthorne's own perspective, however, was different. When he compared Eliot to other historical figures of New England Protestantism, Hawthorne saw him as the "single man, among our forefathers, who realized that an Indian possesses a mind, and a heart, and an immortal soul" (*Grandfather's Chair* 43). Above all, Hawthorne praises Eliot's selflessness and commitment to serving others. "If you should ever doubt," the grandfather counsels his grandchildren, "that man is capable of disinterested zeal for his brother's good, then remember how the Apostle Eliot toiled. And if you should feel your own self-interest pressing upon your heart too closely, then think of Eliot's Indian Bible" (*Grandfather's Chair* 49). With the phrase "disinterested zeal for his brother's good," Hawthorne intriguingly defines Eliot's zeal as a positive trait. In Hawthorne's moral vocabulary, zeal, or passionate intensity, typically carries negative connotations. But because Eliot's intensity is directed toward his "brother's good," not an abstract principle or idea, his zeal becomes a marker of Eliot's moral exemplarity. Additionally, Hawthorne saw his own intense commitments to pacifism reflected in Eliot's rejection of violence as a tool for social good (L. Reynolds 35).

For these reasons, when the Blithedalers preach while atop Eliot's pulpit or in its shadow, they do so in the ghostly presence of a figure defined, for Hawthorne, by his genuine humanitarian concern. Indeed, Coverdale senses Eliot's presence when he gazes upon Pulpit Rock. With his "eyes of sense half shut, and those of the imagination widely opened," Coverdale imagines "the holy Apostle of the Indians, with the sunlight flickering down upon him through the leaves, and glorifying his figure as with the half-perceptible glow of a transfiguration" (*Blithedale* 83–4).

Irony and outrage, thus, suffuse Hawthorne's construction of the novel's initial scene of literary preaching as, during a Sunday afternoon visit to the site, Hollingsworth, a man obsessed with prison reform and driven by personal ambition, usurps Eliot's pulpit and begins to speak. Berlant perceptively notes that in Coverdale's narrative "Hollingsworth's characterization ... hinges on his inheritance of the voice of the utopian past" (350). That voice is, of course, the voice of the preacher. But in Hollingsworth's ascension to Eliot's pulpit, Hawthorne depicts Hollingsworth grasping at an inheritance that he does not rightly deserve. Clearly, Hollingsworth's voice is not the voice of the Hawthorne's ideal anti-Puritanical preacher, John Eliot, but the voice of a dangerous reform-minded preacher whose self-confidence knows no bounds. Hollingsworth embodies precisely the antinatural and self-aggrandizing reform impulses that Hawthorne locates in the Puritan past and consistently critiques with his forays into literary preaching.

These Sunday visits to Eliot's pulpit, which include only four members of the Blithedale community, become a tradition, and, according to Coverdale, Hollingsworth regularly mounts the pulpit and engages in a discourse that Coverdale cagily describes as "not exactly preach[ing]" (Hawthorne, *Blithedale*: 84). The ostensibly secular content of Hollingsworth's addresses seems to block Coverdale from comfortably describing Hollingsworth's orations as "exactly preach[ing]." But it is evident through Coverdale's subsequent description that this moment constitutes another of Hawthorne's high-stakes scenes of literary preaching. An address described as "not exactly preach[ing]," of course, might also be characterized as "nearly indistinguishable from preaching." As both the religious setting and the description of Hollingsworth's auditors as "his few disciples" make clear, Hollingsworth manipulates the sermonic form and seizes on the moral authority vested in Eliot's pulpit (83–4). As he does in *The Scarlet Letter*, Hawthorne draws attention to the address's semiotic quality and aural texture, not its content. Hollingsworth preaches "in a strain that rose and fell as naturally as the wind's breath among the leaves of the birch tree," and Coverdale laments that "a treasury of golden thoughts should thus be scattered, by the liberal handful, down amongst us three, when a thousand hearers might have been the richer for them" (84). Throughout the narrative, Hollingsworth attracts Coverdale, in part, because of his rhetorical skill: "No other speech of man has ever moved me like some of those discourses" (84). Yet, in one of Hawthorne's burning ironies, Coverdale responds to Hollingsworth's sermons far less enthusiastically than Hollingsworth himself. As the self-absorbed Hollingsworth descends from the pulpit, Hawthorne parodies the visceral reactions to open-air preaching that characterized the Second Great Awakening and images Hollingsworth responding to his own sermons by "fling[ing] himself at full length on the ground, face downward" (84). The other members of the congregation, by contrast, debate the sermon's claims.

Reading *Blithedale* filtered through *Grandfather's Chair* allows us to see that Hawthorne's initial characterization of this crucial site measures the distance between Eliot and Hollingsworth, indicating the tensions that will doom the Blithedale experiment. Byron Stay characterizes this initial scene as a moment in which the Blithedalers enjoy "perfect harmony with each other and with their spiritual ancestors" (284). Though Stay offers valuable analysis of this site's role in the novel, I disagree with this assessment for two reasons. First, the scene dramatizes an alarming declension in moral authority as it relates to John Eliot. Hollingsworth immediately appears to be a gifted rhetorician but fails to evince "disinterested zeal for his brother's good" (*Grandfather's Chair* 49). This failure to measure up to the spiritual ancestor leads to the secondary failure of harmony between the Blithedalers: Hollingsworth's preaching leads not to perfect harmony but open disagreement.

Immediately following Hollingsworth's sermon and still in the shadow of Eliot's pulpit, Zenobia launches her own sermon about women's rights, a counter-sermon that eventuates in a tense debate among the community members. This literary pulpit exchange—in which Zenobia usurps the pulpit claimed by Hollingsworth—reveals the fissures that will fracture the community. When Hollingsworth "clamber[s] down from Eliot's pulpit," Zenobia begins to declaim "with great earnestness and passion, nothing short of anger, on the injustice which the world did to women, and equally itself, by not allowing them, in freedom and honor, and with fullest welcome, their natural utterance in public" (Hawthorne, *Blithedale*: 84). Coverdale, as a narrator writing years after the event, remembers only the impassioned tones of Hollingsworth's sermons. By contrast, he has Zenobia's sermon seared in his memory. He recalls her saying,

> It is my belief—yes, and my prophecy, should I die before it happens—that, when my sex shall achieve its rights, there will be ten eloquent women, where there is now one eloquent man. Thus far, no woman in the world has ever once spoken out her whole heart and her whole mind. The mistrust and disapproval of the vast bulk of society throttles us, as with two gigantic hands at our throats! (84)

If a figure in the community emulates Eliot's countercultural humanitarian concern, it is not Hollingsworth but Zenobia. As Eliot fought against the prevailing culture on behalf of Native Americans, Zenobia preaches against the domestic ideology of nineteenth-century America on behalf of women. Hawthorne highlights the words of Zenobia's sermon to contrast her humanitarian ethos with Hollingsworth's ultimately selfish concerns.

Zenobia's literary sermon closes with a jarring statement that, as Joel Pfister notes, demonstrates Hawthorne's rare awareness of the cultural mystification surrounding naturalized sexual difference (321). At the close of the discourse, Priscilla, a caricature of the nineteenth century's cult of true womanhood, objects to Zenobia's claims about women's equality. Zenobia responds bluntly by saying, "Poor child ... She is the type of womanhood, such as man has spent centuries in making it" (Hawthorne, *Blithedale*: 85). Zenobia aims to highlight a long history of cultural violence toward women and suggests that "it shall not always be so!" (84). As the most memorable preacher of the group, Zenobia seems most likely to carry forward Eliot's mantle.

Yet, again like Eliot, Hawthorne depicts Zenobia's mission meeting immediate resistance from those in her own community who deploy deeply entrenched cultural narratives to counter her pragmatic and humanitarian preaching. Priscilla, troubled by both Zenobia's sermon and Coverdale's positive response to it, turns to Hollingsworth for support. Hollingsworth, sensing Zenobia's threat to his mission, refutes Zenobia and Coverdale. He violently reinscribes womanhood within the domestic sphere: "Man is a wretch without woman; but woman is a monster—and, thank Heaven, an almost impossible and hitherto imaginary monster—without man, as her acknowledged principal!" (86). Monstrosity figures prominently in his diatribe because it figures prominently in culture's discussions of women who resist patriarchal control. Drawing on a long cultural history, he types the insubordinate woman as a Medusa-figure, "really neither man nor woman" who must be restrained with physical violence. Hollingsworth announces that he would not hesitate to "call upon my own sex to use its physical force, that unmistakable evidence of sovereignty, to scourge [women] back within their proper bounds" (86) if he believed that there was a genuine prospect of women attaining "wider liberty" (84). With this verbal assault, any possible analogy between Eliot and Hollingsworth comes undone. Hawthorne admired Eliot's insistence on avoiding violence. Hollingsworth, by contrast, immediately suggests its utility as a political tool.

According to Coverdale, Zenobia responds to Hollingsworth's threat with surprising and immediate acquiescence, yet her response suggests resistance that Coverdale cannot detect. After Hollingsworth finishes his violent outburst, Coverdale records that Zenobia responds by saying, "Well; be it so ... I, at least, have deep cause to think you right" (87). The irregular syntax of the phrase's opening draws attention to itself: it is a highly atypical formulation of assent. If the phrase seems more at home on the Elizabethan stage than in rural Massachusetts at the mid-nineteenth century, there is good reason. Zenobia, Coverdale tells us, frequently offers the Blithedalers "readings from Shakespeare" for their entertainment (75). Here, Hawthorne slyly depicts Zenobia delivering a covert performance of Shakespeare that expresses her veiled resistance to Hollingsworth's patriarchal assertion. With the line "Well; be it so," Zenobia strategically quotes Paulina, the fierce critic of patriarchal authority in Shakespeare's *The Winter's Tale*.

Zenobia's allusion to *The Winter's Tale* indicates much about both Zenobia and her perception of Hollingsworth, even at this early stage in the narrative. In Shakespeare's drama Paulina acts in solidarity with her wrongly accused queen, Hermoine, and defends her against Leontes, the misogynistic king who falsely accuses his wife of adultery. Paulina defies multiple men to defend Hermoine in the play's opening acts. In Act II, scene 1, Leontes irrationally accuses his wife of infidelity, verbally abuses her, and has her jailed. In the next scene, Paulina enters the jail to speak with the queen and plan a confrontation with the king. The jailer tells Paulina that, in obedience to the king's desires to surveil his wife, the jailer will listen in on Paulina's conversations. She responds by saying, "*Well, be't so*; prithee / Here's such ado to make no stain a stain, / As passes coloring" (Shakespeare 56; emphasis added). Paulina's line—which Zenobia recontextualizes—indicts Leontes for his irrationality, superstition, and misogyny. Paulina suggests that Leontes's actions have begun a process that will convert an innocent situation ("no stain") into a bloody catastrophe ("a stain / As passes all coloring"). In their subsequent confrontation Paulina attempts to reason with the king. He responds, like Hollingsworth, by verbally abusing her, and his language—"audacious lady," "witch," "crone," "hag," and "callat"—reveals his anxiety with authoritative women (59–61). Indeed, after he fails to intimidate her with his verbal abuse, he turns to her husband, Antigonus, and threatens to hang him if he will not forcefully silence his wife (61). Zenobia's freighted allusion to this drama, which goes undetected by Coverdale, Priscilla, and Hollingsworth, reveals her perception of Hollingsworth's irrational misogyny, proclivity to violence, and threat to the Blithedaler's utopian experiment. He, like Leontes, will turn an innocent situation into a scene of violence and disorder.

With these competing sermons at Eliot's pulpit, Hawthorne establishes the conflicts and tensions that structure the novel. At the novel's conclusion, Hawthorne returns to this symbolically loaded site to voice the central truth he sought to tell in the novel. He does so through the voice of Zenobia, the novel's strongest preacher and the heir to Eliot's legacy.

Coverdale eventually flees Blithedale when he senses that Hollingsworth's personal ambitions are fracturing the community. After a short stay in Boston, Coverdale returns to the community to learn more about the mysterious relationship among Hollingsworth, Zenobia, and Priscilla. He returns to Eliot's pulpit and finds Hollingsworth and Priscilla sitting before Zenobia. This final, pivotal scene of literary preaching completes the drama that remained unresolved in the initial scene of literary preaching. Zenobia claims to be "on trial for her life" and Coverdale sees "in Hollingsworth all that an artist could desire for the grim portrait of a Puritan magistrate, holding inquest of life and death in a case of witchcraft" (Hawthorne, *Blithedale*: 147). Coverdale now sees what was submerged in the initial scene at the pulpit. As Byron Stay memorably puts it, instead of emulating John Eliot, the Blithedalers, especially Hollingsworth, "enact the part of John Endicott," the intolerant and militaristic Puritan that Hawthorne criticizes in "Endicott and the Red Cross" (284). Zenobia's final sermon doubles as her defense of the rights of women against the authority of men. As he did in "The Gentle Boy," Hawthorne characterizes this pulpit contest as a military encounter. Coverdale observes, "My sensations were as if I had come upon a battle-field, before the smoke was as yet cleared away" (*Blithedale* 148). Hawthorne's imagery indicates violence and finality. It also anticipates a clarification, a clearing of the fog or—in one of the novel's central images—a lifting of a veil.

Zenobia's final sermon operates on two fronts. Most obviously, it exposes the antinatural idealism that so troubled Hawthorne, the manner in which reformers sacrificed human kindness for the realization of their ideals. More subtly, it underscores Zenobia's earlier claims about women's rights and men's success in shaping women's self-understanding. With regard to this later claim, she opens her sermon by appealing to a higher law, and she calls on God to judge between her and Hollingsworth regarding "which of us two has most mortally offended Him!" (149). Though Zenobia opens by admitting her "womanly" faults, including her betrayal of Priscilla, she highlights how patriarchal culture leads to these faults. She refers to herself as "a creature, whom only a little change in earthly fortune, a little kinder smile of Him who sent me hither, and one true heart to encourage and direct me" might have realized her full potential as a human (150). Zenobia's opening lines express her frustration at her social context—how her status as woman has profoundly limited her opportunities for growth. For this reason, she argues, she deserves leniency.

As a beneficiary of his culture's deeply institutionalized patriarchy, Hollingsworth cannot beg for a similar mercy. Zenobia turns immediately from self-scrutiny to her indictment against Hollingsworth: "But how is it with you? Are you a man? No; but a monster! A cold, heartless, self-beginning and self-ending piece of mechanism!" (150). Her comment adapts Hollingsworth's earlier assertion that a woman without man is a monster (86), a claim that Coverdale inaccurately believes Zenobia accepts. Here, Hawthorne, through Zenobia, defines monstrosity with a failure to establish sympathetic bonds with others. Hollingsworth attempts to defend himself by saying, "Show me one selfish end in all I ever aimed at, and you may cut it out of my bosom with a knife!" (151). Zenobia replies "It is all self … Nothing else; nothing but self, self, self … you have embodied yourself in a project" (150). This line voices Hawthorne's central moral concern in the novel, the truth of the human heart he sought to tell. For Hawthorne, this egomaniacal conflation of self with a moral or social project, which he detected throughout US culture, led inexorably to a view of other humans as either instruments *for* or obstacles *to* the realization of one's ideals. Thus, when Zenobia describes her relationship to Hollingsworth, she says he's rejected her only because he's realized that she's a "broken tool" (150). In the same manner, he's rejected Coverdale, Zenobia says, only because he would not "be quite your slave" (150).

Unsurprisingly, Hollingsworth, like Leontes in *The Winter's Tale*, attempts to defend himself by asserting the inherent inferiority of women's opinions. Like the Puritan preacher in "The Gentle Boy," he immediately responds to Zenobia's sermon by drawing attention to her gender. Consistently, he refuses to engage Zenobia in rational dispute. "This is a woman's view," he says, "a woman's, whose whole sphere of action is in the heart, and who can conceive of no higher nor wider one" (150), as if this claim does not, in fact, prove Zenobia's point about culture's hostility to women. In Hollingsworth's pathetic rebuttal, Hawthorne highlights how reformers weaponize appeals to "higher spheres of action" to negate the needs of human communities. The imagery through which Hawthorne depicts Hollingsworth—snow, ice, and iron—reveal to the "experienced reader of Hawthorne … that another Puritan has entered the scene" (Baym 193), and at Eliot's pulpit we see Hollingsworth at his most clearly Puritanical.

Readers of "The Gentle Boy" will see in this moment striking parallels to the pulpit exchange at the core of that story, but unlike Catharine, Zenobia refuses to go quietly. With her final sermon, she defeats her rival and gains at least one convert. Coverdale writes that she responds directly to her accuser: "'Be silent!' cried Zenobia, imperiously. 'You know neither man nor woman. The utmost that can be said on your behalf … is, that a great and rich heart has been ruined in your breast'" (Hawthorne, *Blithedale*: 150). The words pierce Hollingsworth and reduce him in a manner that delights Coverdale. No longer the eloquent preacher of "golden thoughts," Hollingsworth now speaks in "the abased and tremulous tone of a man, whose *faith in himself* was shaken" (151; emphasis added). In the first scene of literary preaching, Hollingsworth finds himself so moved by his own sermon that he throws himself on the ground. At the final scene of literary preaching, however, he finds his egocentric "faith" destroyed and departs after being obviously defeated by a rival preacher.

Within the fictional world of *Blithedale*, Hollingsworth's defeat delights Coverdale because this literary pulpit exchange establishes Zenobia's rightful claim to moral authority. When Zenobia effectively silences Hollingsworth, preaches a humanitarian message, and dramatizes humility and self-giving in her exchange with Priscilla, Coverdale believes he's encountered a leader who possesses both authority and kindness. In other words, he begins to rightly see Zenobia. His vision of her, however, remains obstructed by the cultural prism through which he views women. As if partially within a veil, Coverdale sees but does not see clearly. In the subsequent exchange between Zenobia and Coverdale, both still beneath the pulpit, he asks her to distill the moral of her recent discoveries at Blithedale. Characterizing the moral of what she's learned as "a drop of bitter honey," she tells him, "The whole universe, her own sex and yours, and Providence, or Destiny, to boot, make common cause against the woman who swerves one hair's breadth out of the beaten track" (153). Coverdale responds by asking her if she will allow him, as a writer, to "soften" her moral "a little" (154). His response reflects his hesitancy to fully subscribe to Zenobia's feminism, despite his obvious intellectual attraction to her position and respect for her authority.

As she takes leave of both Coverdale and Blithedale, Zenobia once again alludes to Shakespeare saying, "I intend to become a Catholic, for the sake of going into a nunnery" (156). Joel Pfister points out that with this line, an obvious riff on Hamlet's insistence that Ophelia take up residence in a convent, Zenobia alludes not only to her forthcoming suicide by drowning, but, more importantly, mocks the way Ophelia functions as a stereotype "for how [mid-nineteenth-century US culture] was fashioning femininity and representing women and their 'problems' to women" (328). Coverdale, now left alone in front of Eliot's pulpit, senses Zenobia's remaining presence in the space: "I was affected with a fantasy that Zenobia had not actually gone, but was still hovering about the spot, and haunting it" (Hawthorne, *Blithedale*: 156). Earlier in the novel,

Coverdale fantasizes about the abiding presence of John Eliot in this place (83–4), but he now identifies the natural pulpit with the novel's most powerful preacher—Zenobia. Emotion and sympathy overwhelm him and, moved by Zenobia's preaching, Coverdale throws himself on the ground "at the base of Eliot's pulpit" (156).

Coverdale's conflicted and vacillating responses to Zenobia's suicide reveal both his sustained investment in his culture's sentimental ideology and his sincere admiration of Zenobia. On the one hand, he types her suicide as a failed attempt to replicate the beautiful death of the love-stricken Ophelia, a sentimental narrative strategy that Zenobia seems to have anticipated in her prophetic departing line. When the Blithdalers recover Zenobia's body from the river, Coverdale describes "the perfect horror of the spectacle" (161). Her garments hang grotesquely from her already rigid body. Her arms remain bent as if locked in a struggle against "Providence" (161). And, above all, her hands remain clinched "in immitigable defiance" (161). Even the most physically powerful of the Blithedale men, Silas Foster, cannot manipulate her body into a less unsettling pose. Through alluding to nineteenth-century images of Ophelia's "lithe and graceful" drowning in an "Arcadian" setting, Coverdale attempts to mitigate the horror of Zenobia's death (162). Pfister points out that "Coverdale applies literary mythology, a cultural force, to do what Foster cannot do: straighten out Zenobia. He rechristens her Ophelia" (326). Hawthorne, thus, invites his readers to see the incongruity between Coverdale's attempt to mythologize Zenobia's death and the way her rigid corpse expresses an enduring struggle against patriarchal authority.

Coverdale's failed attempt to shroud Zenobia's corpse in a sentimental narrative, however, stands at odds with his genuine insight into the appropriate place for her burial. Though Hawthorne often seems at odds with his narrator, Coverdale seems to show sincere appreciation for Zenobia's intellectual force when he suggests that she be buried beneath Eliot's pulpit.[6] This suggestion

---

[6] In *Hawthorne, Gender, and Death: Christianity and Its Discontents* (Palgrave Macmillan: 2008), Roberta Weldon focuses on the size of Eliot's pulpit rather than its political significance and contends that Coverdale "would have preferred that she be buried at the base of the huge rock that formed Eliot's pulpit and not the pasture land. He would prefer her memory ... never made public" (108-9). Overall, Weldon's study offers many valuable insights into Hawthorne's fiction, but, in my view, her reading of these deliberations about Zenobia's burial overlooks Coverdale's obvious desire to permanently memorialize Zenobia. A detailed examination of the centrality of preaching in this novel enables us to see that Coverdale does not merely want to place Zenobia beneath a "huge rock," as Weldon asserts (108). He wants her name to be "deeply cut" on the face of the large and well-known geological formation that has been the central site of political, cultural, and religious debate during his time at Blithedale. It is, of course, easier to read Coverdale as a figure totally invested in

reveals a dissonant strand within Coverdale's thought, an impulse that conflicts with his embeddedness in his culture's prevailing patriarchal ideology. Coverdale suggests that Eliot's pulpit should become Zenobia's headstone: "It was my own wish, that she should sleep at the base of Eliot's pulpit, and that, on that rugged front of the rock, the name by which we familiarly knew her—ZENOBIA—and not another word, should be deeply cut, and left for the mosses and lichens to fill up, at their long leisure" (Hawthorne, *Blithedale*: 162). Coverdale surprisingly associates Zenobia with the "rugged front of the rock," an association that counters his earlier desire to want to "soften" the "stern" message of her final sermon (154). To underscore the progressive politics of Coverdale's surprising wish, Hawthorne contrasts Coverdale's suggestion with Hollingsworth's desire to bury Zenobia "on the gently sloping hill-side, in the wide pasture, where … Zenobia and he had planned to build their cottage" (163). Hardly the radical reformers they believe themselves to be, the Blithedalers give into Hollingsworth's bucolic domestic ideal and bury Zenobia in a place associated with the home-and-hearth rather than the pulpit.

In *The Blithedale Romance*, Hawthorne's literary preaching enables him to voice a powerful critique of the idealistic projects and cultural formations that he sees as threats to human flourishing—particularly the flourishing of women—but it also generates several narrative problems. Though imperfect, Hawthorne's Zenobia is a sympathetic figure who offers cultural critique in the form of unorthodox sermons, and she's a character Hawthorne invites the reader to identify with one of his intellectual heroes, John Eliot. At the same time, Zenobia's status as an eloquent preacher inevitably introduces the undesirable affordances of literary preaching. Her centrality in the novel, especially as she commands Eliot's pulpit, affirms precisely the clerical ideology and the association of the preacher with the author that Hawthorne labored to resist. To respond to these troubling byproducts of his embrace of literary preaching, Hawthorne draws on the conservatism of the pulpit exchange, aiming to affirm his authority by bracketing Zenobia's sermons.

Hawthorne enacts the conservative phase of the literary pulpit exchange through two moments in the novel's closing chapters. First, the novel's awkward denouement, a chapter that Hawthorne added to the initial manuscript after earlier declaring it finished, underscores the primacy of the literary author. At the novel's closing, both of its central preachers, Hollingsworth and Zenobia,

---

patriarchal ideology. Hawthorne, however, goes to great lengths to demonstrate that his narrator's inner divisions refuse to resolve.

have vanished. And the storyteller who remains asserts massive authority. Immediately after discussing Zenobia's burial, Coverdale offers a surprising metafictional reflection that encourages the reader to reread Coverdale's narrative with an eye for how his desire for Priscilla, a desire he intentionally represses throughout his telling, inflects the narrative's events. This metafictional reflection—a demand that the reader acknowledges the totalizing control of the author—should be understood as one of Hawthorne's attempts to respond to literary preaching's threating affordances. On the closing page, Coverdale admits that his self-protecting attempt to conceal his love for Priscilla shapes the narrative itself: "I perceive, moreover, that the confession, brief as it shall be, will throw a gleam of light over my behavior throughout the foregoing incidents, and is, indeed, essential to the full understanding of my story" (169). In other words, Coverdale tells us that we, the readers, have been manipulated, that we have been victims of an elaborate confidence game. Though the significant social disputes in the novel occur in the shadow of the pulpit and are voiced in the style of the preacher, Hawthorne uses Coverdale's destabilizing confession as an assertion of a more totalizing model authority than that of the preacher. The preacher tells their auditors truths about the world and claims those truths to be grounded in a higher law. The author, however, not only suggests how we should see the world but, more importantly, controls that which comes within our field of vision. In the final chapter of *The Blithedale Romance*, Hawthorne, through Coverdale, reminds us that, as readers of fiction, we submit, at least temporarily, to seeing the world through the veil the author casts over us.

The second narrative development that enacts the conservative phase of Hawthorne's literary pulpit exchange is, of course, Zenobia's unexpected suicide. This element of Hawthorne's plotting continues to frustrate critics. Like Catharine's inexplicable exit from the Puritan meetinghouse in "The Gentle Boy," Zenobia's suicide seems wholly improbable. Perhaps an 1855 critic, Margaret Oliphant, said it best when she wrote, "We do not believe in Zenobia drowning herself … It is a piece of sham entirely, and never impresses us with the slightest idea of reality" (qtd. in Pfister 326). More recently, Hawthorne's brilliant biographer, Brenda Wineapple, refers to Zenobia's storyline as the stuff of "mawkish melodrama" and accuses Hawthorne of sending her to a "surprising and early death" and "precipitously banish[ing] her and her ideas" (248). Yet considered within the long tradition of Western literature, Zenobia's suicide seems, tragically, quite probable—even expected. Ironically, Hawthorne's abrupt removal of Zenobia from the narrative reproduces the way the cultural force that *is* literature conspires, as Zenobia herself puts it, "against the woman who swerves one hair's breadth out of the beaten track" (Hawthorne, *Blithedale*: 153). Additionally, with Zenobia's melodramatic suicide, Hawthorne not only banishes her ideas but, more importantly, removes the novel's central preacher.

As he does in "The Gentle Boy," Hawthorne can attempt to silence this preacher's voice precisely because his central preacher is a woman and may, therefore, be contained though his abrupt mobilization of domestic ideology or familiar patriarchal myth. In this infamous and awkward scene, which doubles Catharine's exile in "The Gentle Boy," Hawthorne opportunistically participates in literature's conspiracy against authoritative women to alleviate his deep anxiety about his embrace of literary preaching. By attending to Hawthorne's efforts to negotiate this form, we can begin to make sense of these perplexing moments in his fiction. In both Catharine and Zenobia, Hawthorne created characters ideally suited for his literary pulpit exchanges, figures that seemed to offer him opportunities for both embracing and rapidly distancing himself from literary preaching.

Yet what Hawthorne attempts cannot be easily accomplished. In US literature, literary preaching acts like a chisel—such as the one Coverdale imagines the Blithedalers using to carve Zenobia's name into Eliot's Pulpit. When authors mobilize the culturally valued form to inveigh against their culture's besetting sins, they deeply cut their literary sermons and their preachers into their narratives' enduring structures. As the comments of critics from the nineteenth century to the present confirm, ZENOBIA and her sermons *are* carved deeply into the cultural imagination of *The Blithedale Romance*. Despite Hawthorne's efforts, he cannot erase what he engraved. In a similar manner, CATHARINE and her preaching remain indelibly etched—by Hawthorne—into the moral center of "The Gentle Boy." In other words, Hawthorne's fiction, like his own imagination, remains haunted by preachers and the echoes of their sermons.

Reforming the Pulpit: Rebecca Harding Davis, James T. Fields, and the Literary Pulpit Exchange

> To preach a sermon or edit a newspaper were the two things in life I thought I could do with credit to myself and benefit to the world, if only I had the chance.
> Rebecca Harding Davis, "One Week an Editor," 1877

Like Hawthorne, Rebecca Harding Davis sensed the sermon's enduring cultural authority and drew heavily on literary preaching throughout her fiction. Yet unlike Hawthorne, Davis regarded literary preaching not as a threat but, rather, as a liberating experience of social power. Philip Gura places Davis among a cadre of nineteenth-century US women writers whose works voice skepticism about both traditional religion and capitalism. "As women, barred from the clergy and the pursuit of wealth," Gura observes, "they were in the perfect position to do so" (*Truth's* 262). On the pages of the high- and middle-brow literary journals that flourished during the mid-nineteenth century, Davis could inhabit spaces that were largely unavailable to her, and, predictably, she chose to inhabit the pulpit and voice her skepticism through literary preaching. Yet Davis's embrace of literary preaching only tells half the story of her most famous novella's engagement with the form and its contradictory affordances.

An examination of the publication history of *Life in the Iron-Mills* (1861)—especially the editorial imposition made by James T. Fields, Davis's editor at *The Atlantic Monthly*—reveals a surprisingly complex engagement with literary preaching. This event in US publishing history exemplifies literary fiction's long-standing struggles with clerical authority because of Davis's and Fields's opposing attitudes toward literary preaching. Davis intended to confront her readers with a literary sermon, and in the original manuscript, which she submitted to *The Atlantic Monthly* in 1860, she included a scene that suggests the initial move of the literary pulpit exchange—the hostile replacement of a conservative preacher with a radical preacher who critiques dominant religious orthodoxies. In Davis's original manuscript, she offers a pointed sermonic response to a genteel sermon. Unlike her literary idol, Hawthorne, Davis elects not to follow this counter-sermon with any recuperative effort that diminishes the preacher's authority. The story's engagement with literary preaching, however, is far from straightforward. In a groundbreaking study, Janice Milner Lasseter demonstrates that without Davis's permission Fields excised the manuscript's central scene of literary preaching, a passage that Lasseter rightly describes as crucial to the "social activism Davis intended to effect" (185). Fields's heavy-handed editing, a dramatic containment of the preacher's voice, evinces a desire to suppress literary preaching because the form resists the development of a secular model of authority in which literary authors function as the nation's moral arbiters. The promotion of such a post-clerical literary culture was one of the primary aims of *The Atlantic Monthly* during Fields's tenure as editor.

In Davis's most studied work, she employs the initial phase of the literary pulpit exchange to indict and correct the abuses of middle-class Protestantism, a religious formation that she understood as a perverted form of Christianity that abetted industrial capitalism. In contrast to Whitman, Davis did not long for a new religion but rather for a recovery of what she saw as the neglected heart of

Christianity, a secret "that has lain dumb for centuries" (*Life* 41). Davis's literary preaching promotes a vision of Christianity as an anticapitalist social praxis that demands solidarity with the economically oppressed. However, Davis's engagement with the form resists triumphalism or the projection of a utopian future. Instead, it functions under the sign of vulnerability because her socialist Christianity depends on the actions of humans within an economic system that seemed nearly totalizing in its effects.

Davis's insistence on engaging directly with the culture's pressing social problems seems, at first glance, out of step with Hawthorne's more elliptical pattern of performing cultural work through inviting the reader to consider analogues between the US past and present. Hawthorne, however, served as a vital model for Davis and was her most important literary influence. And her tactic of engaging with literary preaching strongly suggests her reception and adaptation of Hawthorne's strategic engagements with the form. Davis's admiration for Hawthorne began at a young age. In Davis's autobiography, *Bits of Gossip* (1904), she notes that as a child she delighted in hiding in her tree house and reading Hawthorne's sketches, in which "commonplace folks and things ... took on a sudden mystery and charm" (37). She also recalls writing to him shortly after she published *Life in the Iron-Mills* and remembers her thrill at receiving a reply that he would like to visit her: "Well, I suppose Esther felt a little in that way when the king's scepter touched her," she gushes (*Gossip* 37). Later that year, Confederate forces captured the Western portion of the Baltimore and Ohio railroad, preventing Hawthorne's visit. But the two writers met the following year when Davis accepted Hawthorne's invitation to visit him in Concord.

Davis's recollection of her visit to Concord sheds light on the cultural work of her literary preaching because it discloses her response to New England Transcendentalism. Put briefly, it disgusted her. She writes that "to the eyes of an observer, belonging to the commonplace world" the leading figures of Transcendentalism looked quite different than "they do in the portraits drawn of them for posterity by their companions, the other Areopagites, who walked and talked with them apart—always apart from humanity" (38). "They thought they were guiding the real world," she writes, but "they stood quite outside of it, and never would see it as it was" (38). The metaphor of sight, so crucial for Davis's project, takes center stage here and the conditional verb form suggests a willful refusal. Emerson and Bronson Alcott especially repulsed Davis. She humorously recalls sharing a meal with Alcott in which he "heartily" ate a beef sirloin before offering a long-winded lecture on the importance of a vegetarian diet that prominently features pears, a fruit that Alcott believed exerted a powerful "spiritual influence" (39). Davis notes, with appreciation, that Hawthorne, her literary idol, "laughed like a boy" during Alcott's bizarre lecture on the "direct and ennobling influence" of pears (39).

The humor, however, barely veils Davis's irritation. By 1862, Davis had seen enough of the catastrophes of the Civil War, slavery, and industrial capitalism to reject what she saw as the insulated theorizing of the Concordians. As the following passage from her autobiography reveals, she was grateful that Hawthorne shared her opinions:

> Whether Alcott, Emerson, or their disciples discussed pears or the war, their views gave you the same sense of unreality, of having been taken, as Hawthorne said, at too long a range. You heard much sound philosophy and many sublime guesses at the eternal verities; in fact, never were the eternal verities so dissected and pawed over and turned inside out as they were about that time, in Boston, by Margaret Fuller and her successors. But the discussion left you with a vague, uneasy sense that something was lacking, some back-bone of fact. Their theories were like beautiful bubbles blown from a child's pipe, floating overhead, with queer reflections on them of sky and earth and human beings, all in a glow of fairy color and all a little distorted. (39–40)

In this indictment of Transcendentalism she identifies her own literary project's key aims. First, she wants to establish "a back-bone of fact," a rigorous assessment class and economics in American culture. Secondly, she wants to offer a cultural critique that accurately depicts real persons and events, not dreamy distortions. Davis's fiction turned to the commonplace and the contemporary to present a literature that engaged the culture's issues, cast them in a realistic light, and proffered, often through sermonic appeals, a means of addressing the social damage effected by industrial capitalism.

The full significance of Davis's literary preaching emerges when one reads it as a rejection of both New England Transcendentalism *and* an accommodationist Protestantism in the thrall of industrial capitalism. She believed that Transcendentalism and culturally dominant forms of Protestantism mirrored one another in their liberal tendency to enshrine the individual's development or salvation and, concomitantly, to marginalize social concerns.[7] Davis's frustration

---

[7] For a perceptive account of Davis's anti-Transcendentalist perspective, see Sharon M. Harris *Rebecca Harding Davis and American Realism* (U of Pennsylvania P: 1991), 12–19 and 81–90. Harris notes that Transcendentalism's tendencies toward solipsism and the cultivation of "dangerously blind allegiance" to Emerson especially rankled Davis (86). Despite the usefulness of this account, it is worth noting that Harris's discussion of Davis's "life-long distain of Transcendentalism" focuses primarily on the wing of that movement that prized self-culture and intuition (13). In *American*

with Transcendentalism pales in comparison to her fury concerning mainstream American Protestantism. Transcendentalism represented, for her, a doomed reform impulse that relied on a narcissistic ethos and was blind toward its own class bias. Far worse, American Protestantism represented a form of Christianity that had betrayed its most essential mission—solidarity with the poor. Time and again, Davis pressed her readers to consider the meanings of Christianity if it failed at its basic charge. In distinction to a hierarchical model of charity-based services, Davis advocated for a form of Christian socialism that through both its structure and broader political activity would combat economic formations that thrived on the oppression of the laboring class (Lasseter 183). Davis's writing attempted to address this social crisis. And because of her view of Christianity, this social crisis was also a theological crisis.

Drawing on literary preaching's affordance of moral authority, Davis addresses this crisis in her most famous work, *Life in the Iron-Mills*. The novella focuses on the tragic death of Hugh Wolfe, a Welsh immigrant and iron puddler. Wolfe lives with his ailing father and his cousin Deborah, a laboring woman who loves him but knows that Wolfe does not return her love. Wolfe represents the entire laboring class, but he is also individuated because he possesses artistic talent that he expresses through sculpting korl, the porous waste product of pig iron manufacturing. When three middle-class men visit the iron mill, they discover one of Wolfe's creations—a sculpture of a grasping woman with a "wild, eager face, like that of a starving wolf's" (53). The face of "a starving wolf" suggests *Wolfe's* physical, psychological, and aesthetic starvation. Most significantly, the sculpture's face asks "questions of God" and provokes the visitors to debate social responsibility, religion, and politics (Davis, *Life*: 54). When the men ask Wolfe what idea he intended to express through the sculpture, he says that the figure hungers for "summat to make her live, I think,—like you" (54). As the men debate the implications of Wolfe's sculpture, Deborah steals a roll of money from a visiting Yankee scholar named Mitchell. She gives the money to Wolfe because she believes it will liberate him.

As Wolfe wrestles with the ethics of keeping Mitchell's money, he enters a church and hears an unconvincing preacher deliver a sermon tailored to the tastes of his genteel parishioners. The sermon fails to speak meaningfully to Wolfe's needs, and the preacher's failure seals Wolfe's fate. All that follows, the

Transcendentalism: A History (Hill and Wang: 2007), Philip Gura provides a nuanced history of New England Transcendentalism that reveals the variety of positions and priorities within Transcendentalism, some of which Davis would surely have been more sympathetic with than she was with the strain of Transcendentalism associated with Alcott and Emerson.

narrator notes, "was mere drifting circumstance" (65). Wolfe despairs and takes the money. After being arrested, tried, and jailed, he kills himself by slitting his wrists with a piece of tin that, as Sharon M. Harris notes, he ironically sharpens on the jail cell's iron bars (47). Deborah serves a three-year prison sentence and then joins a Quaker community because a Quaker invites her to live with them.[8] At the story's conclusion, the first-person narrator reveals that they keep the korl woman in their office, behind a curtain. The mysterious narrator concludes by admitting that the statue continues to haunt them.

Throughout *Life in the Iron-Mills*, Davis's narrator employs a preacherly voice that speaks directly to the reader, engages in religious debate, and incessantly alludes to scripture. At the outset of the narrative, for instance, Davis's narrator tells the reader,

> I am going to be honest. This is what I want you to do. I want you to … come right down with me,—here, into the thickest of the fog and mud and foul effluvia … There is a secret down here, in this nightmare fog, that has lain dumb for centuries: I want to make it a real thing to you. You, Egoist, or Pantheist, or Arminian, busy in making straight paths for your feet on the hills, do not see it clearly,—this terrible question which men have gone mad and died trying to answer. (*Life* 41)

The trope of veiling informs the narrator's project of making visible political realities that remain invisible to the reader. The narrator refers to the mill as the site of a "veiled crime" (46). Likewise, the "key-note to solve the darkest secrets of a world gone wrong" are "veiled" but nevertheless present within the "solemn music" of the town's church bells (52). The narrator aims to stir the audience by suggesting that both a social crime and the seeds of its remedy remain shrouded by ideology. The narrator targets a trio of intellectual or religious types—"Egoist, or Pantheist, or Arminian"—who seem, above all, joined by their focus on self-improvement. The narrator sees the "Egoist, or Pantheist, or Arminian" as essentially similar because they pursue the common aim of "making straight paths" for their own feet (41). The narrator's cutting allusion to the frequently repeated injunction in the scriptures to "prepare ye the way of the Lord, make his paths straight" (Isa. 40:3, Mt. 3:3, Mk 1:3, and Lk. 3:4) denounces the self-worship and social blindness that Davis saw as the defining feature of mid-nineteenth-century religion in both its Transcendentalist and traditional Protestant forms.

---

[8] Like her mentor, Hawthorne, Davis uses Quakers to critique Protestantism. For an insightful discussion of Davis's representation of Quakers, see James Emmett Ryan, *Imaginary Friends: Representing Quakers in American Culture, 1650–1950* (U of Wisconsin P: 2009), 167–74.

The narrator's opening engagement with literary preaching also suggests that Davis's unnamed first-person narrator is also one of the novella's central characters—Mr. Mitchell.[9] Throughout *Life in the Iron-Mills*, Mitchell, the character, frequently quotes from scripture and offers scriptural commentary to challenge the other men who visit the mill. These moments function as condensed literary sermons, moments in which Mitchell preaches but only in a telegraphic manner. For instance, in a scene in which a mill owner absolves himself of any responsibility for the laborers' well-being, Mitchell responds by quipping, "I am innocent of the blood of this man. See ye to it!" (Davis, *Life*: 55). Here, Mitchell directly quotes Mt. 27:24, a scriptural passage that contains Pontius Pilate's spurious claim to be innocent of Jesus's crucifixion. The mill owner recognizes the passage and responds testily, "You quote scripture freely" (56). Mitchell answers, "Do I not quote correctly? I think I remember another line, which may amend my meaning: 'Inasmuch as ye did it unto one of the least of these, ye did it unto me' … Bless you, man, I was raised on the milk of the Word" (56). The mill owner's observation about Mitchell's habitual quotation of scripture is as accurate as it is significant. Mitchell, as both a character *and* the unnamed narrator, does quote scripture freely. More significantly, as he does in the novella's opening, Mitchell consistently applies scripture in discomfiting ways. Even with these passing quotations, Mitchell compares the mill owner to one of scripture's most ruthless leaders, Pontius Pilate, and suggests that the owner's mistreatment of the mill workers is an act of cruelty toward Jesus himself.

In addition to Mitchell's ironic use of scripture, as both character and narrator, the presence of Wolfe's statue in the narrator's apartment confirms that Mitchell narrates *Life in the Iron-Mills*. At the end of the story, the unnamed narrator reveals that he possesses the statue of the korl woman, a textual clue that the narrator appears as a character in the story itself. Critics who insist that Davis's narrator is an anonymous middle-class woman struggle to explain the presence of the korl woman in her apartment.[10] With regard to Mitchell, however, there are numerous clues that he would desire to possess it. The statue

---

[9] In "*Life in the Iron-Mills*: A Nineteenth-Century Conversion Narrative," William Shurr shows convincingly that Mitchell is not only a character in the novella but also the novella's narrator. My analysis builds on Shurr's work and buttresses his argument by identifying Mitchell, both as character and narrator, as invested in the project of literary preaching. The reading offered in this chapter also corrects Shurr's claim that Mitchell converts to a form of Transcendentalism inflected by Emerson and Whitman, a claim that, if true, would put Mitchell at odds with Davis's religious vision.

[10] See, for example, Jean Pfaelzer, *Parlor Radical: Rebecca Harding Davis and the Origins of American Social Realism* (U of Pittsburgh P: 1996), 27–8.

"touch[es] him strangely," clearly impressing Mitchell more than the other men who visit the mill (53). He reacts powerfully to the statue by gasping for breath and admiring it silently (52–3). Later, the narrator notes that Wolfe believes that Mitchell "saw the soul of the thing" (54). Finally, Mitchell visits Wolfe in prison, apparently having abandoned his plans to explore "the institutions of the South" to take up residence in the mill town and tell this story (51). Davis seems to be suggesting that during their private conversation in prison, Mitchell asks Wolfe for permission to take possession of the statue because it plays such an important role in the story he now feels compelled to tell America. Read this way, *Life in the Iron-Mills* can be seen as Mitchell's confession, as a record of his religious and moral growth. It is also a narrative in which, at least in the version Davis intended for publication, Mitchell preaches a veiled truth that has caused him to transform his life.

Like Hawthorne, Davis begins to emplot Mitchell's sermon by evoking a failed sermon that highlights a cultural crisis. Davis's depiction of the failed sermon, however, contrasts sharply with Hawthorne's pattern of presenting a flawed preacher. In this scene, Davis wants the reader to see how even the best performance of Christianity culturally available leads to tragedy. The failed preacher in *Life in the Iron-Mills* is not a sadist (the Puritan in "The Gentle Boy"), a cowardly adulterer (Arthur Dimmesdale in *The Scarlet Letter*), or an egomaniac masquerading as an altruistic reformer (Hollingsworth in *The Blithedale Romance*). In fact, and this is Davis's devastating point, the preacher represents American Protestantism at its best. He is "a Christian reformer; he had studied the age thoroughly" (64). Davis amplifies this preacher's failure by contrasting the sermon with the church architecture's effect on Wolfe. Wolfe enters a gothic church as he wrestles with himself about stealing Mitchell's money. As a repressed artist, Wolfe thrills to the "far-retreating arches" and the "distances, the shadows, the still, marble figures, the mass of silent kneeling worshippers, the mysterious music" (64). The sublime experience causes him "wonderful pain," and he seems poised for a moment of spiritual epiphany (64). The preacher, however, fails to deliver.

According to Mitchell, this preacher fails because his class-based assumptions operate as a veil that distorts his view of the world and the gospel. Mitchell initially characterizes the preacher in what appear to be undeniably positive terms: "The voice of the speaker ... was clear, feeling, full, strong. An old man, who had lived much, suffered much; whose brain was keenly alive, dominant; whose heart was summer-warm with charity" (64). He preaches the necessity of philanthropy (i.e., "charity") to the congregation and offers a program of reform, and the sermon resonates with his middle-class congregation. The representation begins to shift toward critique, however, when Mitchell relays that in "burning, light-laden words he painted, the incarnate Life, Love, the universal Man" (64). But Wolfe, though affected by the tones and cadences of the sermon, cannot understand the preacher's "light-laden" words. Because the preacher seeks to address "another class of culture," Wolfe regards the sermon as "a very pleasant song in an unknown tongue" (64). Here, literary preaching's affordance of a sensual, quasi-musical "language before language" appears as valuable but ultimately incomplete. Without a clear and accessible articulation of proper theology, the sermon functions merely as another aesthetic experience for the middle class whose pursuit of material gain is never questioned. Indeed, it seems that the preacher's aesthetic commitment to crafting his eloquent sermon mirrors his resistance to interacting with the urban poor. He embodies the personality that Mitchell notes among both "political" and "private reformers" who go among the poor "with a heart tender with Christ's charity, and come out outraged, hardened" (42). He wants to effect reform, Mitchell suggests, while remaining insulated from suffering or giving up the aesthetic delights of his culture.

With this scene of failed preaching, Davis's novella tilts toward naturalism and suggests that the collusion of traditional Protestantism and industrial capitalism leads inexorably to Wolfe's death. Mitchell describes the preacher's failure as the event that seals Wolfe's fate: "The trial-day of [Wolfe's] life was over, and he had lost the victory" (65). Throughout the novella, Davis points out how token religious observance obscures the violence of industrial labor and, thus, exacerbates a cultural situation in which that violence remains unchecked. Davis dramatizes this hypocrisy most vividly by noting that on Sundays the "fires [in the iron furnaces] are partially *veiled*" from the townsfolk out of deference to religious sensibility (45; emphasis added). The coverings placed over the mouths of the furnaces obscure the reality that beneath the veil the fires remain burning and require the laborer's constant attention. At the moment the mock Sabbath ends, Mitchell writes, the "furnaces break forth with renewed fury, the clamor begins with fresh, breathless vigor, the engines sob and shriek like 'gods in pain'" (45). The final simile—"like 'gods in pain'"—reveals Davis's theology of divine passibility, or the belief that God can and does suffer. More significantly, Davis suggests that the contemporary collusion of industrial capitalism and Christianity leads to a situation in which both God and man "sob and shriek" in pain.

In the original manuscript of *Life in the Iron-Mills* that Davis sent to *The Atlantic Monthly*, she engages in literary preaching in a manner that resembles

Hawthorne's deployment of the literary pulpit exchange. Like Hawthorne, Davis constructs a scene in which a mysterious preacher offers a counter-sermon to the fictional preacher who voices the dominant ideological position. The key difference, however, rests in the fact that because the narrator and "visiting" preacher merge in Davis's novel, there is no readily available technique through which she can recuperate autonomous literary authority. Nor does she desire such an authority. As Lasseter has shown, in the original manuscript, Mitchell's counter-sermon appears after the paragraph in which Mitchell discusses the reform preacher, the paragraph that concludes with the sentence "In this morbid, distorted heart of the Welsh puddler he had failed" (64). Because, as I discuss further on, Davis's editor, James Fields, suppressed Davis's engagement with literary preaching without her permission, I wish to quote the crucial paragraph in full:

> Years ago, a mechanic tried reform in the alleys of a city as swarming and vile as this mill town, who did not fail. Could Wolfe have seen him as He was, that night, what then? A social Pariah, a man of the lowest caste, thrown up from among them, dying with their pain, starving with their hunger, tempted as they are to drink, to steal, to curse God and die. Theirs by blood, by birth. The son, they said, of Joseph the carpenter, his mother and sisters there among them. Terribly alone, one who loved and was not loved, and suffered from that pain; who dared to be pure and honest in that devil's den; who dared to die for us though he was a physical coward and feared death. If He had stood in the church that night, would not the wretch in the torn shirt there in the pew have "known the man"? His brother first. And then, unveiled his God. (qtd. in Lasseter 176)

This paragraph, Mitchell's counter-sermon, begins with antithesis, the characteristic opening move of literary preaching. Like Catharine in "The Gentle Boy" and Zenobia in *The Blithedale Romance*, Mitchell begins his sermon by challenging the preacher who proceeds him. Mitchell compares the "mechanic ... who did not fail" to the preacher who "failed" Wolfe. By typing Jesus as a sort of mechanic, Mitchell proffers a vision of Jesus as a working-class figure who can repair "machinery," a provocative notion in a novella that aims to expose the "vast machinery of a system by which the bodies of workmen are governed" (45). Mitchell's representation of Jesus intentionally critiques the representation offered by the genteel Christian reformer. The established preacher uses "burning, light-laden words" to "paint" Jesus as an ethereal paragon of virtue. Mitchell's clipped language offers a jarring contrast that underscores the particularity of Jesus's physical embodiment among the economic and ethnic underclass. Mitchell's Jesus is not "the universal Man." He is a "social Pariah," a member of the "lowest caste," a "mechanic," "a physical coward," and the "son ... of Joseph the carpenter." Moreover, Mitchell's Christ does not speak; he is a physical presence and a person of action. Mitchell imagines that if Wolfe had encountered *this* Jesus—the Jesus who was hungry, urban, and thoroughly identified with the sufferings of the economically and ethnically marginalized—he might have begun to understand Jesus as both "his brother first" and then "*unveiled* his God" (qtd. in Lasseter 176; emphasis added).

This final sentence of Mitchell's counter-sermon serves as a key that unlocks his frequent references to a veiled secret, a piece of knowledge that has, in Mitchell's estimation, remained hidden and obscured. Lasseter is surely right when she argues, "This is the core of the matter, the secret undisclosed in the *Atlantic Monthly* text ... [This paragraph] identifies Christ as a member of the human community, a part of the people to whom he ministered, unlike the members of this church, none of whom is his brother" (182). The secret Mitchell would have his readers see is that the church has rejected Jesus's call to a life of solidarity with the economically oppressed, a call he embodies throughout his ministry. In the novella's terms, the church has "veiled" this call beneath cultural assumptions about power and economics. The Christian reformer's sermon insists that economic suffering might be alleviated through philanthropy that would demand nothing from the congregants but their increased financial generosity. Clearly, this conservative mode of reform maintains sociocultural hierarchies and systems of economic exploitation. It is a Christianity, as Mitchell notes, "toned to suit" a particular "class of culture" (64). Mitchell's sermon, however, suggests a mode of Christian socialism modeled on divine kenosis—Jesus's self-emptying and radical identification with humanity. In other words, he promotes an alternative model of sociality based on solidarity and celebrated throughout the scriptures he quotes "freely."

Mitchell's sermon allows us to reread the narrative with an eye toward a Christian socialist project. The question the korl woman asks—"What must we do to be saved?" (55)—operates on two registers. Most obviously, it confronts the reader with the veiled suffering of the laboring class in a deterministic universe, prodding, "Is there anything else available to us? Anything to answer our hunger?" But the korl woman's question, framed by Mitchell's sermon, is also eminently concerned with the moral obligation of the wealthy and powerful. It echoes the question that a rich young man asks Jesus: "Good Master, what shall

I do that I may inherit eternal life?" (Mk 10:17).[11] Jesus answers the would-be disciple by telling him he should sell all he has, redistribute his wealth, and then join Jesus and his disciples in their patient work. The man responds by walking away: "And he was sad at that saying, and went away grieved: for he had great possessions" (Mk 10:22). It is, therefore, especially significant that Mitchell follows his narration of the korl woman's question by indicting the rich young mill owner's inability to empathize with Wolfe. Mitchell's sermon underscores Davis's central theme in *Life in the Iron-Mills*: the failure of the traditional protestant church to follow their "carpenter" Lord in operating in radical solidarity with the poor.

In *Life in the Iron-Mills*, Davis refuses to offer a programmatic method of reform for the social ills it discusses, but she gestures toward the possibility of discovering such a remedy through the arc of Mitchell's life. If we understand that Mitchell narrates the story, then James Emmett Ryan's assertion that "none of [the upper-class characters] extends anything other than mere sympathy and prayers to the oppressed victims of subsistence wage-slavery" seems inaccurate (170). In fact, in Mitchell's life trajectory, we see the seeds of precisely the sort of social reform that Davis imagines. Mitchell transforms from the fast-talking, cigar-smoking, and ironic Yankee who is visiting the mill into someone so impacted by his encounter with Wolfe, Deb, the korl woman, and a new vision of a working-class Christ that he moves into the same dilapidated building the workers inhabit and commits to relaying the theological and political significance of their story to all who will listen. In short, Mitchell extends himself and his talents to the effort for labor reform, at the cost of his comfort and social status. His use of literature—and especially literature steeped in scripture and evocations of the sermon—as a means of social reform mirrors Davis's own.

According to Davis, Fields's excision of the work's counter-sermon "scarred" her original text and marred its purpose (qtd. in Lassester 179). We should note that when *Life in the Iron-Mills* was republished as part of a collection of stories in 1865, Davis insisted on reinserting a minimally revised version of the original sermon. Though substantively the same, the sermon in the 1865 version is two paragraphs instead of one and includes numerous revisions of phraseology.[12]

---

[11] Several verses later Jesus's disciples rephrase this question and substitute the phrase "be saved" for the rich young man's class-based formulation "inherit eternal life" (Mk 10:26). This substitution echoes perfectly the korl woman's question.

[12] For more on the discrepancies between the manuscript version and the 1865 version, including the full text of both literary sermons, see Lasseter 176. Lasseter insists that the original version is the superior version because it more clearly engages the novella's trope of veiling/unveiling. In the 1860 manuscript version, Davis writes that a sense of Jesus's economic oppression would have "unveiled"

Clearly, she understood this engagement with literary preaching as essential to her social aim and the meaning of her story. But Fields's literary aims were different than Davis's.

From its founding moment in the spring of 1857, *The Atlantic Monthly* set its sights high. The magazine's founding members—including Moses Phillips, Ralph Waldo Emerson, Henry Wadsworth Longfellow, Oliver Wendell Holmes, and James Russell Lowell—sought to fashion it as a vehicle through which literature, broadly defined, might shape American culture and morality. Susan Goodman argues that by 1857 "a Boston-based literary magazine seemed overdue. Readers associated the new magazine with the attributes of its mother city, the imaginative center of the nation's literary life … [T]he city had the reputation of a latter-day Athens" (4). Oliver Wendell Holmes memorably suggested that "a man can see further … from the top of the Boston State House, and see more worth seeing, than from all the pyramids and turrets and steeples in all the places in the world" (qtd. in Goodman 4). The association of the church ("steeple") with feudalism ("turrets") and ancient religion and ritual ("pyramids") reveals much about both the magazine's liberal view of human progress and Brahmin provincialism.

At its inception, the magazine was not antireligious per se, but it clearly suggested that Boston's literary culture offered the most enlightened structure of meaning for citizens of a modern democracy. James Russell Lowell served as the first editor of the magazine. In a prefatory note in the first issue of *The Atlantic Monthly*, Lowell described the magazine's commitment to being "the exponent of what its conductors believe to be the American idea" (qtd. in Goodman 6). Ellery Sedgwick describes "the American idea" constructed in the first issues of the *Atlantic* as "Yankee humanism," a Cambridge Brahmin ethos that valued intellectual freedom, dissent, progress, and Emersonian self-reliance (9). One can detect the founders' diminished emphasis on traditional religious matters in the magazine's billing as a "journal of literature, politics, science, and the arts." It would be more accurate, however, to say that for the architects of *The Atlantic Monthly*, guided by Emersonian thought, "literature" and "the arts" occupy the place formerly filled by religion. These discourses, in other words, offer readers a structure of meaning and exert significant moral influence.

God's solidarity with the poor to Wolfe. The 1865 version carries forward this precise theme but does not use the word "unveiled." Instead, Davis writes about God's solidarity with the poor being a "covered truth." These changes do not suggest that Davis changed her stance, though she perhaps felt that she had overused the word "veil" in the first version and sought a more subtle expression of the same theo-political point.

When he became the *Atlantic's* second editor in 1861, Fields sought to continue Lowell's essential vision for the magazine's cultural project. That cultural project, however, had shifted and become more explicitly anti-clerical. In the early years of circulation, it became clear that the magazine's claims for the authority of literary culture rankled New England clergy. Calvinist and evangelical pulpits took offense and engaged the *Atlantic* in a series of public controversies about religion and culture. Oliver Wendell Holmes seems to have especially relished these controversies and blasted New England Calvinism in the early issues of the *Atlantic* in both satirical fiction and nonfiction (Sedgwick 59). Fields inherited an editorship of a magazine that existed in mutual hostility with Calvinist and evangelical pulpits. Partially motivated by financial concerns, Fields included pieces of fiction and literature that he believed might allow the magazine to win a broader appeal. This attempt to court a larger audience, however, never seriously threatened to derail the magazine's consistent advocacy of Yankee humanism.[13] During Fields's tenure as editor, *The Atlantic Monthly's* treatment of religion evinced hostility toward religious dogma in general and emphasized the evolutionary nature of religious thought. In the pages of the *Atlantic*, Emerson's insistence on discovering and celebrating the "god within" often represented the highest pinnacle of religious speculation thus far (Sedgwick 99). But even this seemed provisional. The future surely contained new insights, and the *Atlantic* circle strove to promote humanistic reason over and against notions of religion that demanded subservience to historical religious teachings.

For this reason, Davis's intense literary preaching of a Christological message "hidden for centuries" suggested a dogmatic cultural affiliation at odds with the magazine's stated aim. Criticism of Christian hypocrisy—such as that which fills the pages of *Life in the Iron-Mills*—was standard-issue fare for the *Atlantic* in the 1860s. The same cannot be said, however, of Mitchell's counter-sermon, the one-paragraph sermon in which he unironically offers an alternative reading of Jesus's ministry, suggests its implications for contemporary Christian praxis, and its importance as a response to the violence of industrial capitalism in America. Rejecting the Emersonian claim that Jesus's ministry, above all, reveals the God within each individual, Mitchell insists that Jesus's poverty and solidarity with

---

[13] For more on Fields and the culture work of *The Atlantic Monthly*, see Ellery Sedgwick, *The Atlantic Monthly, 1857-1909: Yankee Humanism at High Tide and Ebb* (U of Massachusetts P: 1994), 69–113 and Susan Goodman, *Republic of Words the Atlantic Monthly and Its Writers, 1857-1925* (UP of New England: 2011), 51–9.

the poor are the most crucial aspects of his identity and mission.[14] What is radical about Jesus, according to Davis, is not that he reveals that God is within each human, but that the God "unveiled" by Jesus consistently resides among the economically marginalized. Mitchell preaches that properly identifying Jesus as a man who, above all, lived in solidarity with the poor and called those who would follow him to do likewise might be the starting place for the discovery of resistance to the industrial violence that brutalized American men and women.

This was too much preaching and theology for the *Atlantic*. What American readers needed was not more pulpit discourse or meditation on the particularity of Jesus's social class. For the early contributors and editors of the *Atlantic*, the key to the future was to be found in the future, not through a rereading of the gospels. By excising this key paragraph, Fields sought to transform *Life in the Iron-Mills* from a story that underscores the authority of a prophetic preacher and calls for a powerful reformation of dominant visions of Jesus's ministry into a story that exposed middle-class callousness to the plight of the laboring class. In Davis's original version, Mitchell undeniably preaches a counter-sermon as he attempts to reform Christianity. In Fields's version, Mitchell appears, primarily, as a gadfly who happens to know scripture. The deleted paragraph shifts into the sermonic voice in a manner that Fields sees as inappropriate for the pages of a magazine that aims to cultivate the moral authority of US literary culture. This, and this alone, marks the paragraph as unique. Fields understood that clerical authority resisted the development of autonomous literary authority and literary preaching resisted narrative efforts at containment. In other words, Fields's editorial decision reflects precisely the anxiety toward literary preaching that gripped Fields's dear friend and most famous writer—Nathaniel Hawthorne. Davis shared Hawthorne's attraction to the pulpit; Fields shared Hawthorne's

---

[14] Davis's sense that Jesus's radical solidarity with the poor was *the* defining feature of his work remained central to her understanding of Christianity throughout her career, and she often measured her contemporaries' claims to admire Jesus by their financial lives. Few things angered Davis more than claims to admire Jesus from people whose finances suggested to her that they did not understand what she believed was the crucial aspect of his identity and ministry. When incited, Davis could be merciless. For example, in her assessment of Walt Whitman in *Bits of Gossip* she writes, "[Whitman] saluted Christ as 'my comrade,' declaring that 'we walk together the earth over, making our ineffaceable mark upon the time and the eras' while he, Whitman, was loafing in a comfortable house in Camden, provided for him by charity, accepting weekly the hard-earned money of poor young men, while he had thousands hoarded which he spent in building a tawdry monument to himself" (123). Davis's portrait suggests that she did not know of Whitman's work in the Civil War hospitals, a kind and sustained act of solidarity with the suffering that surely would have softened her often unfair assessment of his work and life. See Rebecca Harding Davis, *Bits of Gossip* (1904) in *Rebecca Harding Davis: Writing Cultural Autobiography*, edited by Janice Milner Lasseter and Sharon M. Harris (Vanderbilt UP: 2001), 23–113.

anxiety about the pulpit's enduring moral authority over and against the moral authority of literature.

We better understand Fields's editorial decision by regarding it, above all, as an attempt to stifle Davis's unapologetic embrace of literary preaching. If an attempt to minimize the gritty, offensive, and sordid motivated Fields, as Lasseter argues, it is difficult to understand the text that Fields *did* publish (178). The version of *Life in the Iron-Mills* that appeared in *The Atlantic Monthly* features a narrator who critiques the genteel class (the *Atlantic's* readers) and leads the readers on a tour through an iron mill where half-nude women's bodies bear witness to the violence of Northern industry. It observes the laborers' "kennel-like rooms" and meals of "rank pork and molasses" (42). It features one of the most chilling and moving portrayals of suicide in American literature as, confined in an adjoining jail cell, Deb listens helplessly to Wolfe slitting his wrists, his iron manacles clicking against each other. It is hard, if not impossible, to imagine that these elements of the story remained if respect for the sensibilities of his readers motivated Fields. What *was* unique about the one paragraph that did end up on the cutting room floor was not its sordidness. What threatened Fields was Davis's unabashed embrace of Christianity's enduring social relevance and the way in which she suggested that the presence of the working-class Christ, summoned by the literary preacher, would be essential to redressing economic disparity.

This study of Hawthorne's and Davis's engagements with literary preaching discloses their shared interest in deploying the form to address the cultural problems that they believed most threatened the nation during the middle decades of the nineteenth century. Both authors relished including outsider preachers in their fictions—preachers not unlike the unconventional revivalists who defined the Second Great Awakening—who boldly denounce prevailing theological, cultural, or political ideologies. Yet despite these strong parallels between their engagements with this privileged form in US literature, attention to their use of literary preaching also reveals a sharp dissimilarity between the two writers. Throughout his career Hawthorne fought against his strong attraction to the pulpit in an attempt to mark off his own vocation. His literary pulpit exchanges reveal his desire to fashion a vocational identity that allowed him to wear the mantle of moral authority without wearing the minster's collar or strengthening the grip of the clerisy on the national imagination. Davis, by contrast, was surely writing about herself in an essay entitled "Women in Literature" (1891) when she observed that a "few women" write not out of desire for income or prestige but because "there is in them a message to be given, and they cannot die until they have spoken it" (402). Such women, Davis continues, "help themselves and the world by so writing" (402). Delivering such burning messages often blurred the distinction between the literary author and the preacher, but Davis did not mind that at all. In the violent and fragile mid-nineteenth century, the nation needed fearless preachers like her—and she knew it.

3

Reprising *God's Trombones*: The Novel Sermons of William Faulkner and Zora Neale Hurston

In 1919, James Weldon Johnson, then a field secretary for the National Association of Colored People (NAACP), traveled to Kansas City as part of a speaking tour to recruit additional members to the recently founded organization. While in Kansas City, Johnson worked tirelessly. On one evening, after four public speaking engagements, the tour organizers told Johnson that he had one more church to address. Johnson recalls that it was after nine o'clock, and he was completely exhausted. But he agreed to make one more speech. The organizers led Johnson to a church where a famous visiting preacher was scheduled to preach before Johnson spoke to the congregants. After three preliminary sermons, "mere curtain raisers," the visiting preacher stepped behind the pulpit (Johnson 8). The preacher began reading a sermon from a prepared text, and, predictably, the exhausted congregation "sat apathetic and dozing" (8). But then something remarkable happened that profoundly affected Johnson and, by extension, exerted a significant influence on twentieth-century US literature.

In the preface to *God's Trombones: Seven Negro Sermons in Verse* (1927), Johnson recalls that the preacher discerns the audience's disinterest, casts aside his text, and launches into an inspired folk sermon. The preacher—who remains nameless in Johnson's text—becomes a figure for whom Johnson expresses both admiration and professional envy. He records this scene of folk preaching in prose so vivid that any summary would diminish its brilliance:

> Suddenly he closed the Bible, stepped out from behind the pulpit and began to preach. He started intoning the old folk-sermon that begins with the creation of the world and ends with Judgment Day. He was at once a changed man, free, at ease and masterful. The change in the congregation was instantaneous. An electric current ran through the crowd. It was in a moment alive and quivering;

and all the while the preacher held it in the palm of his hand. He was wonderful in the way he employed his conscious and unconscious art. He strode the pulpit up and down in what was actually a very rhythmic dance, and he brought into play the full gamut of his wonderful voice, a voice—what shall I say?—not of an organ or a trumpet, but rather of a trombone, the instrument possessing above all others the power to express the wide and varied range of emotions encompassed by the human voice—and with greater amplitude. He intoned, he moaned, he pleaded—he blared, he crashed, he thundered. I sat fascinated; and more, I was, perhaps against my will, deeply moved; the emotional effect upon me was irresistible. Before he had finished I took a slip of paper and somewhat surreptitiously jotted down some ideas for the first poem, "The Creation." (8–9)

This narrative account recalls numerous scenes of preaching examined in this study, but Johnson's subsequent attempt to capture the folk sermon's energy in verse form represents a novel approach to literary preaching. In the preface, Johnson celebrates the preacher as an artist, an intellectual, and a political leader, and he describes *God's Trombones* as an attempt to document, in verse form, the African American folk sermon's poetry and music (6). Crucially, Johnson does not engage in literary preaching to deliver powerful sermon-poems that speak against specific social ills. Indeed, the sermons Johnson records in verse represent a unique moment in American literary preaching because they are so ordinary, so thematically apolitical, and because they so closely resemble sermons that were preached throughout America.

Throughout the preface, Johnson praises "old-time" Black church preachers as men of "positive genius" by whom "people of diverse languages and customs who were brought here from diverse parts of Africa and thrown into slavery were given their first sense of unity and solidarity" (6–7). The preachers were, in other words, like Johnson, leaders and organizers in the African American community, and no stable boundary existed between political and religious leadership. Indeed, Johnson notes that as a byproduct of the segregation of worship spaces in US culture, the Black church functioned as a unique space where "race leadership might develop and function": "These scattered and often clandestine groups have grown into the strongest and richest organizations among colored Americans" (7). At the center of these churches and hush harbors were men who, above all, knew "the secret of oratory, that at bottom it is a progression of rhythmic words more than it is anything else" (7). The seven poems that comprise *God's Trombones* aimed to represent the rhythmic modulations of the preacher's voice, the sermons' arresting imagery, and the form's narrative structures (9).

Though the preface functions largely as a paean to the folk preacher's artistry and leadership, Johnson does not shy away from critiquing preachers or their role in African American culture. In these passages, Johnson marks a distinction between his work and the preacher's, attempting to block the identification that he establishes throughout the preface. In a jarring moment, Johnson identifies the preacher as a sort of drug dealer and the sermon as a form that serves an anaesthetizing function: "It was also he who instilled into the Negro the narcotic doctrine epitomized in the Spiritual, 'You May Have All Dis World, But Give Me Jesus'" (6). We should note, therefore, the conflicted posture toward the preacher's influence that appears in the subsequent passage where Johnson describes the preacher as "the greatest single influence among the colored people of the United States" and African Americans as "the most priest-governed group in the country" (6). Clearly, Johnson's positive regard for the preacher does not protect him from also being a target of Johnson's scorn.

Furthermore, Johnson aims to distance himself from the preacher by casting the folk preacher as an anachronism, a figure whose role is rapidly vanishing. Positioning himself as a salvage anthropologist, Johnson describes one of his principle aims in *God's Trombones* by prophesying the folk preacher's extinction: "The old-time Negro preacher is rapidly passing. I have here tried sincerely to fix something of him" (12). These ideologically freighted lines, the closing lines of Johnson's preface, represent Johnson's fantasy of inhabiting a cultural moment in which the preacher's power fades. He is not, he suggests, capturing an active language that will continue to shape the nation but "fixing" (i.e., documenting) one that is already "rapidly passing." Indeed, Johnson's celebration of the sermon depends on its waning status in the cultural imaginary.

Though African American preaching informs numerous US literary texts that were published prior to 1927, Johnson established the African American folk sermon as a previously overlooked product of genius and catalyzed new literary engagements with the form. This chapter considers the literary preaching of William Faulkner and Zora Neale Hurston, authors whose evocations of the sermon were spurred by the publication of *God's Trombones*. Faulkner and Hurston have often been understood as sharing a literary kinship because of their shared interest in the legacies, folkways, and environmental concerns of the rural South. But Faulkner and Hurston also shared a fascination with preaching and preachers in Southern culture. In their novels, they sought to reprise *God's Trombones*, and they found literary preaching irresistible as they advanced their cultural projects and imagined their identities as artists.

Though the cultural work of each author's literary preaching differs, Faulkner's and Hurston's novels show a similar development of responsiveness to the form. As they wrestle with the sermon across their novels, both authors move from relatively straightforward evocations of the sermon in their early novels to significant refigurations of the form in subsequent works. By attending to each author's negotiations of the form, across multiple texts, we can glimpse new structuring principles of their works and gain a stronger sense of the cultural work they aimed to accomplish through literary preaching. For Faulkner, a strong authorial identification with the African American folk preacher at the climax of *The Sound and the Fury* (1929) led him, in *Light in August* (1932), to stage a rejection of the US tradition of literary preaching. Hurston's engagement with literary preaching follows a similar, though not identical, trajectory. *Jonah's Gourd Vine* (1934), Hurston's first novel, involves a strong authorial identification with an African American folk preacher, a figure that Hurston, like Johnson, celebrates as a folk artist of the highest order. Yet this initial fictional engagement with literary preaching raised critical questions about the imbrications of religious oratory and gender oppression. In *Their Eyes Were Watching God* (1937), Hurston, the daughter of a Baptist preacher, turns her sights to these questions and imagines the novel itself as a liberatory sermon by and for African American women.

Shegog's Sermon and the Splendid Failure of Faulkner's Literary Preaching in *The Sound and the Fury*

Frederick Gwynn: Do you remember any kind of feeling of satisfaction when you finally finished *The Sound and the Fury*? I think most readers feel a—a great equilibrium at the end there. Do you recall any such feeling yourself?

Faulkner: No, I don't. That's the—the one that I love the best for the reason that it was the most splendid failure. I think that—that they all failed. Probably the reason the man writes another book is that he tried to—to tell some very important and very moving truth and failed. He's not satisfied, so he tries again.

William Faulkner, comments in "Frederick Gwynn's Literature Class," 1957[1]

---

[1] From "Frederick Gwynn's Literature Class – 15 February 1957," MSS 6187 Readings by William Faulkner, Small Special Collections Library, University of Virginia. Stephen Railton and The University of Virginia Library have graciously made transcripts of Faulkner's sessions when he

If Faulkner's attendance record provides any indication, it seems that he did not especially enjoy going to church as an adult. Faulkner was not a religious man, but as his fiction makes clear, preaching and preachers fascinated him. During his childhood, Faulkner and his mother, Maud, often attended a local Methodist church. When he did not attend church with his mother, he sometimes accompanied his grandmother, Leila Butler, to the First Baptist Church of Oxford (Williamson 145). As a boy, he attended camp meetings where he listened with rapt attention to the theatrical preaching of traveling evangelists (Parini 21), and as a young writer he studied African American preaching (Bleikasten, *Ink*: 141). In time, like many US novelists before and after him, Faulkner sought the thrill of performing from the pulpit, even if only as a fictional character. At a climactic moment in his breakthrough novel, *The Sound and the Fury* (1929), Faulkner offers a textualized sermon, Rev. Shegog's Easter sermon, one of US literature's most well-known and overdetermined instances of literary preaching.

Though Faulkner drew on his first-hand knowledge of Southern religious culture to construct this scene, the Shegog scene also underscores Faulkner's enthusiastic reception of *God's Trombones*, a book that garnered positive reviews during the years Faulkner composed *The Sound and The Fury*.[2] Robert Fleming identifies *God's Trombones* as one of Faulkner's sources for the Shegog scene and points out that "Faulkner, in touch with Sherwood Anderson's New Orleans literary set, could hardly have been unaware of a book that was reviewed in the *Saturday Review*, *The New York Times Book Review*, *Bookman*, *The Nation*, and *Poetry*" (24–5). Shegog's sermon appears in the final section of *The Sound and the Fury*, and its similarities to the scene of preaching imaged in Johnson's preface to *God's Trombones* are unmistakable.

On Easter morning in 1928, Dilsey Gibson, the Compson's domestic worker, takes her daughter Frony, her son Luster, and Benjy Compson with her to church. During the service, Rev. Shegog, a famed visiting preacher from the Midwest, delivers the sermon. Initially, the congregants remain unimpressed by the visiting preacher's diminutive stature and his "level and cold" voice that

---

served as a writer-in-residence publicly available at the online archive *Faulkner at Virginia: An Audio Archive*.

[2] For a still widely cited study of Faulkner's familiarity with the African American preaching, see Bruce Rosenberg's "The Oral Quality of Rev. Shegog's Sermon in William Faulkner's *The Sound and The Fury*," *Literatur in Wissenschaft und Unterricht* 2, no. 1 (1969). See also André Bleikasten's analysis of this scene as a successful mimesis of actual preachers in *The Ink of Melancholy: Faulkner's Novels, from The Sound and the Fury to Light in August* (Indiana UP: 1990), especially pages 137–43. For an opposing view of this scene, see Thadious M. Davis's *Faulkner's "Negro": Art and the Southern Context* (Louisiana State UP: 1983). She argues that the scene fails to capture the energy and eloquence of actual folk sermons that were recorded during the era.

sounds like a "white man" (Faulkner, *Sound*: 293). After a few minutes of lifeless preaching, however, Shegog undergoes a dramatic transformation; shifts into the idioms, rhythms, and tones of the African American folk sermon; and delivers an Easter sermon that electrifies and unites the congregation. This sermon affects Dilsey powerfully, far more than any other congregant. But the text refuses any straightforward account of precisely how or why the sermon moves her. When questioned by Frony about her weeping, Dilsey answers ambiguously, "I seed de beginning, en now I sees de endin" (297). André Bleikastan notes that this scene presents "the only experience of spiritual enlightenment recorded in the whole book" and then, crystalizing one of recurrent questions about this novel, asks whether the vision shared by Shegog and Dilsey is "illumination or illusion" (*Ink* 142). To address this persistent question and analyze the sermon's complex role in the novel, I wish to highlight the three reasons that Faulkner turned to literary preaching and evoked an African American folk sermon.

First, an awareness of Faulkner's frustration with linguistic representation enables us to grasp his interest in *God's Trombones* and one of his central aims with this high-stakes scene of literary preaching. In an introduction Faulkner wrote for a later edition of the novel, he recalls that writing *The Sound and the Fury* filled him with "that emotion definite and physical and yet nebulous to describe: that ecstasy, that eager and joyous faith and anticipation of surprise which the yet unmarred sheet beneath my hand held inviolate and unfailing, waiting for release" (*Essays, Speeches, and Public Letters* 297–8). This oft-cited account discloses Faulkner's abiding irritation with language's inability to transmit the fullness of intensely felt human experience. The moment one utters or writes a word, the "definite" reality of the event, experience, or idea becomes diminished, and other possible meanings are repressed. One of Faulkner's characters, Addie Bundren, who also strains against symbolic language and longs for the immediacy of extralinguistic communication, voices Faulkner's anguish when she says, "Words are no good … words dont ever fit even what they are trying to say at" (*As I Lay Dying* 171). *The Sound and the Fury* pulses with this dissatisfaction with linguistic representation, and Faulkner responds to this situation by writing a literature of abundance. He piles clauses on clauses, employs multiple narrators, and stretches grammar's limits. He writes and rewrites the Compson story from different perspectives and in different styles to both display *and* challenge symbolic language's limitations and the alienation they produce.

Thus, though Faulkner deploys literary preaching for multiple reasons, the form's affordance of performative sensuality figures among the form's most attractive affordances. Shegog's sermon enables Faulkner to entertain an authorial fantasy of transcending symbolic language's constraints and to construct a scene that tilts toward the musical. Summoning the preacher's rhythmic voice and the impassioned responses of the congregants, Faulkner's text begins to *sound* and to gain semiotic force. Like Johnson, Faulkner not only evokes the preacher's voice but also explicitly compares the sound of Shegog's post-transformation voice to a brass instrument: "[His voice] was as different as day and dark from his former tone, with a sad, timbrous quality like an alto horn, sinking into their hearts and speaking there again when it had ceased in fading and cumulate echoes" (Faulkner, *Sound*: 294). Additionally, he likens the sound of one woman's verbal response to Shegog's preaching as a "single soprano" (295) and describes one congregant's moaning affirmation as floating toward the pulpit "without words, like bubbles rising in water" (296). Shegog himself compares a heavenly chorus of voices to "golden horns" (297). At once speech, chant, and music, Shegog's sermon transcends the divisions generated by language and gathers congregants into a space in which "their hearts were speaking to one another in chanting measures beyond the need for words" (294). Figured alternately as the miraculous intrusion of the Lacanian Real into the realm of the symbolic (Tebbetts 137) or as evidence of Faulkner's assent to "the Modernist premise that true insight is most often grounded in intense experience and cannot be adequately transmitted through mere words or logic" (Singal 140), Faulkner embraces the form at the novel's conclusion to suggest what salvation might sound like for subjects who have been alienated by a fall into language.

Literary preaching summoned Faulkner for a second reason as well. As is often the case when authors evoke the sermon in their early works, Shegog functions as an idealized authorial double, a master artist through whom Faulkner performs cultural work, imagines his vocation, and fantasizes about his power. Multiple textual details, besides the brilliance of his language-based artistry, confirm Shegog's status as Faulkner's double. Shegog's diminutive stature and "shabby" clothing, which contrast with his impressive power with language, speak to Faulkner's tremendous anxiety about his own height and clothing, as well as his pride in his skill with language (Faulkner, *Sound*: 293).[3] Additionally, Shegog's transformation from an unimpressive orator into a

---

[3] In *William Faulkner: Self-Presentation and Performance* (U of Texas P: 2000), James G. Watson notes that Faulkner populates his fiction with "physically small, inconspicuous" men who perform grand actions of courage or artistry (7–8). When Shegog arrives at the church, Dilsey's daughter, Frony, sizes him up and, unimpressed, says "En dey brung dat all de way fum Saint Looey" (293). Dilsey responds that she's "knowed de Lawd to use cuiser tools dan dat" (293). We should hear Faulkner's self-protective rejoinder embedded within these lines.

master artist, which occurs as, like a writer, "His arm lay[s] ... across the desk," parallels Faulkner's sense of the self-erasing procedure the author must endure (294). Faulkner describes Shegog's transformation by, ironically, comparing it to demonic possession. The preacher's unimpressive appearance changes when he begins to "feed" his body to a "voice" that overtakes him and begins to preach the folk sermon through him:

> He was like a worn small rock whelmed by the successive waves of his voice. With his body he seemed to feed the voice that, succubus like, had fleshed its teeth in him. And the congregation seemed to watch with its own eyes while the voice consumed him, until he was nothing and they were nothing and there was not even a voice but instead their hearts were speaking to one another in chanting measures beyond the need for words. (294)

Though the sermon enables the congregants' hearts to communicate "beyond the need for words," their experience depends on the preacher's suffering. Here, the artist becomes a self-giving figure as a succubus-like voice devours Shegog's individuality in order that artistic and cultural work might be performed. Like a rock on the shore, the narrator notes, Shegog bears the marks of being repeatedly seized on by a voice that has chosen him as its instrument. The image echoes Faulkner's claim that "an artist is a creature driven by demons. He doesn't know why they choose him and he's usually too busy to wonder why" ("Stein" 36). Similarly, in an interview with Malcolm Cowley, Faulkner described his process of composition by saying "I listen to the voices ... and when I put down what the voices say, it's right. Sometimes I don't like what they say, but I don't change it" (Cowley 114). In Shegog's self-sacrifice to the demon-like voice, Faulkner offers a flattering (and dramatic) self-portrait that reveals his ambivalent relationship to the voices that he claimed compelled him to write and hoped would enable him, as Shegog does with his art, to break through language itself.

Because Faulkner presents Shegog's sermon as an ecstatic communal event in which meaning does not depend wholly on words but also on sound and ceremony, critics tend to overlook the way the sermon indicts racial injustice, arguing instead that, as Bleikasten puts it, "what matters here is not so much the message conveyed as the collective ceremony of its utterance and its sharing" (*Ink* 141). Indeed, many critics have disregarded the content of Shegog's sermon or its potential as a message that, like other scenes of literary preaching, leverages the form's affordance of moral authority to perform prophetic unsettlement. Noel Polk, for instance, calls the sermon "a hodgepodge of pseudo-eloquence and non sequitur and nonsense theology" (Polk 134). In a similar vein, Daniel Singal claims, "There is no real narrative or argument to what he says and little order or cohesion—just a montage of phrases and images conveying the sufferings of Jesus" (141). Critics are not entirely incorrect in their negative assessment of the ambiguous scene. At one level, the worship scene may communicate, to some listeners, a problematic illusion of ultimate well-being amidst a culture of systematic racial violence.

Casting Shegog's sermon as "nonsense theology," however, preempts precisely the sort of critical analysis that this passage demands and obscures the third reason the form attracted Faulkner—its affordance of moral authority. The sermon's message is hardly nonsensical or irrelevant, either to Dilsey or to the scathing prophecy about white Southern culture that Faulkner advances. Dilsey's reaction to Shegog's sermon becomes intelligible when we shift our attention away from the sermon's performative sensuality and its conventional promise of religious salvation and, instead, attend to how Faulkner's most famous textualized sermon performs a theological critique of the South's systematic practice of racial violence. Crucially, Dilsey's response does not represent the entire community of congregants. Dilsey's response represents a minority report. As a model auditor, who also functions as a model reader, she rightly values the sermon's content as well as its aesthetic force.

Shegog's political genius depends on his ability to defamiliarize Christianity's central narratives—to play fast-and-loose with the scriptural sources—to offer a narrative that arrests the attention and intersects the attentive congregants' communal history. In Shegog's sermon, Faulkner represents racially motivated violence—especially violence against women and children—as a recapitulation of the ethnic cleansing that King Herod orders after learning of Jesus's birth and identifying him as a potential rival (Mt. 2:16-18).[4] In a sermonic moment that anticipates the trauma at the heart of Morrison's *Beloved*, Shegog directs the congregants' attention to a group of children sitting among them:

> "Jesus wus like dat once. He mammy suffered de glory en de pangs. Sometime maybe she helt him at de nightfall, whilst de angels singin him to sleep; maybe she look out de do en see de Roman po-lice passin." He tramped back and forth, mopping his face. "Listen, breddren! I sees de day. Ma'y settin in de do wid Jesus

---

[4] For another account of the meanings of Shegog's pattern of historical analogy, see David Hein, "The Reverend Mr. Shegog's Easter Sermon: Preaching as Communion in Faulkner's *The Sound and the Fury*." *The Mississippi Quarterly* 58, nos. 3-4 (2005): 572. Though he treats this passage differently, Hein perceptively regards this moment as a sign of Shegog's firm embeddedness in the practice of Black preaching and Faulkner's intimate knowledge of that tradition: "A leitmotif of African-American preaching has been the presence of suffering and redemption in the interlocking stories of the ancient Hebrews, of Jesus, and of blacks themselves" (572).

on her lap, de little Jesus. Like dem chillen dar, de little Jesus. I hears de angels signin de peaceful songs en de glory; I see de closin eyes; sees Mary jump up, sees de sojer face: We gwine to kill! We gwine to kill! We gwine to kill yo little Jesus!" (Faulkner, *Sound*: 296)

In this passage, Shegog's repeated "maybe" invites the congregants to join him in an act of gothic imagination. His description of the Roman soldiers as "po-lice" collapses the ethno-political violence of first-century Palestine and the racialized violence of twentieth-century Mississippi. The Romans' threat to sever the mother–child dyad conjures the cultural history of the auction block and slavery's systematic anti-maternal violence. Additionally, Shegog marks the policemen as ethnically distinct from the people they terrorize by identifying them as "Roman." These are not just policemen; these are policemen whose power and authority derive from their ethnicity. Thus, as Shegog recounts the Passion week drama, he counterintuitively blocks the African American congregants from identifying with the guilty party, those who crucify Christ, and marks a clear distinction between the oppressed and the oppressor.

After making this crucial move, Shegog transitions rapidly to a depiction of Jesus's crucifixion that compares it to a lynching, a topic never far from Faulkner's haunted imagination.[5] Shegog again revises the scriptural accounts and imagines "boastin" and "braggin" men mocking Jesus as they kill him on one of Calvary's "sacred trees" (296). The words "cross" and "tree" are often used synonymously in hymnody and religious poetry, but Shegog's usage requires analysis because of his highly conspicuous repetition of the word "tree" when he imagines one of the "boastin" men shouting: "Ef you be Jesus, lif up yo tree en walk!" (296). To account for this strange line some critics have suggested that Shegog confuses "two quite different New Testament passages, one a taunt quoted in the Passion narrative and the other a command uttered by Jesus during a healing miracle" (Hein 573). Shegog, however, is not confused. The soldier's taunt conjures a surreal, nightmarish image of a victim of ritualized violence struggling to find his footing and believing that he might survive this atrocity if only he could uproot the tree upon which he is being murdered. In the sermon, this macabre ritualized killing—perhaps a grotesquely altered crucifixion or, more likely, a

---

[5] In 1908, when Faulkner was eleven, a man named Nelse Patton was lynched in Oxford not far from Faulkner's home. Faulkner knew of this atrocity and likely saw Patton's mutilated body the following morning. Faulkner's fictions obsessively evoke lynchings or near-lynchings, and the horrors of lynching and what it revealed about Southern culture were never far from Faulkner's mind. For more on Faulkner, lynching, and Nelse Patton, see Joseph Blotner's *Faulkner: A Biography* (UP of Mississippi), 113–14 and Doreen Fowler's "Beyond Oedipus: Lucas Beauchamp, Ned Barnett, and Faulkner's Intruder in the Dust," *MFS Modern Fiction Studies* 53, no. 4 (2007): 790–2.

hanging—leads Shegog to describe a vision in which he "hears de weepin en de cryin en de turnt-away face of God: dey done kilt Jesus; dey done kilt my Son!" (296).[6]

Shegog's sermon ends with a traditional affirmation of faith, but prior to this conclusion he describes God's refusal to tolerate the wickedness the sermon catalogues. The sermon's penultimate movement deeply affects Dilsey and leads to her rejection of the Compson family. Dilsey's close observation of the Compson's generational selfishness, elitism, and racism, uniquely prepares her to hear Shegog's message. The God that Faulkner depicts through Shegog's sermon is a God who will not be mocked, a "widowed God" that "aint gwine overload heaven" by allowing the unjust to enter (296). Put bluntly, the deity that Shegog describes does not hesitate to damn those who deserve it. He tells the congregation, "I sees de darkness en de death everlastin upon de generations" (296). We should see a direct linkage between this imprecatory line and Dilsey's overdetermined statement: "I seed de beginnin, en now I sees de endin" (297). Shegog's sermon enables Dilsey to glimpse both the justice and the inevitability of the Compson family's destruction. It also compels her to see her moral obligation to separate her fate from theirs. Philip Castille rightly emphasizes the importance of Dilsey's epiphanic "*now* I sees de endin" (428). In this moment, Dilsey comes to see the Compsons as "beyond salvation, beyond even help, because God has turned 'His mighty face' and 'shet His do' to them for their cruelty and hatred" (Castile 428). In "1699-1945. Appendix: The Compsons," the appendix to *The Sound and the Fury* that Faulkner published in 1945, we learn that Dilsey refuses to speak to Jason Compson again after this Easter morning, moves to Memphis, and remains unmoved by hearing of Quentin's subsequent trouble (640-7). One must ignore the sermon's transformative influence on Dilsey's life to suggest that its content does not matter.

After the sermon, Dilsey tries to communicate her new insight to Frony. "You tend to yo business," she tells her daughter, "en let the whitefolks tend

---

[6] Shegog's formulation of this Good Friday scene anticipates precisely the parallel between lynching and Jesus's crucifixion that Faulkner's other famous preacher, Gail Hightower, suggests in *Light in August*. When Hightower understands that Joe's capture ignites Jefferson's racist mania, he anticipates Joe's lynching and says that in Joe's "crucifixion they too will raise a cross ... They will do it gladly, gladly. That's why it is so terrible, terrible, terrible" (368). The town's murderous impulse confirms and concretizes its shaping narratives of racial identity. Hightower understands that for the white citizens of Jefferson to "pity" Christmas would be tantamount to an admission of "self-doubt" regarding the racial hierarchy upon which their identity depends (368). The connection that Faulkner, through both Shegog and Hightower, suggests between Jesus's crucifixion and postbellum lynching is that these ritualized murders enable politically empowered members of ethnically stratified societies to shore up their threatened confidence in the existing social order.

to deir'n" (Faulkner, *Sound*: 298). Castille astutely notes that these are lines of resistance that articulate a new separation from the Compsons (429). James Weldon Johnson lamented the way African American preaching too often led Black Americans to embrace a religion that celebrated patient suffering under oppressive social structures, a Nietzchean morality of the weak represented by the title of the hymn "You May Have All Dis World, But Give Me Jesus" (6). Dilsey's post-sermon attitude, however, would be epitomized by a decidedly political sort of hymn, one that claims the value of this world and her life within it. After hearing Shegog, she seems to be singing something like "You Can All Go to Hell, But I'm Going to Memphis."

All this, however, hardly confirms the sermon's status as an unqualified success or, more broadly, Shegog's sermon as a tool for advancing something like Black liberation theology. Faulkner's scene records the other congregants' religious ecstasies *and* the sermon's failure to do more than offer them a momentary reprieve from the everyday orderings of their lives. At the sermon's conclusion, Dilsey, a convert to a new mode of being, cannot stop weeping. The other congregants, however, begin to talk casually as if nothing has changed. After the intense aesthetic experience that provides a short-lived sense of union and transcendence, they divide and begin "talking easily again group to group" (Faulkner, *Sound*: 297). Commenting on the congregants' response, Castille observes "there is no evidence that anyone else is deeply affected by the homily" (428). Frony, obviously unchanged, tells Dilsey to stop crying "wid all these people lookin. We be passin white folks soon" (297). In the other congregants' responses and Frony's anxious desire to hide her mother's emotion from "white folks," Faulkner confirms Johnson's fears about the narcotic tendency of African American folk preaching.

What, then, should readers make of the sermon? To return to Bleikasten's formulation, what do we make of a sermon that seems to provide liberatory illumination to one congregant but ideological illusion to the others? Is it "splendid" because it dramatizes the transcendence of symbolic language, indicts racist violence, and enables Dilsey Gibson to seize a new future? Is it a "failure" because, aside from offering the other congregants a fleeting reprieve from the alienation wrought by language, it makes little difference to a world shaped by potent social forms such as caste, gender hierarchy, and economics? Is it a "failure" because Faulkner, like many authors before and after him, chooses to enter the pulpit to address his culture's moral failures and display the power of his art, thereby abetting an already entrenched clerical ideology and courting an affiliation of himself with the preacher? Or, worse, is it a failure because it suggests that the real-world matters little in light of the promises of Christian eschatology? Faulkner understood the sermon as affording, as part of its structure and cultural heritage, all these possibilities. It is a literary form of "splendid failure" that offers possibilities for liberatory resistance alongside mystification and, relatedly, affords moral authority as it simultaneously sustains an ideology in which the preacher is vested with tremendous symbolic power. Faulkner remained troubled by the problematic connections he sensed among the sermon, cultural authority, and Southern history, and, shortly after publishing *The Sound and the Fury*, Faulkner returned his attention to the form.

"And Him in the Pulpit Cursing God": Contested Pulpits and Anti-Preaching in *Light in August*

It has become a critical commonplace to acknowledge *Light in August* (1932) as Faulkner's most sustained reflection on the perversity of Southern religion; however, neither the novel's complex engagement with literary preaching nor the manner in which this preoccupation extends the ambiguity that defines the literary preaching of *The Sound and the Fury* has been sufficiently addressed. It is no accident that Faulkner's bloodiest novel revolves around the pulpit. As in Hawthorne's oeuvre, violence and religious rhetoric seem inextricably intertwined in Faulkner's fictional Yoknapatawpha because the Southern pulpit often licenses dominant culture's violence while simultaneously promoting the long-suffering of the oppressed. Faulkner understood the African American sermon as a potent performance genre that, as in the rare case of Dilsey Gibson, might offer the subject liberation. But Faulkner also understood that sermons often abetted and lent theological support to the South's most dangerous ideologies. In *Light in August*, Faulkner repudiates literary preaching, despite its alluring possibilities, because US culture's continual deference to the sermon, which literary preaching encourages, propagates dangerous idealisms and consistently provides theological cover for people who leverage the form to serve their own ends. *Light in August* reveals Faulkner's reception of Hawthorne, reflects his bitter analysis of the sermon's function in Southern culture, and, most importantly, makes clear his determination to break from the tradition of literary preaching.

Faulkner's inventive rejection of literary preaching, an approach that involves what I refer to as the *anti-sermon*, represents a critical development of the form in US letters. Faulkner's anti-sermons appear as intentionally stylized and dramatic interruptions of sermons. They answer ideologically loaded sermons with something like performative terrorism. Less public oratory than performance art, anti-sermons differ from what I have referred to in Chapter 2 as counter-sermons because an anti-sermon does not aim to correct or reform, only to intimidate and silence. An anti-sermon denounces, rejects, and curses, and it resists the temptation to fill the vacuum of ministerial authority that it creates. The anti-sermon does not engage in the sermonic voice, but rather silences it with a primal cry that indicts the sermon for its role in catalyzing violence and licensing oppression.

Recent historical studies of Southern religion enable a clearer perception of the cultural work Faulkner performs though the novel's anti-sermons. According to Rosemary Magee, in the wake of the Union's victory, white Southern preachers gathered tremendous cultural authority by providing congregants with theological rationales for the Confederacy's fall (120). The answers from the pulpit were not easy, but they were authoritative. According to Southern ministers, though the Southern cause was morally right and Northerners waged an unjust war against the Confederacy, God punished the South in order to chasten it and refine it for his own inscrutable purposes. According to this line of thought, scripture often revealed that God tested those he loved, not just as individuals but as communities, and the Confederacy's defeat might be understood as an act of such divine testing. John Adger, an influential Southern theologian in the years after the Civil War, articulated what became a common theme of the postbellum Southern pulpit: "There was one error … into which we acknowledge that some Southern ministers sometimes fell … that God must surely bless the right … Yes! the hand of God, gracious though heavy, is upon the south for her discipline" (qtd. in Noll 77–8). Faulkner clearly knew of this ideologically freighted sermonic tradition and engaged it throughout his fiction. Though they are not ordained preachers, Ike MacCaslin in *Go Down, Moses* (1942) and Quentin Compson in *Absalom, Absalom!* (1936) entertain theological speculation on the outcome of the Civil War and imagine framing the South's defeat as a sign of divine chastening.

In *Light in August*, Faulkner explores the theological framing of the Confederacy's defeat most fully through the novel's central preacher—the Rev. Gail Hightower. As a young minister who comes "straight to Jefferson from the seminary," Hightower emerges as a figure fixated on the confederate past and determined to use the sermon to ensconce his grandfather's death during the Civil War within a larger religious drama (Faulkner, *Light*: 61). Though the townspeople find his repetitive, unhinged discussions of his grandfather's mock-heroic actions troubling, they note how he seemed to talk that way in the pulpit too, wild too in the pulpit, using religion as though it were a dream. Not a nightmare, but something which went faster than the words in the Book; a sort of cyclone that did not even need to touch the actual earth … It was as if he couldn't get religion and that galloping cavalry and his dead grandfather shot from the galloping horse untangled from each other, even in the pulpit. (61–2)

In Hightower, Faulkner creates a character who practices and preaches what Charles Reagan Wilson describes as a pervasive "Southern civil religion"—often referred to as "The Lost Cause"—that "made Robert E. Lee into a saint, Stonewall Jackson into a prophet, and the Confederacy itself into a sacred memory" (33). His cyclonic, otherworldly preaching indicates his disregard for "the church and the people who composed the church" (Faulkner, *Light*: 61). He, thus, emerges as a postbellum idealist with both a regional and personal obsession.

As his ministry develops, the congregants worry that Hightower's wife has stopped attending church and that he seems oblivious to her absence. For the townspeople, Hightower's failure to register his wife's breach of etiquette confirms his unnatural fixation and the intensity of his perverse idealism:

> They would look at him and wonder if he even knew that she was not there, if he had not even forgot that he ever had a wife, up there in the pulpit with his hands flying around him and the dogma he was supposed to preach all full of galloping cavalry and defeat and glory just as when he tried to tell them on the street about the galloping horses, it in turn would get all mixed up with absolution and choirs of martial seraphim, until it was natural that the old men and women should believe that what he preached in God's own house on God's own day verged on actual sacrilege. (62–3)

Like Hawthorne's Puritan preacher in "The Gentle Boy" and Hollingsworth in *The Blithedale Romance*, Hightower's idealism leads him to neglect the needs of both his wife and the community he serves. Despite their concern, the congregants, seemingly out of respect for Hightower's office, appear reluctant to resist him.

Hightower's wife, however, refuses to accept her husband's disregard or the perverse theology that underwrites his preaching. After returning from one of her ambiguous trips to Memphis, Mrs. Hightower interrupts her husband's sermon. The narrative that Byron Bunch recalls records two interlocking functions of her disturbance, both of which are critical to Faulkner's analysis of religious oratory in *Light in August*:

> She came to church that Sunday and took her seat on a bench at the back, alone. In the middle of the sermon she sprang from the bench and began to

scream, to shriek something toward the pulpit, shaking her hands toward the pulpit where her husband had ceased talking, leaning forward with his hands raised and stopped. Some people nearby tried to hold her but she fought them ... she stood there, in the aisle now, shrieking and shaking her hands at the pulpit. (64–5)

At one level, Mrs. Hightower undercuts her husband's ministerial authority, "shrieking" over his sermon and mimicking his shaking hands. Her rhetorical ambush forces him to pause with "his wild face frozen in the shape of the thundering and allegorical period which he had not completed" (65). Her dramatic interference, thus, scrambles Hightower's propagation of Southern civil religion. At another level, though, her interference carries a larger cultural critique because she implicates not just this sermon, perverse though it may be, but the Protestant imagination of the pulpit as a space of enduring symbolic authority. Three separate times in Byron's account, the text identifies the pulpit as a focus of Mrs. Hightower's anger.[7] Moreover, by the end of her disturbance, the congregants cannot tell "whether she was shaking her hands at [Hightower] or at God" (65). With Mrs. Hightower's anti-sermon, Faulkner implicates Southern civil religion and, more broadly, remonstrates against the Protestant religious tradition in which the preacher functions as one of "God's Trombones," a spokesperson installed in the pulpit and, thereby, vested with the immense power to speak on God's behalf.

Mrs. Hightower, Faulkner's adaptation of Hawthorne's Catharine, becomes the novel's first *anti-preacher*, a marginalized figure who interrupts a sermon to disrupt and unsettle the religious ideologies that structure the novel. She does not attempt to offer an alternative sermon to reform or redirect religious sentiment—as many figures in US literature do—but only to drown out and shut down the preacher with a pre-linguistic scream. And she succeeds—at least temporarily. Her performance silences Hightower and causes him to "come down" from the pulpit (65). Despite her success, however, the church elders enlist local institutions and send Mrs. Hightower to a sanitarium. In the elders' participation in Mrs. Hightower's forced institutionalization, Faulkner indicts a culture in the thrall of priestcraft. Though they know better, the elders choose

---

[7] The word *pulpit*, often rendered in the phrase *in the pulpit*, appears a staggering fifteen times in Faulkner's narration of young Gail Hightower's career (61–70). The obsessive repetition often controls the passage's pacing and communicates Rev. Hightower's obsession with capturing and protecting this authoritative space. Therefore, within the novel's analysis, Mrs. Hightower's attack rightly implicates not just her husband but also the pulpit itself because she senses that Protestant ideology's problematic construction of the pulpit dangerously blurs the boundary between divine revelation and all-too-human speech.

to punish the anti-preacher rather than the man who wields the sermon to further what they understand "verge[s] on actual sacrilege" (63). Hightower, a man characterized by "wild" speech and sociopathic tendencies, travels with his "crazed" wife to the sanitarium and then returns promptly to Jefferson. He preaches from the pulpit on "the next Sunday, as usual" (65). Thereafter, following each of his biweekly visits to her, he appears "in the pulpit again ... as though the whole thing had never happened" (65).

Mrs. Hightower's anti-sermon reveals Faulkner's assessment of literary preaching at this stage of his career. In Emerson's journal's, Whitman's poetry, Hawthorne's novels, and Davis's *Life in the Iron-Mills*, scenes featuring dangerous preachers or failed sermons unfailingly prepare the way for artistic mobilizations of literary preaching that enact prophetic resistance. As Faulkner constructs young Hightower, he seems to be creating an easy target for precisely this sort of displacement by a character or narrative voice closely aligned with Faulkner's sensibilities and cultural concerns. Yet, in *Light in August*, Faulkner only silences the idealist's sermon through a cry that gives voice, but not words, to human suffering. He censures both Hightower's specific ideology and the larger theological imagination that enables him, but he resists the temptation to offer a counter-sermon, and, thus, tests a novel approach to the form that troubled so many US writers. This iconoclastic approach demonstrates Faulkner's principled refusal to engage fully with a form that creates as many problems as it solves. And the experiment seems to have pleased him because he replicates it precisely in the novel's second scene of anti-preaching—Joe Christmas's disruption of an African American folk sermon.

To discern how Joe's anti-preaching contributes to the cultural work of *Light in August*, the scene needs to be understood in relationship to the three other scenes of literary preaching that precede it in the novel's chronology. Joe's anti-preaching, in other words, takes on its full significance when one considers not only its obvious doubling of Mrs. Hightower's anti-preaching but also its resonance with the novel's two other evocations of the sermon: the racist sermons of Joe's maternal grandfather, Doc Hines, and Joanna Burden's violent attempt to convert Joe.

Doc Hines's sermons occur first in the novel's chronology, but Faulkner withholds them until the novel's conclusion. Though Hines's neighbors know almost nothing about his professional life, they do know that he "went on foot about the country, holding revival services in negro churches" (341) and believe "that he once had been a minister" (343). Only later do the townspeople discover the truth:

> This white man ... was going singlehanded into remote negro churches and interrupting the service to enter the pulpit and in his harsh, dead voice and at times with violent obscenity, preach to them humility before all skins lighter than theirs, preaching the superiority of the white race, himself his own exhibit A, in fanatic and unconscious paradox. (343–4)

Hines's usurpation of the pulpit, Faulkner's satirical adaptation of Hawthorne's literary pulpit exchanges, anticipates young Gail Hightower's determination to similarly capture Jefferson's pulpit and preach sermons that conflate Confederate ideology and Christianity (61). Charles Reagan Wilson rightly links Hines and Hightower, arguing that through this pairing, "Faulkner shows that [these preachers'] beliefs are, in fact, central to the Southern culture he inherited" (35). Like Hightower, Hines's speech in public, not just in religious spaces, veers toward the sermonic and demonstrates the dangers of religious enthusiasm wedded to racist fantasy. Faulkner later reveals that just prior to his daughter's death, Hines repeats his custom of interrupting a sermon and usurping a pulpit, this time in a white prayer meeting where he "went to the pulpit and begun to preach ... for the white folks to turn out and kill" the Black members of their community (Faulkner, *Light*: 378). When the congregants tell him to "come down from the pulpit," Hines "threatened them with the pistol, there in the church, until the law came and arrested him and him like a crazy man for a while" (378).

In this oft-overlooked scene where he images Hines preaching while brandishing a firearm, Faulkner provides a textual clue through which we might reconsider Joe and Joanna Burden's final encounter, a scene that condenses the novel's excavation of the linkages between violence and religious oratory. At the end of their affair, Joanna plans to convert Joe to Christianity and then kill both him and herself. When he enters her room, she asks him to kneel with her. "I don't ask it," she says, "It is not I who ask it. Kneel with me" (282). Joanna's implication is clear: she speaks not on her own behalf, but on behalf of a God who demands Joe assume a submissive posture. She claims for herself something akin to theological authority by employing what Caleb Smith refers to as a "self-abnegating" manner "of address" (xi) and suppressing "the private self so that the commandments of some transcendent, impersonal power [can] speak through [her]" (5). Like Doc Hines, with whom she shares an obsession with racial difference, Joanna believes so blindly in the righteousness of her warped theological mission that she points an "old Civil War, cap-and-ball" pistol at the man she aims to convert (Faulkner, *Light*: 298). In the detail that the weapon recalls the Civil War, Faulkner also ironically links Joanna's violent religious oratory to Hightower's preaching. For these reasons, Joe's subsequent attack on

Joanna, in which he slices her throat, should be read as a symbolic silencing of the novel's three white preachers—Hines, Hightower, and Burden—figures linked by a racist ideology that embraces violence and finds expression through religious oratory. Joe's attack on Joanna is not his last attack on a preacher for he, like Faulkner and Johnson, identifies the sermons often preached from African American pulpits as oppressive rhetorics that call for the submission of the marginalized.

Immediately after killing Joanna, Joe interrupts a rural African American revival meeting and delivers the novel's second anti-sermon. The text does not detail the sermon being preached by Brother Bedenberry on the evening of Joe's attack, but Faulkner designs this scene to represent an evangelical revival meeting involving calls for personal conversion. Faulkner suggests the nature of this religious gathering by describing one of the congregants startled by Joe as a "woman on the mourners' bench, already in a semihysterical state" (322). Imaged as both submissive and somewhere between madness and sanity, the woman assumes a posture and emotional state that hint that this revival service participates in the form of Christianity that James Weldon Johnson typifies as instilling "narcotic doctrine[s]" that encourage political quietism (6).

Faulkner combines numerous images from the novel's other pulpit contests to construct this scene. Like his maternal grandfather, Doc Hines, Joe's sudden appearance carries the threat of gunplay. The witness tells the sheriff that "the man had apparently grasped [the door] by the knob and hurled it back into the wall so that the sound crashed into the blended voices [of the congregants] like a pistol shot" (Faulkner, *Light*: 322). Joe moves deliberately "toward the pulpit where the preacher"—in an image that precisely replicates Hightower's reaction to his wife's anti-sermon—"leaned, his hands still raised, his mouth still open" (322). Joe's disruption causes so much "screeching and hollering," one witness reports, "you couldn't hear what Brother Bedenberry was saying" (323). Unlike Mrs. Hightower, however, Joe seizes the privileged site of cultural authority. As a witness to the attack recalls, Joe reaches "into the pulpit," grabs Brother Bedenberry "by the throat," and attempts "to snatch him outen the pulpit" (323). As he does in his attack on Joanna, Joe attacks the preacher's throat in an attempt to silence religious oratory that suggests that the oppressed should assume a posture of submission. After silencing and stunning the preacher, Joe climbs "into the pulpit where Brother Bedenberry had done clumb out the other side and stood there ... with his hands raised like a preacher" (323). Yet Joe does not preach. He begins, like Mrs. Hightower, to deliver an anti-sermon "curs[ing], hollering it out, at the folks, and he cursed God louder than the women screeching" (323). While the congregants flee, Joe remains "in the pulpit cursing God" (324). As a member of the congregation rides into town to alert the police, Joe ironically celebrates his anti-sermon, the culmination of his silencing of both Black and white Southern preaching traditions, by saying, "A mule ... bound for town with the good news" (325).

An awareness of the anti-sermons that structure *Light in August* allows us to see Mrs. Hightower and Joe Christmas as allies in a common struggle against an oppressive social order that promulgates itself through religious ideology. Faulkner deploys anti-preaching to perform a significant strand of the novel's cultural work—the implication of Southern preaching in the region's violence—but he nimbly sidesteps the undesirable affordances of literary preaching as he does so. With his anti-preachers, Faulkner upstages the sermon without embracing the sermonic voice or buttressing clerical ideology. Anti-preaching represents a significant departure from Faulkner's engagement with the form in *The Sound and the Fury*. And what he gains seems to compensate for what he loses.

In Hightower's belated confession, which occurs in the novel's closing pages, Faulkner expresses a final assessment of Southern religion and confirms his rejection of literary preaching. Against the backdrop of the novel's anti-sermons, the aging Gail Hightower describes his youthful, egotistical mobilization of the sermon as "the greatest social sin of all ... perhaps moral sin" (486–7). He incriminates himself as a man who, like Hines, stole the pulpit, "a charlatan preaching worse than heresy, in utter disregard of that whose very stage he preempted, offering instead of the crucified shape of pity and love, a swaggering and unchastened bravo, killed with a shotgun in a peaceful henhouse" (488). As Hightower continues to reminisce, his unspoken confession critiques Southern preachers for perverting their office:

> It seems to him that he has seen it all the while: that that which is destroying the Church is not the outward groping of those within it nor the inward groping of those without, but the professionals who control it and who have removed the bells from its steeples. He seems to see them, endless, without order, empty, symbolical, bleak, skypointed not with ecstasy or passion but in adjuration, threat, and doom. He seems to see the churches of the world like a rampart, like one of those barricades of the middleages planted with dead and sharpened stakes, against truth and against that peace in which to sin and be forgiven is the life of man. (487)

Hightower's silent confession validates the rage voiced more powerfully, though less articulately, by both his young wife and Joe Christmas. Here, Faulkner identifies literary preaching as a doomed project because it inexorably links the author with preachers who purport to speak as "God's Trombones" but, in fact, again and again, leverage the sermon to fulfill their own fantasies, a compulsion doomed to destroy what beauty, truth, and peace religion might offer. Moreover, as these scenes of anti-preaching make clear, Faulkner intuits literary preaching's tendency to reify the preacher's already-immense—and often dangerous—cultural authority. And in *Light in August*, he determines to remove the preacher from the pulpit and silence the sermon.

Zora Neale Hurston's Literary Preaching: The Art of the Folk Sermon, the Work of the Novel, and Hurston's Vocation

Like Faulkner, Zora Neale Hurston, the daughter of a folk preacher, responded powerfully to James Weldon Johnson's literary preaching. Her debut novel *Jonah's Gourd Vine* (1934) celebrates the folk sermon, and her correspondence with Johnson makes clear that *God's Trombones* encouraged her to center her first novel on a minister (*Letters* 298, 303). Throughout her career as an author, Hurston sought to capture the vitality, beauty, and significance of African American folkways and traditions. In doing so, she believed that she was presenting a more accurate and politically valuable portrait of African American experience than was offered in the overtly political literature championed by W. E. B. Du Bois in "Criteria of Negro Art" (1926) and represented by Alain Locke's edited collection *The New Negro* (1925) (Hemenway 38–43). For Hurston, such literature suffered serious flaws. First, it often aimed to present African Americans as exemplary to the extent that they cherished white, bourgeois values. Secondly, Hurston believed that the protest literature of the 1920s and 1930s falsely represented racism as totalizing in its deleterious effects on African American individuals and communities. Hurston rejected this naturalistic, propagandistic impulse in African American writing and sought to counter it by providing an alternative portrait of African American folk culture.

Hurston's finest biographer to date, Robert Hemenway, shows that Hurston strategically highlighted the richness of Black folkways to resist the myth that African American culture was degraded and existed only as a reaction to white oppression (221). As a young author, Hurston located the prime example of the power and beauty of Black folk culture in the African American church and, more specifically, in the African American folk sermon. In *Jonah's Gourd Vine*, Hurston puts this cultural form on display, seizing on the folk sermon's performative artistry to explode white stereotypes of Black folk culture. Moreover, throughout the novel, Hurston offers the preacher as a model for the contemporary African American literary artist and, through her engagement with literary preaching, limns not only how and why the artist succeeds but also how they fail.

Fully alert to the form's tendency to suggest an identification of the author with the preacher, Hurston discerned a clear parallel between the Black folk preacher's role and her role within contemporary African American literary culture. Consider, for example, the cultural dynamics at play in Hurston's description of Rev. John Buddy Pearson, the protagonist of *Jonah's Gourd Vine*. The following description appears in a letter that Hurston wrote to James Weldon Johnson on April 16, 1934, several weeks prior to the publication of the novel:

> I have tried to present a Negro, preacher who is neither funny nor an imitation Puritan ram-rod in pants. Just the human being and poet that he must be to succeed in a Negro pulpit. I do not speak of those among us who have been tampered with and consequently have gone Presbyterian or Episcopal. I mean the common run of us who love magnificence, beauty, poetry and color so much that there can never be too much of it ... I see a preacher as a man outside of the pulpit and so far as I am concerned he should be free to follow his bent as other men. He becomes the voice of the spirit when he ascends the rostrum. (*Letters* 298)

Hurston makes clear she intends to focus on the sermon's "magnificence, beauty, and poetry" to counter the long-standing racist stereotypes of African American preaching, such as those that appeared conspicuously in Marc Connelley's *The Green Pastures*, a popular drama that won the Pulitzer Prize for Drama in 1930 (M. West 58). At the same time, Hurston wants her protagonist to have feet of clay, to speak in the community's idioms, and to accurately reflect the pressures of pastoral leadership. The letter's most telling moment, however, occurs where she casts aspersions on African American preachers "who have been tampered with and consequently have gone Presbyterian or Episcopal." To Hurston, this denominational shift demonstrates a willful assimilation into norms of white middle-class Christianity, a move away from "the common run of us." This defection reflects, in religious terms, a rejection of Black folk culture, and Hurston sees this as an analogue to the defection of a generation of Black writers who aimed to succeed in the literary marketplace by accepting white literary culture's expectations and norms.[8] With this line, the parallel between the folk preacher and Hurston's nascent understanding of her own literary vocation comes into focus. The preacher remains wedded to the particularities of African American religious expression and resists the temptation to assimilate into allegedly dignified (i.e., white, bourgeois) expressions of Christianity. The ideal African American novelist or poet, likewise, resists cultural pressures to produce art that conforms to the prevailing norms of a white aesthetic.

Like the folk preacher, Hurston understood her literary work as responsive to and representative of African American folk culture. Hurston's letters to Johnson make clear that she sought to align herself with him through her embrace of literary preaching. But her letters also highlight her insistence on establishing the primacy of the preacher in the Black aesthetic imaginary. In a letter to Johnson, dated May 8, 1934, Hurston writes that the folk preachers are "the first artists, the ones intelligible to the masses ... a voice has told them to sing of the beginning of things" (*Letters* 303). For Hurston, the performative art that *is* preaching recalls the tradition of the Homeric bard who chants the communal myths to the populace. African American literary art, Hurston insists, should take the rich tradition of Black preaching as its starting place because preachers' sermonic poems represent African American literature's foundational texts. For this reason, Hurston initially dedicated *Jonah's Gourd Vine* to "the first and only real Negro poets in America—the preachers, who bring barbaric splendor of word and song into the very camp of the mockers" (qtd. in Hemenway 195). This original dedication points not only to the preacher's art but the also the preacher's courage to offer public testimony amid a hostile culture. And, clearly, Hurston was not speaking only of the preachers she witnessed and admired. As a young artist intent on deploying literary preaching to evince the splendor of Black folk culture before an often-mocking audience, she was speaking into the mirror.

In *Jonah's Gourd Vine*, a künstlerroman of the preacher, John Pearson's rise from poverty depends on his absorption of folk traditions of dance, song, and, especially, religious oratory. Through his absorption of these traditions, John discovers his talent as an orator and his role within his community. John's ascension to church leadership depends on his community's support, as well as

---

[8] For an especially useful and concise account of the debates surrounding the form and function of African American literary art during this period and Hurston's relationship to these debates, see M. Genevieve West, *Zora Neale Hurston & American Literary Culture* (UP of Florida: 2005), 17–23. For Hurston's classic statement of the relation of the African American artist to her community and its cultural practices, see her editorial, "Race Cannot Become Great Until It Recognizes Its Talent," published in the *Washington Tribune* on December 29, 1934.

his genius. At a church meeting, John offers a prayer that impresses the deacons. Hurston represents this prayer as a work of performative art by representing it in verse form. She uses this strategy, which she borrows from Johnson, throughout the novel to represent the laborer's folk songs and, especially, John's final sermon. The prayer-poem runs to thirteen lines, and the following excerpt reveals John's use of both domestic imagery and anaphora, as well as Hurston's attempt to capture the texture, imagery, and breath patterns of the oral performances that structure folk Christianity:

> You are the same God, Ah
> Dat heard de sinner man cry.
> Same God dat sent de zigzag lightning tuh
> Join de mutterin' thunder.
> Same God dat holds de elements
> In uh unbroken chain of controllment.
> ...
> We thank Thee that our sleeping couch
> Was not our cooling board. (*Jonah's* 88–9)

After hearing this image-laden prayer, Deacon Moses tells another church elder, "Dat boy got plenty fire in 'im and he got uh good strainin' voice. Les' make 'im pray uh lot" (89). John's eloquent prayers—"his barbaric poetry to his 'Wonder-workin' God"—become the centerpiece of the community gathering, and the church elders acknowledge that John "done more'n de pastor ... Dat boy is called tuh preach and don't know it" (89). Before long, John discovers his gift, becomes ordained, and preaches sermons that "set de church on fire" (112).

The communal and political significance of John's folk preaching—and its dramatization of Hurston's literary aesthetic—becomes evident when Hurston contrasts John with a rival preacher. Eventually, John's extramarital affairs, an element of the novel that I analyze below, cause several church members to insist on cutting ties with him. Before they do, however, they want to be sure they have a suitable replacement. The church arranges a preaching contest in which John preaches at a morning service and his would-be successor, Rev. Felton Cozy, preaches the evening sermon. Though comic, this scene of literary preaching dramatizes what Hurston understood as a serious contest for the proper form of African American literary art.

John's sermon reflects his deep embeddedness in African and African American folk traditions. Though Hurston does not provide the text of John's sermon, she invokes a long tradition of folk preaching—and strengthens the bond of literary kinship that links her and Johnson—by merely indicating the sermon's title. John chooses to preach his "far-famed 'Dry Bones' sermon" (158). This selection advances the contrast between John's art and his rival's because sermons on Ezekiel's vision were a regular feature of folk Christianity from the mid-nineteenth to the mid-twentieth century. "Dry Bones" sermons suggested the possibility of individual and communal healing in the wake of catastrophic trauma. In the narrative from Hebrew Scripture, God gives Ezekiel a vision of a valley of dry bones, an image of Israel's oppression, communal trauma, and hopelessness. In the vision, God commands Ezekiel to preach to the bones and tell them that God will rearticulate and animate them. As Ezekiel begins speaking, the bones begin to take on flesh. He notices that the bodies, however, are not breathing. God instructs him to speak again, and the bodies arise and form into an army. In his preface to *God's Trombones*, James Weldon Johnson identifies "Valley of Dry Bones" sermons as one of several frequently preached sermons that passed "from preacher to preacher and from locality to locality" (5). In this sense, these set-piece sermons bear significant resemblance to folk songs or folk stories that circulate through a community and remain recognizable despite the adjustments each performer makes to the inherited material.

During the preaching contest, therefore, John performs less as a creative artist in the Romantic mode than a brilliant, culturally rooted musician riffing on a cherished song. According to Richard Lischer, in the folk church, the individual preacher often demonstrated his artistry by (1) his sense of timing for when to select a particular sermon from the repertoire he inherited and (2) how he modified both the content and delivery of the source sermon (114). Lischer writes, "The effectiveness of folk preachers depends on the dexterity with which they manipulate their sources ... [Folk preachers depend on] a prodigious memory in which they store thematic set pieces that they have 'almost' memorized, the Spirit-given freedom to create new thematic sections on their feet, and the inspired gift of doing it all in poetic meter" (114). John's virtuosic performance of the "Dry Bones" sermon electrifies the congregants: "The church was alive from the pulpit to the door ... He brought his hearers to such a frenzy that it never subsided until two Deacons seized the preacher by the arms and reverently set him down. Others rushed up into the pulpit to fan him and wipe his face with their own kerchiefs" (Hurston, *Jonah's*: 158). Here, in the image of the congregation's sudden quickening, Hurston suggests that John's inspired oratory gives new life to the congregants in precisely the manner that Ezekiel's prophecy brings life to the dry bones. It is artistic, folkloric speech, Hurston insists, that brings life to the dead and hope to the oppressed.

Hurston's portrayal of Rev. Cozy's sermon, by contrast, indicts artists who prize the trappings of white academic culture and vector their works toward explicitly addressing issues of racial injustice, with little sense for either artistry or folk tradition. Cozy prefaces his sermon by telling the congregants "Ahm a race man! Ah solves the race problem! One great problem befo' us tuhday is what is de blacks gointer do wid de whites?" (158) His opening misfires as the congregants realize that this "preacher" has rejected the folk sermon's conventions, including identifying what scriptural passages inform his sermon. One of the bewildered congregants leans toward her friend and says, "Ah ain't hear what de tex' wuz." Her friend whispers back, "Me neither" (158). Cozy offers a twelve-point sermon in which he attempts to instill racial pride by identifying Africans' cultural achievements. The congregation sits in relative silence. At one point, Cozy, sensing his pending failure, implores the congregation to respond to him: "Y'all say 'Amen.' Don't let uh man preach hisself tuh death and y'll sit dere lak uh bump on uh log and won't he'p 'im out. Say 'Amen'!!" (159) After the service, a deacon asks the two church ladies what they thought of the sermon. One of the ladies makes a disapproving noise and says, "Sermon? ... dat wan't no sermon. Dat wuz uh lecture" (159). For Hurston, the parishioner's description of Cozy's sermon as a "lecture" carries an implication of racial betrayal as well as a withering evaluation of his performance.

In her anthropological writings about Southern religion, Hurston notes that members of African American folk churches deride African American preachers who adopt the style of white preachers. According to Hurston, "They say of that type of preacher, 'Why he don't preach at all. He just lectures.' And the way they say the word 'lecture' make it sound like horse-stealing" (*Sanctified Church* 106–7). In this comedic but crucial scene in *Jonah's Gourd Vine*, then, Hurston offers her aesthetic theory by drawing a distinction between didactic literature that fails the appeal to the masses and the cultural authority of the poet who remains tethered to folk culture. She also suggests that artists will produce the most aesthetically rich and durable works of art if they revel in the resources of African and African American folk culture.

As a final example of the aesthetic richness of Black folk culture, Hurston offers her readers the entire text of John's farewell sermon, a poem that spans more than two hundred lines and seven pages of text. Like Johnson, Hurston represents this sermon in verse form—with a significant exception. Hurston breaks from the pattern she appreciated in Johnson's work by altering the sermon's beginning. Hurston's representation of John's sermon begins in standard paragraph form to capture her sense that it often took folk preachers several lines to transition from speaker to preacher-poet.[9] Her textual representation, in other words, aims to celebrate and identify the moment in which the preacher warms to the text and audience. John's opening lines, appearing in paragraph form, identify his scriptural texts and make a moralizing commentary about the danger of playing cards, but then, like both the Kansas City preacher who inspired *God's Trombones* and, by extension, Faulkner's Shegog, John's performance changes dramatically as he embraces the form's performative sensuality:

> Jesus have always loved us from the foundation of the world
> When God
> Stood out on the apex of His power
> Before the hammers of creation
> Fell upon the anvils of Time and hammered out the ribs of the
>   earth
> Before He made any ropes
> By the breath of his fire
> And set the boundaries of the ocean by the gravity of His
>   power
> When God said, ha!
> Let us make man. (Hurston, *Jonah's*: 175).

John's sermon-poem sweeps from an account of creation, through sacred history, to the present day, locating his congregants in a theological narrative as he demonstrates an inventive use of metaphor and simile. John describes his conversion experience as "where I got off de damnation train" (181) and white caps on a stormy ocean as "walk[ing] out like soldiers goin' to battle" (178). Additionally, as Eric Sundquist notes, the cadences of John's sermon correspond with his evocation of drumming imagery (i.e., "the hammers of creation / Fell upon the anvils of Time") to produce a form of "verbal art" that "echoes African ancestry" (57). John relays his visions to his people, and in so doing they can hear and see their communal history afresh. John's richly textured sermon opens with a celebration of God's creation of the world by the power of his speech. With this passage, however, Hurston makes clear that humans—and perhaps especially preachers and literary artists who take their cues from the preacher—share this power of making and remaking their audiences' worlds through language.

---

[9] In *The Preacher King: Martin Luther King, Jr. and the Word that Moved America* (Oxford UP: 1995), Richard Lischer identifies the same phenomenon and writes, "Most [folk preachers] speak the first part of their sermons, but their real power comes from the rhythmic chant with which they intone the main body and climax" (114).

Reception History and Receptivity to History

While contemporary Hurston critics argue that the novel's climactic sermon evinces Hurston's emerging confidence as a writer of fiction,[10] one especially important critic in 1934 identified it as one of the novel's failures. John Chamberlain, a well-regarded critic writing for *The New York Times*, reviewed *Jonah's Gourd Vine* on May 3, 1934. He begins by praising the novel for its "excellent anthropology" and describing John's sermon as "moving and picturesque" (17). After quoting eleven lines from John's sermon, he suggests that it recalls "James Weldon Johnson's Whitmanesque biblical rhythms" (17). On the one hand, Chamberlain rightly places Hurston in the company of two pioneers of literary preaching. On the other, he problematically suggests that Whitman serves as Johnson's aesthetic catalyst and more problematically erases the primary artistry of the actual preachers whose eloquence enabled the literary sermons of Whitman, Johnson, and Hurston alike. He then infamously writes, "Mrs. Hurston is writing poetry and giving us anthropology; her sermon ... is too good, too brilliantly splashed with poetic imagery, to be the product of any one Negro preacher" (17).

Five days after Chamberlain's review was published, Hurston, understandably frustrated, wrote to James Weldon Johnson:

> [Chamberlain] means well, I guess, but I never saw such a lack of information about us. It just seems that he is unwilling to believe that a Negro preacher could have so much poetry in him. When you and I (who seem to be the only ones even among Negroes who recognize the barbaric poetry in their sermons) know that there are hundreds of preachers who are equalling [sic] that sermon weekly. He does not know that merely being a good man is not enough to hold a Negro preacher in an important charge. He must also be an artist. He must be both a poet and an actor of a very high order, and then he must have the voice and figure. He does not realize or is unwilling to admit that the light that shone from GOD'S TROMBONES was handed to you, as was the sermon to me in *Jonah's Gourd Vine*. (*Letters* 302).

---

[10] For example, in *Zora Neale Hurston: A Biography of the Spirit* (Roman & Littlefield: 2011), Deborah Plant writes that John's "words moved [his congregants] through dimensions of space and time, and empowered them to see the unseen, bear witness to a past that was thousands of years old ... Through his words he could bring them face to face with God" (107). Robert Hemenway calls the sermon-poem a "linguistic tour de force" and argues that this sermon "is directed away from the self and toward the communal celebration" (196–8). It is not merely a moment in the developing narrative, Hemenway rightly argues, but "the important literary event at this point in the novel ... one could remove the sermon, place it in another context, and the language would command virtually the same response" (197).

This letter highlights both Hurston's specific response to Chamberlain and her larger understanding of her literary preaching. First, Hurston complains that Chamberlain's racism blocks the cultural work she intends to accomplish through her embrace of literary preaching. Chamberlain is "unwilling" to acknowledge the beauty of African American folk preaching because he cannot imagine Black preachers to be capable of producing powerful art. Chamberlain's entrenchment in white ideology compels him to reject John's sermon as an inauthentic representation of Black folk culture. It is, as Chamberlain writes, "too good" to come from "one Negro" in the American South. Hurston hoped that the beauty of African American folk culture might begin to erode white readers' misconceptions, but Chamberlain's response suggested that, in fact, racist presumptions were so deeply fortified that such a process was unlikely to succeed.

Second, Hurston's letter casts both herself and Johnson as receptive messengers who relay local folk performances to a broader audience. Though Hurston's use of verse form highlights the sermon's status as literary art, Hurston insists that it is the *preacher's* art not her own. Indeed, John's final sermon is an almost verbatim copy of a sermon originally preached by Rev. C. C. Lovelace, which Hurston recorded during her anthropological fieldwork in Eau Gallie, Florida, in 1929 (Hemenway 197).[11] Moreover, Hurston insists not only that her literary preaching accurately reflects the realities of African American sermonic performance but also that the power of that particular sermon is not unique. Hurston was furious that her use of literary preaching was discredited at precisely the moment she'd remained as close to her sources as possible. And, as Hurston insisted again and again, the Black preacher's art compared positively to even the most elite works of classical literature: "The masses do not read literature ... The truth is, the greatest poets among us are in our pulpits," she wrote in a letter she sent to Lewis Gannett four days after writing to Johnson, "and the greatest poetry has come out of them. It is merely not set down. It passes from mouth to mouth as in the days of Homer" (*Letters* 304).

Attention to the cultural work of Hurston's literary preaching in *Jonah's Gourd Vine* clarifies the novel's ambiguous title. The title refers to a biblical story found in the book of Jonah. Jonah—a powerful preacher—reluctantly converts the city of Nineveh and then takes up residence in a desert. God

---

[11] Eric Sundquist speculates that Hurston may have adapted Lovelace's sermon more than she admits but rightly insists that regardless of Hurston's alterations of the sermon, if any, "it is Hurston who set the sermon in verse, marking Lovelace's straining ... choosing orthographic signals of his dialect" (63).

miraculously provides a leafy vine to give Jonah shelter from the heat. When Jonah complains because God has shown mercy to people that Jonah deems worthy of damnation, God sends a worm to eat the vine. The vine withers and dies in less than a day. Jonah expresses fury at this loss, and God rebukes Jonah because he cares more for a plant and his own comfort than he does for the people of Nineveh.

Hurston scholars continue to debate about how, precisely, the events of the novel map onto this biblical myth.[12] Lovalerie King perceptively argues that "collectively, Lucy, home, family, and community serve as the most obvious parallel to the sheltering vine" beneath which the preacher thrives (*Zora* 44). Clearly, for Hurston, "community" implied not just a network of interpersonal relationships, but, perhaps more importantly, folk traditions, tales, and rituals—including centrally the folk sermon. Yet as King searches for a textual analogy for the worm, her otherwise insightful analysis misses the heart of Hurston's cautionary tale about the downfall of an African American artist. King suggests that "the obvious parallel to the destructive worm is John's unbridled libido, which leads to the collapse of the shelter's foundation" (*Zora* 44). King's reading fits well within the body of criticism that regards John's sexual promiscuity as the key threat to community in the novel. Such readings, however, threaten to perpetuate the "exploitive and demeaning discourse on black male sexuality" that M. Genevieve West identifies as one of the pervasive aspects of America's racist mythology that Hurston sought to counter in *Jonah's Gourd Vine* (59–67). West rightly notes that "John is far more complex than the stereotype would allow," but the fact that his personal failures are sexual in nature "may for some readers have too closely aligned him with stereotypical images of black men" (59). In *Jonah's Gourd Vine*, Hurston offers more than the banal assertion that men invested with authority often use their power to satisfy their sexual appetites regardless of the communal consequences.

John's temptations and subsequent infidelities should be considered primarily as a Hurston's extended metaphor for the temptation of the African American artist, imaged here as a gifted poet-preacher, to rupture their union with African American folk communities. By reading John's infidelity as primarily a figure for abjuring the sustaining and generative force that *is* folk culture in favor of more modern, "universal" values, not merely as an index of moral failing and sexual impulsivity, we gain a stronger understanding of Hurston's project and how it

---

[12] For a review of the variety of ways that Hurston critics have interpreted this title, see M. Genevieve West, *Zora*, 57–8.

relates to her own sense of a parallel between the work of the preacher and the work of the literary artist.[13]

To underscore this point, Hurston indicates that John's sudden downfall occurs not solely because of his sexual promiscuity but also because of his unquestioned embrace of technologies that rapidly remove him from the sources of his shelter. John's acts of infidelity, after all, are also acts of flight mediated by modern technology—the locomotive and the automobile. The locomotive engine, in particular, functions as the novel's trope for modernity as a force of cultural dislocation, a force of communal rupture.[14] The train functions as the analogue for the worm in Jonah's story because it opposes the stable, nourishing forces of John's community and eventually makes possible his liaisons. As a young man, John intends to honor his marriage. But when he takes his first ride on a train, his encounter with modern technologies of transit clearly suggests a rival to the community represented by his union with his childhood love, Lucy. The overtly sexual imagery of the passage underscores this point: "Nothing in the world ever quite equalled that first ride on a train. The rhythmic stroke of the engine ... the red plush splendor ... the long mournful howl of the whistle" (Hurston, *Jonah's*: 104). In the glory of this "ride" on the train, "John forgot the misery of his parting from Lucy" (104). The distinctly modern thrill of John's technologically aided flight, not his later sexual activity, erodes his relationship to the folk community.

Even more than the train, the Cadillac that John acquires enables him to distance himself from his communal foundations. Like the train, the Cadillac plays the double role of symbolizing phallic power as well as communal dislocation. Hurston describes John's first drive in a manner that registers both meanings: "The next morning he turned the long nose of his car northwards and pulled up at Hambo's gate" (194). Here the phallic imagery becomes indistinguishable from John's northward travel away from his third and final wife, Sally. John's flight results in an embarrassing liaison with a young woman. John experiences deep shame about this infidelity and attempts to return home

---

[13] This metaphorical reading of John's infidelity helps clarify *why* Hurston chose sexual infidelity as her protagonist's primary flaw. The vehicle (marital infidelity) aptly suggests the tenor (the rejection of folk culture for the attractions of modernity) in a way that another conventional vice such as either gambling or alcoholism does not.

[14] In the opening section of "The Music of God, Man, and Beast: Spirituality and Modernity in *Jonah's Gourd Vine*," Anthony Wilson advances a reading of the novel along these lines (68–72). My analysis of the novel's title builds on Wilson's fine analysis of John's fraught relationship to the locomotive engine. Wilson rightly points out that "the train plays a double role in the novel's symbology: it signifies both sexuality and phallic power and the encroachment of technological modernity and its attendant threats to community and self" (74).

to "be in the shelter of Sally's presence" (200). As he speeds through the night, a train strikes his Cadillac and he dies instantly. At the superficial level, this ending seems like the work of a young novelist who does not know how she wants to conclude the story. Yet in the collision of the train and the automobile, the novel's figures for dislocation, Hurston suggests the fate that awaits African American artists if they flee the foundational African American artistic forms—sermons, prayer, song, and folklore—that provide them with their richest and strongest aesthetic moorings.

The Pulpit, the Porch, and the Shared Sermon: Literary Preaching in *Their Eyes Were Watching God*

Hurston's experience of writing *Jonah's Gourd Vine* amplified her interest in the imbrications of religious oratory, patriarchy, and the symbiotic relationship between the congregants and the preacher. If the folk preacher was the Black community's great poet, as she believed, would that vital cultural role be available only to men? What did the authority accorded to the preacher mean for African American women? In what ways did the voice of the preacher either represent or drown out their voices? These issues fascinated Hurston, and they take center stage in her most well-known novel, *Their Eyes Were Watching God*.

Published three years after *Jonah's Gourd Vine*, *Their Eyes Were Watching God* opens with a meditation on gender oppression and religious oratory. As Janie begins to enter adulthood, her grandmother, Nanny, directs her toward a marriage that will provide relative material security and physical protection. Nanny's panic about Janie's nascent sexuality derives from Nanny's firsthand experience of sexual slavery in the antebellum South and her horror at learning of her daughter's rape at the hands of a schoolteacher. As Janie listens, Nanny traces a genealogy of violence that begins with white men's brutality toward Black men. These men respond to their oppression by, in turn, oppressing their "womenfolks" (Hurston, *Eyes*: 14). According to Nanny, this process results in a social situation in which the African American woman "is de mule uh de world" (14). Nanny's lesson crushes Janie because she realizes that culture threatens to foreclose her future at the moment she has begun to imagine it.

Yet, in precisely this vulnerable moment, Hurston suggests that this pattern might be resisted through the formation of mutually transformative relationships between women. Such relationships, the novel suggests, create spaces for women to speak about matters of religion and women's experience of the world. In a textual *pieta*, Hurston images Nanny cradling her devastated, adolescent granddaughter: "For a long time she sat rocking with the girl held tightly to her sunken breast. Janie's long legs dangled over one arm of the chair and the long braids of her hair swung low on the other side" (14). Critically, the comfort Nanny offers in this moment flows from her performance of religious oratory: "Nanny half sung, half sobbed a running chantprayer over the head of the weeping girl" (14).

Nanny's "running chantprayer" suggests the folk sermon's poetry and anticipates Nanny's confession of her thwarted vocational desire. Multiple critics address Nanny's dream to secure Janie's physical safety and material comfort (King, *Zora*: 58–9 and Wall 90), but the manner in which Nanny's frustrated vocational dream structures Janie's narrative has not been adequately explored. Nanny desires much more for her daughter and her granddaughter than lives devoid of poverty and sexual oppression, more than lives of respectability. With a proper awareness of Hurston's vision of the preacher as an artist of the masses, Nanny's confession startles us and reorganizes our thinking about *Eyes* as a "speakerly text" (Gates, "Eyes": 165):[15]

> Ah didn't want to be used for a work-ox and a brood-sow and Ah didn't want mah daughter to be used dat way neither. It sho wasn't mah will for things to happen lak they did. Ah even hated de way you was born. But, all the same Ah said thank God, Ah got another chance. *Ah wanted to preach a great sermon about colored women sittin' on high, but they wasn't no pulpit for me.* Freedom found me wid a baby daughter in my arms, so Ah said Ah'd take a broom and a cook-pot and throw up a highway through de wilderness for her. She would expound what Ah felt. But somehow she got lost offa de highway and next thing Ah knowed here you was in de world. So whilst Ah was tendin' you of nights *Ah said Ah'd save de text for you. Ah been waitin' a long time, Janie, but nothin' Ah been through ain't too much if you just take a stand on high ground like Ah dreamed.* (Hurston, *Eyes*: 16; emphasis added)

---

[15] Gates famously identifies Hurston as the first example in African American literature "whose rhetorical strategy is designed to represent an oral literary tradition, designed 'to emulate the phonetic, grammatical, and lexical patterns of actual speech and produce the "illusion of oral narration"'" ("Eyes" 165). For Gates, the key feature of the "speakerly text" is that "all other structural elements seem to be devalued, as important as they remain to the telling of the tale, because the narrative strategy signals attention to its own importance, an importance which would seem to be the privileging of oral speech and its inherent linguistic features" ("Eyes" 165). M. Cooper Harriss helpfully suggests that "preacherly texts" might be a more appropriate term for Hurston's literary strategy because such a term underscores how Hurston "stresses preaching as oral tradition foundational to her own literary enterprise" (279). Harriss's fine analysis differs sharply from the reading I advance here because he focuses primarily on Hurston's anthropological writings in order to advance provocative arguments about "Hurston's status as an original religious thinker" (278).

Nanny dreams of preaching a "great sermon" that rejects the cultural situation in which African American women figure as the "mule[s] uh de world" (14). The problem, according to Nanny, is that, due to her gender and her life circumstance, no pulpit, the "high ground" she mentions here, is available to her.[16] In response to her disappointment, Nanny prepares her offspring to fulfill her artistic vision. She alludes to the same scriptural passage that Mr. Mitchell, the narrator of *Life in the Iron-Mills*, quotes ironically in the opening of his tale and casts herself as a female prophet who cries out "in the wilderness prepare ye the way of the Lord, make straight in the desert a highway for our God" (Isa. 40:3). She tells Janie that she has not preached her sermon but determined to "save de text" for Janie. Thus, we should note that Nanny refers to something like a pulpit, an elevated place of religious authority, when she tells Janie that she desires, above all, to see her "take a stand on high ground like Ah dreamed" (Hurston, *Eyes*: 16).

This scene complicates any simplistic reading of the problem represented by Janie's first marriage to Logan Killicks. The problem is not merely, as Cheryl Wall puts it, that the utilitarian marriage "fulfills Nanny's dreams … [but] … the old woman's dreams are not [Janie's] own" (90). Neither is the problem that Nanny accepts the "dominant ideology of true womanhood" and seeks to place Janie "on a pedestal that served both to protect and constrict" (King, *Zora*: 59). The "high ground" that Nanny speaks of in this moment—a pulpit-like space that confers authority and licenses truth-telling—differs markedly from the genteel "pedestal" King describes. This critical tendency can be understood, however, because Janie herself represses Nanny's prophetic ambition for her later in the novel. For instance, when she describes her decision to pursue Tea Cake, Janie says "Ah done lived Grandma's way, now Ah means tuh live mine" (Hurston, *Eyes*: 114). She clarifies her point by telling Pheoby that Nanny's sole ambition was "sittin' on porches lak de white madam … Dat's what she wanted for me— don't keer whut it cost. Git up on uh high chair and sit dere" (114). Janie describes genteel marriage as a "high chair," suggesting the infantilizing construction of femininity that she rejects. Yet the "high chair" that Janie describes here eclipses Nanny's stated desire to see Janie "tak[ing] a stand on the high ground." In this moment, Janie misrepresents her grandmother's wishes so that she can present

---

[16] With Nanny's comments, Hurston identifies the pulpit as a space of further gender oppression. Broadly speaking, this is, of course, a historically accurate claim. It's worth noting, however, that some African American women such as Sojourner Truth, Jarena Lee, and Julia A. J. Foote defied this cultural norm, were ordained, and preached powerfully. For a detailed discussion of pioneering African American women preachers in the nineteenth and twentieth centuries, see Bettye Collier-Thomas, *Daughters of Thunder: Black Women Preachers and Their Sermons, 1850-1979* (Jossey-Bass: 1998).

herself as an autonomous woman who pursues her own desires and not her grandmother's.

The confusion that emerges in Janie's—and the critics'—discussions of Nanny's goals exists because Nanny wrestles with two competing dreams. Prior to her powerful confession, Nanny reveals that her "daily prayer" is that she might live to see Janie "safe in life" (15). Surprised by Janie's sudden sexual awakening, Nanny must quickly decide which matters more—Janie's immediate safety or the "great sermon of black woman sitting on high" that she'd hoped her granddaughter might preach. Nanny chooses to try to secure Janie's safety. The decision makes sense, given Nanny's status as a survivor of and witness to unchecked sexual violence, but that does not mean it occurs without emotional pain. She cedes her life's dream (preparing a child to deliver the "great sermon") to the rival longing of her old age (Janie's safety). Thus, the novel's opening establishes one of its defining tensions—will Janie seek the safety proffered, but certainly not guaranteed, by conventional marriage relations or will her life be a fulfillment of Nanny's deferred dream? Will she seek safety in capitulation or attempt to preach a sermon of liberation, freedom, and power?

Contesting the Preacher in Eatonville

Janie's second marriage to Joe Starks devolves from a passionate romance into a contest for verbal power. The sermonic form figures prominently in their marriage dynamic because Joe dominates Eatonville through his successful manipulation of the folk sermon. Joe, the mayor of Eatonville, purchases the first streetlamp for the fledgling community, installs it at the crossroads, and gathers the town for a dedication "speech" (45). Like Ahab on the *Pequod*'s quarterdeck, Joe invests his private ambition with theological significance through his repurposing of the sermon. He describes God as "De Sun-maker" who ordains darkness and light. Joe tells the crowd, however, that they must "make some light ourselves" if humans want light when God ordains darkness (45). Allusions to biblical passages, traditional spirituals, and liturgical conventions saturate his closing lines: "De first street lamp in uh colored town. Lift yo' eyes and gaze on it. And when Ah touch de match tuh dat lampwick let de light penetrate inside of yuh, and let it shine, let it shine, let it shine. Brother Davis, lead us in a word uh prayer" (45). With his eye for the theatrical, Joe waits to light the lamp's wick until Brother Davis brings his "traditional prayer-poem with his own variations" to a conclusion, touching the flame to the wick as Davis says "amen" (45). The scene suggests both the malleability of sermonic idioms and Joe's keen understanding of the sermon's cultural authority.

This event immediately precedes Joe's meteoric rise, and Eatonville's citizens begin to resent Joe's ability to manipulate sermonic forms to control and belittle them. "You kin feel a switch in his hand when he's talkin' to yuh," one of the men complains (49). Sam Watson agrees and describes Joe's power by saying, "He's de wind and we'se de grass. We bend which ever way he blows" (49). The Eatonville community begins to long for an orator who might rival Joe's cleverness and rhetorical skill. Amos Hicks, one of the town's leaders, mentions that his brother serves as a minister in a nearby town and longs for a preacher to challenge Joe: "If he wuz here, Joe Starks wouldn't make no fool outa him lak he do de rest uh y'all" (49).

Joe's appropriation of the sermon corresponds to his exclusion of Janie from *any* space of public speech. Huston underscores this throughout the Eatonville section by describing Joe's refusal to allow his wife to participate in the variety of conversations that occur on the porch. When Joe forbids her from participating in these discussion, he attempts to bully her through preacherly rhetoric: "I god, Ah can't see what uh woman uh yo' stability would want tuh be treasuring' all dat gum-grease from folks dat don't even own de house dey sleep in. 'Taint no earthly use. They's just some puny humans playin' round de toes uh Time" (54). The startling metaphor "de toes uh Time" and the highly ironic critique of "treasuring" things that "taint no earthly use" (Mt. 6:19-21) seem out of place in a domestic argument. This is the stylized language of folk preaching, the language of Rev. John Pearson, used by Joe Starks to subjugate Janie. The rhetorical similarity between Joe Starks and John Pearson—the central preacher in *Jonah's Gourd Vine*—is no accident. In fact, later in the novel Joe Starks participates in a mock funeral for mule. After Joe delivers a humorous eulogy, Sam Watson "set his hat like John Pearson and imitated his preaching" (60). This act of imitation, Hurston hints, reveals Joe's pattern of appropriating the sermon. On the one hand Sam seems to be merely entertaining the audience and perhaps poking fun at the local preacher. On the other hand, because he immediately follows Joe, he seems to signify on Joe's eulogy, pointing out Joe's habit of mimicking the local preacher to the gathered crowd.

Because Joe's status depends on his ability to speak with quasi-religious authority, no episode more disturbs him than Janie's surprising emergence as a rival religious orator. During his tenure as mayor, Joe purchases an old mule only to free it, parading his wealth and false generosity. As Joe absorbs the praises of the crowd, Janie uncharacteristically speaks from the porch, traditionally a place of male authority, and challenges her husband. "Abraham

Lincoln," she says, "he had de whole United States tuh rule so he freed de Negroes. You got uh town so you freed uh mule. You have tuh have power tuh free things and dat makes you like uh king uh something" (58). Pearlie Fisher Peters describes this as Janie's first "assertion of her talking voice" (139). One of the porch talkers, Hambo, hears Janie and remarks that the town never knew Janie was "uh born orator": "She put jus' de right words tuh our thoughts" (Hurston, *Eyes*: 58). In this key scene, Hurston indicates that Janie understands the community's suffering and possesses the verbal talent to beat Joe. She is, in fact, emerging as the preacher that Amos Hicks imagines to be capable of resisting Joe's rhetorical force.

First, however, Janie preaches against the porch talkers, the very men who rightly identify her as a "born orator" (58). This scene represents the first clear sign that Janie will fulfill Nanny's deferred dream. Shortly after praising Janie's eloquence, the porch talkers witness an Eatonville woman who complains bitterly that her husband has not been providing for his family but using his wages to buy food for another woman. Her public shaming of her husband registers as rejection of the patriarchal injunction against women's dissent. The men on the porch respond to her violation with escalating linguistic violence. "If dat wuz *mah* wife," one of the men says, "Ah'd kill her cemetery dead" (74). Another responds, "Ah'd break her or kill her. Makin' uh fool outa me in front of everybody." A third man says, "Ah'd kill uh baby just born dis mawnin' fuh uh thing lak dat" and suggests that only "low-down spitefulness" can account for this woman's anger (75). The final porch talker, Jim Stone, brings this litany of threats to an end by suggesting that its "God's truth" that only "low-down spitefulness" could motivate the woman's decision to speak out against her husband (75). This seemingly banal idiomatic expression—"God's truth"—exposes the porch talkers to Janie's counter-sermon. Janie detects in Stone's utterance the entanglement of patriarchy with religious discourse that her Grandmother lamented.

Janie first preaches on the porch to defend this abject woman, a representative of women's low value in Eatonville's culture. Signifying on one man's assumption to speak "God's truth" about the matter, Janie says, "Sometimes God gits familiar wid us womenfolks too and talks His inside business. He told me how surprised He was 'bout y'all turning out so smart after Him makin' yuh different; and how surprised y'all is goin tuh be if you ever find out you don't know half as much 'bout us as you think you do" (75). Janie closes by taunting the porch talkers' inability to resist Joe's powerful oratory. She says, "It's so easy to make yo'self out God Almighty when you ain't got nothin tuh strain against but women and chickens" (75). By identifying the porch talkers as "strain[ing]" against women and chickens, Janie delivers a painful reminder of their inability to counter Joe's successful appropriation of the sermonic voice. In Hurston's work, "straining" refers to the most prized aspect of a strong preacherly voice, the verbal display of labor marked by audible breathing (Sundquist 49). Therefore, Janie's brief literary sermon mocks the porch talkers' threats as "strain[ing]" (i.e., preaching) against the community's weakest members because they know that they cannot "strain" against the man who oppresses them. Diana Miles argues that this attempt to speak "on the male-owned porch in defense of women" leads to Janie being silenced (59); Dale Pattison agrees and notes that Janie's "attempt fails" (15). At one level, this is true because Joe responds by telling Janie that she's become "too moufy" and sending her inside (Hurston, *Eyes*: 75). Considered differently, however, the text reveals that Janie's mini-sermon finds its mark. After Janie concludes, all of the men except Joe remain silent, recognizing both her insight and a verbal power that might rival Joe's. Additionally, the rapidity of Joe's intervention indicates that Janie's mobilization of theological language against the town's men disturbs him. If this is not a moment of unqualified triumph for Janie, it is, nevertheless, a moment of significant transgression.

After silencing the men on the porch, Janie eventually directs her newfound voice at Joe and breaks his grip on the Eatonville community. Janie's verbal battle with Joe occurs in the general store and begins when Joe decides to demean Janie, opening his insults with "I god almighty," an idiom that underscores his attempt to speak with divine authority (78). Consistent with the pattern of his rhetoric, Joe weaponizes biblical idioms to shame her. He calls her "old as Methusalem," makes a crude comment about her body, and asserts that she retains no value because she, according to Joe, no longer stirs male desire (78). Janie's dramatic move into the center of the storeroom floor—"something that hadn't been done before"—suggests an attempt to claim Joe's territory (78). Though Janie directs her comments to Joe, she speaks with an orator's awareness of her audience. Janie tells her audience what they already know—that Joe's power relies on his "big voice" (79). But then she reveals that when he undresses he looks "lak de change uh life" (79). Commenting on this key verbal battle, M. Genevieve West notes, "Much to everyone's surprise, Janie responds [to Joe's sexual insult] in kind, implying that [he] is impotent" (99–100). West usefully directs our attention to the response of the crowd, a feature of this scene often overlooked in Hurston criticism.

Hurston's portrayal of the audience's response demonstrates the way Janie's image-laden truth-telling smears the boundaries of two folk genres—the folk sermon and the dozens. Janie's verbal sparring in this moment should not be characterized as literary preaching; however, when Janie finishes her response to Joe, Sam Watson, who has been hoping for a preacher to dismantle Joe's rhetorical power, responds with a jubilant exclamation typical of a call-and-response sermon, "Great God from Zion!" (Hurston, *Eyes*: 79). Though it is ambiguous, there is a sense in which Janie's bold, public denunciation of the local tyrant initially registers with Sam as an something like the folk sermon. Perhaps Sam's response derives from the fact that Janie's prior breech of the cultural injunction against women speaking on the porch clearly *does* engage the sermonic voice. Perhaps it derives from the fact that Janie's comments speak truth to power and artfully liberate the oppressed. Perhaps it derives from the fact that the community believes that only another preacher could beat Joe at his own game. But Sam, understandably, seems uncomfortable with his initial exclamation. He shifts registers away from the call-and-response discourse and says, "Y'all really playin' de dozens tuhnight," (79) a comment that identifies the exchange he's witnessed as an exemplary instance of the African American "folkloric speech event" of "interactive insult" (Garner 80). Yet, traditionally, playing the dozens entails a simulated conflict that serves the "community by promoting attitudes, modes of action, and solutions to recurring social problems" (Garner 81). Janie and Joe clearly engage in a real verbal conflict with far-reaching consequences, and, thus, typifying this verbal contest as an instance of the dozen's seems not-quite-right either. Ultimately, Janie's dramatic response resists being neatly categorized, but it confirms her status as a powerful speaker whose art will be leveraged on behalf of the community, especially women.

"The Dream Is the Truth": Janie, Pheoby, and Hurston on High

The early Eatonville drama, which centers on preaching, should be seen as a crucial training ground for Janie's eventual fulfilment of Nanny's deferred dream of preaching "a great sermon about colored women sittin' on high" (Hurston, *Eyes*: 16). This "great sermon" *is* Janie's liberatory conversation with Pheoby: the morally authoritative sermon begins in the novel's opening pages and concludes only at the novel's closing. As Janie offers her extended personal (and political) testimony to Pheoby, the two women engage in a dialogic mode of storytelling patterned on a call-and-response sermon. In *Their Eyes Were Watching God*, Hurston imagines a shift from a monological sermon toward one marked by dialogue, cooperation, and encouragement, casting the sermon as a liberatory communal production by and for women, not an individual man's artistic performance.[17] This shift represents the most innovative aspect of Hurston's development of literary preaching as a form in the novel.

The frame narrative of *Their Eyes* unfolds as Janie, Pheoby, and the narrative voice collaborate to voice a personal testimony with significant political ramifications for African American women. Picking up the sermonic resonance of Janie and Pheoby's conversation *and* Hurston's narrative voice, Dolan Hubbard claims that "Janie intends to convert Pheoby, and Hurston intends to convert the reader-participant" (49). Similarly noting the trio of voices that mingle in the framing narrative, Edwidge Danticat helpfully points out that "Janie, Pheoby, and Zora Neale Hurston form their own story telling chain" and that Hurston's narrative voice, like Pheoby's, "becomes Janie's echo by picking up the narrative thread in intervals, places where in real life, or in real time, Janie might have grown tired of talking" (x). This narrative pattern mirrors the practice of "bearing up the preacher," a practice through which the audience participates in the sermon by verbally encouraging the preacher (Thomas 220).

For a woman to preach and testify, however, Hurston suggests the necessity of not only finding a voice but also of creating new spaces. We might read Janie's relocation to the *back* porch as a tactical move that provides the female speaker(s) with the secrecy necessary for refashioning their identities through language. Dale Pattison perceptively notes that Janie's back porch functions as a something like a hush harbor, a religious space that enables a quasi-public performance of "subversive rhetoric unique and exclusive to the African American experience" (13). This space provides protection from the misogynistic (front) porch talkers' verbal abuse. And, indeed, Hurston renders Pheoby's arrival at Janie's porch as a compressed escape narrative, a journey from oppression to a site of safety and transformation. She "hurries on off" into the evening, carrying a small food supply, and feels the porch talkers' cruel questions "pelting her back" (Hurston, *Eyes*: 4). She arrives at Janie's house, walks around the side, passes through an "intimate gate," an image of rebirth, and enters the backyard, where she finds Janie waiting for her (4).

At both the beginning and conclusion of the frame tale, Hurston underscores its status as a feminist spiritual testimony through religious imagery. When Pheoby arrives, she finds Janie sitting on the back porch in a domestic shrine. Small oil lamps flicker around Janie as she soaks her feet in a bowl of water.

---

[17] For more on the sermonic resonance of Janie and Pheoby's conversation, see Hubbard *The Sermon and the African American Literary Imagination* (U of Missouri P:1994), 47–63.

The multivalent image suggests the Catholic practice of lighting votive candles around a statue of a saint. Additionally, Janie's act of washing her own feet with a basin and towel after the meal—an act Hurston repeatedly highlights (4–5)— recalls the Christian practice of foot washing, a highly contentious practice in Southern religion during the 1930s (Humphrey 323).[18] In the Gospel of John, Jesus washes his disciples' feet after a meal in order to underscore the centrality of self-giving and servanthood to his mission (Jn 13:12-20). Janie's act of washing her own feet after completing her meal, by contrast, models ethical self-love and questions cultural narratives that delimit African American women's lives by insisting on their roles as servants of others.

Janie's initial rhetorical moves establish her as a female preacher poised to offer Pheoby a transformative lesson. As Hubbard rightly notes, Janie "taps into the responsive mythology of the black sermon as she assigns meaning to her experience" (62). After mocking the porch talkers by referring to them as "Mouth-Almighty," Janie deploys a series of metaphors to tell Pheoby that she has a life-changing testimony to deliver. "Ah could then sit down and tell 'em things," Janie tells Pheoby (Hurston, *Eyes*: 6). Sounding as if she's channeling Rev. John Pearson, she announces, "Ah been a delegate to de big 'ssociation of life. Yessuh! De Grand Lodge, de big convention of livin' is just where Ah been dis year and a half y'all ain't seen me" (6). As she warms to her topic, Janie tells Pheoby, "'Taint' no use in me telling you somethin' unless Ah give you de understandin' to go 'long wid it" (7). These opening lines signal her appropriation of sermonic formulas and prepare Pheoby for participation in the call-and-response performance. If Janie's recourse to sermonic idioms seems conservative, we should note that by seizing on these formulas as she begins her tale, she violates patriarchal norms against women speaking with religious authority and fulfills Nanny's dream, delivering an epic sermon about a Black woman's joy, suffering, wisdom, love, and new-found independence and power. The cultural work that Janie aims to effect mirrors Hurston's own. In *Their Eyes Were Watching God*, literary preaching no longer simply displays African American folk culture's aesthetic beauty; it also dramatizes Hurston's linked arguments about the potential richness of African American women's lives and the need for female solidarity in challenging conformist modes of living.

---

[18] Richard Alan Humphrey notes that during the 1930s, questions about the practice of foot washing were a matter of significant debate among many Southern denominations. See Humphrey "Foot Washing" for a concise and helpful discussion of the practice and its significance in Southern religion during the years Hurston worked on *Their Eyes Were Watching God*.

In the figure of Pheoby, Huston offers the reader a model for how they should respond to her art. Carla Kaplan avers that frame tales "interpolate their readers into the text" (152). She writes, "Ideal listeners such as Pheoby, then, are there as heuristic models for the reader; they teach us what we need to learn and how we ought to read" (152). Pheoby's importance as a sympathetic respondent comes into focus when we contrast her with the porch talkers who berate Janie and the all-white jury who misunderstands her. Like the preachers Hurston so admired for their courage amidst "the camp of mockers," Janie endures the crowd's mockery. When she returns to Eatonville, the porch talkers make "burning statements with questions, and killing tools out of laughs. It was mass cruelty" (Hurston, *Eyes*: 2). Pheoby, by contrast, brings Janie a meal and sits at her feet to learn from her friend. Gurleen Grewal reads Pheoby as a symbolic listener and argues that she "enacts the ideal of a reciprocal, nourishing relationship between an artist and her community" ("Beholding" 109). As Grewal and other commentators indicate, Pheoby's listening involves much more than just listening; she participates in the performative event. Given literary preaching's tendency to concretize clerical authority, it would be difficult to overstate the significance of Hurston's portrayal of the sermon as a dialogic form.

The seamlessness of their intersubjective narrative exchange affirms Janie's claim that the women can collaborate in the intimate, but nevertheless political, sermonic performance because they share both an oral culture and an experience of the world. Janie informs Pheoby that, at present, she has no intent to address the porch talkers. She empowers Pheoby, however, to take her message where she sees fit: "You can tell 'em what Ah say if you wants to. Dat's just de same as me 'cause mah tongue is in mah friend's mouf" (Hurston, *Eyes*: 6). Here Hurston identifies Janie's search for a voice as fulfilled not through possessing and hoarding her own story but through dispersing it and inviting her friend to propagate her message. Moreover, Pheoby contributes significantly to the message, embellishing and clarifying moments in Janie's story. Her status as a co-participant in the call-and-response structure depends largely on the fact that her subject position is nearly identical to Janie's. She responds because she understands Janie in a way that numerous other audiences in the novel refuse to or cannot. Janie, sensibly, counsels Pheoby not to waste time trying to convince the misogynistic porch talkers. This is not, she suggests, a message for everyone but only for those ready to celebrate a sermon of this sort (16).

These warnings reveal Hurston's perceptive sense that her fiction was before its time, often at odds with the dominant fictional modes of "social or critical realism" that the largely male African American literary establishment promoted (Gates, "Zora": 200). In her detailed review of numerous contemporary reviews of *Their Eyes Were Watching God*, M. Genevieve West notes that only three reviewers comment on what contemporary critics regard as the novel's most significant social theme—the quest for female subjectivity (126). After the male arbiters of the African American literary establishment wrote blistering critiques of the novel, Hurston found herself "pushed to the periphery of the African American literary community" (M. West 126). Janie's sermon, the fulfillment of Nanny's deferred dream, would eventually find a broader audience, and Hurston would come to be regarded as a matriarchal figure in African American women's writing. None of this, however, would happen in Hurston's lifetime.

In the closing scene of the novel, however, Hurston imagines her sermon receiving a thrilling reception. Aware that the porch talkers will judge her for her nonnormative love with Tea Cake, Janie, a gifted orator, offers Pheoby a poetic image of what she's learned about love: "You must tell 'em dat love ain't somethin' lak uh grindstone dat's de same thing everywhere and do de same thing tuh everything it touch. Love is lak de sea. It's uh movin' thing, but still and all, it takes its shape from de shore it meets, and it's different with every shore" (Hurston, *Eyes*: 191). Hurston registers Pheoby's response to Janie's testimony in the ecstatic language of religious conversion: "'Lawd!' Pheoby breathed out heavily, 'Ah done growed ten feet higher from jus' listin' tuh you, Janie. Ah ain't satisfied wid mahself no mo'. Ah means tuh make Sam take me fishin' wid him after this. Nobody better not criticize yuh in mah hearin'" (192). Pheoby's conversion realizes Hurston's fantasy of authorial reception, and within the narrative logic of *Their Eyes Were Watching God*, the sermon succeeds so brilliantly because Janie aims to preach a sermon *not* for everyone but *specifically* for Pheoby or women like her. Pheoby's announcement signals an important transformation because she had previously aspired to achieve a life of relative luxury characterized by sitting on the front porch like the white women Nanny envied (Hubbard 62). After listening to Janie, Pheoby trades the dream of better approximating bourgeois, white femininity for a more egalitarian marriage with her husband. Pheoby describes her change by rejecting her old self ("Ah ain't satisfied wid mahself no mo"), acknowledging her growth ("Ah growed ten feet higher from jus' listin' tuh you"),[19] and committing to a new course of action that

---

[19] Pattison astutely notes that Pheoby's "spatially connotative higher (as opposed to taller) suggests that Janie's narrative has freed her from static conceptions of identity grounded in physical place" (25). Moreover, Pheoby's description of growing "higher" signals "spirituality or transcendence" (25).

affirms bodily pleasure and adventure ("Ah means tuh make Sam take me fishin' wid him after this"). Janie responds with a final benediction that emphasizes an Emersonian ethic of self-reliance and nonconformity. "It's uh known fact," she says to her novitiate, "you got tuh *go* there tuh *know* there ... Two things everybody's got tuh do fuh theyselves. They got tuh go tuh God, and they got tuh find out about livin' fuh theyselves" (192).

Janie has found out about living for herself and testified to what she's learned; however, after Pheoby leaves, the preacher immediately faces a test of her faith. When Janie enters her bedroom, her traumatic experiences begin to flood her: "The day of the gun, and the bloody body, and the courthouse came and commenced to sing a sobbing sigh out of every corner in the room" (192). As her trauma gathers destructive force, a vision of Teacake appears before her, seemingly resurrected by her narration of their love story. As he "pranc[es] around her" in a manner both protective and playful, the traumatic memories take flight, and the room fills with "peace" (193). Having spent her evening converting Pheoby, Janie turns her attention to herself and urges herself to attend to her own sermon. Riffing on Jesus's final miracle in the Gospel of John, in which the resurrected Jesus miraculously helps the disciples net more fish than they can land (Jn 21:1-11), Janie imagines herself "pull[ing] in her horizon like a great fish-net. Pull[ing] it from around the waist of the world and drap[ing] it over her shoulder. So much life in its meshes! She called in her soul to come and see" (193). Janie's miraculous catch, an image of the richness of her unorthodox life, bears witness to her own gospel.

In adapting the miracle recorded in the final chapter of the Gospel of John, Hurston's image suggests the completion of a religious narrative, but the novel's final phrase, "come and see," also indicates a new beginning. With this closing scriptural allusion, Hurston jumps from the final chapter of John back to its first chapter. The phrase appears twice in the first chapter of the Gospel of John. It is the first declarative utterance attributed to Jesus as he invites his first two disciples to "come and see" where he lives (Jn 1:39). Several verses later, the disciples repeat Jesus's line as they, in turn, recruit other followers and encourage them to "come and see" Jesus (Jn 1:46). Thus, Hurston's novel closes by suggesting the open-endedness of Janie's future, the individual work necessary for her to remain fast to her vision, and the possibility of her secular ministry spreading.

Though the novel ends on an uplifting note, ambiguity surrounds Pheoby's conversion and Janie's future. Religious history teaches many lessons, and among the most important are that conversion experiences do not necessarily inaugurate lasting change of either personal behavior or social situations. For instance, how will Sam respond to his wife's requests to join him on fishing trips? How will the porch talkers respond when Pheoby defends Janie and propagates her message? Most importantly, will Janie herself be able to sustain her hard-won identity in the face of the challenges that surely await her in Eatonville? The lingering presence of her traumas, which hover "in the top of the pine trees" outside of Janie's bedroom, suggests that Janie's memory will remain conflicted, a site of competing narratives (193). What happens, we might wonder, if the liberatory sermon dies out and no congregants respond to the call? What traumas can the sermon relieve and where are the limits of its narrative power? Or, more threateningly, what becomes of a sermon if the speaker no long remains convinced by her own rhetoric, can no longer rally herself to "come and see" the truths of her vision? These questions, which remain unanswered at the end of *Their Eyes Were Watching God*, resurface in the literary preaching of one of Hurston's literary daughters and the author I examine in the subsequent chapter—Toni Morrison.

4

Toni Morrison, the Anxieties of Literary Preaching, and the Circulated Sermon

In a 1981 interview with Charles Ruas, Toni Morrison describes her novels with a comparison that discloses one of her fiction's aesthetic touchstones. She explains her novels' "multiple endings" by insisting that the novels do not "stop" or "shut" because the meaning of the novel, as in an oral folktale, rests in her readers' responses. To explain this authorial sensibility further, she likens reading her novels to participating in a call-and-response sermon: "Being in church and knowing that the function of the preacher is to make you get up, you do say yes, and you do respond back and forth … [S]omething is supposed to happen so the listener participates" (101). In this arresting explanation, Morrison acts as precisely the sort of critic that she would later claim to "long for," a critic who understands African American cultural forms, their "function in the black cosmology," and their status as "moorings" and "anchors" in her novels (Morrison, "An Interview with Toni Morrison," by McKay 151). This vision of the novel as something like a call-and-response sermon that requires audience participation for its success is no fleeting vision for Morrison. In another 1981 interview, Thomas LeClair asks Morrison what makes her work distinctive, and she responds by saying, "the language, only the language" (Morrison, "Language" 123). Morrison scholars with a special interest in her style frequently cite the first part of her answer: "The language must be careful and must appear effortless. It must not sweat. It must suggest and be provocative at the same time." Rarely, however, does her further elaboration receive critical attention, perhaps because it suggests a puzzling identification of her style with that of the preacher. After saying that the language "must not sweat," Morrison says that her stylized language's "function is like a preacher's: to make you stand up out of your seat, make you lose yourself and hear yourself" (124). In other words, her language, like her strategic refusal to "shut" her novels, is designed to provoke a response, and, curiously, Morrison compares both of these aesthetic commitments to the art of preaching.

Despite Morrison's attraction to the energy, openness, and sensuality of the sermon, she has an intensely ambivalent relation to invoking the sermon for several interlocking reasons. First, Morrison holds the form at arm's length because it tends to reify highly centralized structures of authority and, more broadly, to fortify culturally dominant modes of Christianity that fail to address the communal needs of African Americans, especially women and children.[1] Second, although Morrison compares her literary style with that of a preacher, her intricate strategies of characterization reveal an attempt to navigate a dialectic of desire and repulsion as she constructs her vocational identity in relation to her numerous fictional preachers. Morrison rightly senses that the form inexorably affords an identification of the author with the preacher, a complex affordance that both enables and frustrates her project. Her attraction to the preacher's artistry, moral authority, and willingness to voice countercultural truths exists in dialectical tension with her repulsion at the preacher's hubris, elitism, and tendency to privilege abstractions over the needs of the body. Consequently, Morrison's intentionally multivalent scenes of preaching throw the reader into interpretive crisis and demand patient critical attention.

No single chapter could treat each of Morrison's engagements with literary preaching, a recurring feature of her novels, in their full complexity. Given this study's interest in the contradictory affordances of literary preaching, I focus on two novels in which Morrison's engagements with literary preaching contribute most significantly to the novels' cultural work and Morrison's sense of authorial identity. Tracing the development of Morrison's literary preaching from *The Bluest Eye* to *Beloved*, we see her moving from an ambivalence about literary preaching to a dramatic revision of the literary sermon in which, startlingly, the figure of the preacher absconds in order that the sermon may flourish. This chapter discloses Morrison's strategy of deploying open-ended literary sermons

---

[1] For a useful account of Morrison's rejection of mainstream Christianity, see Shirley A. Stave, "From Eden to Paradise: A Pilgrimage through Toni Morrison's Trilogy," in *Toni Morrison: Memory and Meaning*, edited by Adrienne Lanier and Justine Tally (UP of Mississippi: 2014). Stave emphasizes Morrison's pattern of revising Christianity by rejecting its "metaphorization of God as the father" (110), its privileging of the "spirit over flesh" (117), and the "pettiness of God … as he is portrayed in the Old Testament (113). Frequently, Morrison shows that flaws in Christian theology and practice contribute to the political crises and personal tragedies that define her character's lives. At the same time, Morrison understands the African American church's historical significance and regards it as an institution that provided crucial space for community bonding, political formation, and personal encouragement (Morrison, "Toni": 116). See Toni Morrison, "Toni Morrison," by Charles Ruas.

to merge the reader with the writer, a strategy that builds upon the tradition of call-and-response preaching in which the congregants and preacher become coworkers in an ongoing project. Through her intensely democratic engagement with literary preaching in *Beloved*, Morrison suggests that revival and the healing of community are the work of the community of readers as well as the literary artist. But before she advances this democratic vision, Morrison grapples with the sermon in *The Bluest Eye*.

By treating Soaphead Church's sermon, one of the culminating scenes of *The Bluest Eye*, as a complex literary palimpsest, we can begin to discern the significance of Morrison's multivalent engagement with literary preaching in her first novel, an engagement that inaugurates her career-long practice of evoking the sermon in her narratives and reveals her reasons for resisting *and* embracing the form. On the one hand, Soaphead Church—a mixed-race pedophile who loathes "all that suggest[s] Africa" (including his own body) and uses the sermon to defend his sexual predation and praise his own power as a storyteller—embodies the antithesis of Morrison's entwined cultural projects of affirming the Black body's sanctity and giving voice to the African American girls who are often the silent casualties of structural racism (Morrison, *Bluest*: 167). It is not surprising, then, that through this satirical scene of literary preaching, Morrison reveals the deleterious results of Church's arrogance and internalized racism—and the community's tolerance of him. Yet, alarmingly, Church functions as an authorial surrogate, an imaginative writer who, like Morrison, captures the pulsations and cadences of the preacher's voice and possesses an acute sense of the historical-ideological processes that give birth to the psychological and physical violence that the novel dramatizes. And, curiously, the novel's initial, vertiginous engagement with the sermon catalyzes Morrison's second engagement with literary preaching in *The Bluest Eye*: Claudia MacTeer's prophetic pronouncement of the community's sinful response to Pecola's misery, a concluding sermon that adapts Church's sermon and anticipates the literary preaching that reverberates throughout Morrison's fiction. We should understand Church's call and Claudia's response as trajectory-setting and nettlesome engagements with the form that Morrison identifies as one of her central cultural touchstones.

Furthermore, because the sermon serves as an aesthetic touchstone for numerous American writers, Morrison's adaptations of the sermon in her first novel enable her not only to comment on the role of religious oratory in US culture but also to revise the US literary tradition she writes herself into in *The Bluest Eye*, a tradition in which, across the color line, literary preaching flourishes. Most obviously, Morrison's literary preaching signifies on and departs from the twentieth-century Black male traditions of literary preaching encoded in the works of Ralph Ellison and James Baldwin. In *The Sermon and the African American Imagination*, Dolan Hubbard analyzes the sermon's radical and restrictive effects in African American religious culture and argues persuasively that "the very idea of examining the sermon and the African American literary imagination means that one must acknowledge the political conservatism of black religion—its tendency to promote a submission to authority in the face of subversive impulses of the will" (21). Though their emphases vary, both Ellison and Baldwin deploy literary preaching primarily to critique its conservative, ideological function within the African American cultural imaginary.

Throughout *Invisible Man*, Ellison's multiple scenes of public speaking draw explicitly on the tropes and dynamics of Black preaching. The novel features a storefront preacher's call-and-response sermon on the "Blackness of Blackness," the conservative Rev. Homer A. Barbee's Founder's Day sermon, the unnamed narrator's attempt to preempt a riot by offering a public speech that mimics the call-and-response sermonic form, and a closing eulogy in which the narrator, increasingly exhausted by the failure and manipulation of his eloquence, announces "there's no one here to preach a sermon" (455). As H. William Rice has shown, despite the sermon's rhetorical power, it consistently fails to liberate either the individual speaker or his auditors in *Invisible Man*, and, at the novel's conclusion, eloquence is temporarily "rejected as a mode of self or community definition" (20). When, toward the end of the novel, the narrator impales the jaw of Ras the Exhorter/Destroyer, he silences his double and catalyzes his own movement away from a world defined and disfigured by speech toward a world that privileges the untapped possibilities of literary writing (Rice 20). For Ellison, the sermon is a form of undeniable artistic and consensus-making power. But, as is dramatized by the ironic revelation of Rev. Barbee's blindness, the sermon offers no truly liberatory vision, no radical insight.[2] Rather, as

---

[2] In *Juneteenth*, Ellison's posthumously published novel, he takes a more ambivalent stance on the sermon's value. In her sensitive treatment of Ellison's relationship to African American Christianity, Laura Saunders regards the novel's central literary sermon, a dialogic sermon performed by Rev. Hickman and Rev. Bliss, as "Ellison's *credo*, his understanding of the African-American role in US history" (47). H. William Rice suggests, however, that though the sermon performs significant cultural work and evinces Ellison's sensitivity to the "improvisational language of the minister," it ultimately fails as Bliss/Sunraider "misappropriates the voice of the black sermon into the race-baiting political rhetoric that we encounter on the first pages of the novel," see *Ralph Ellison and the Politics of the Novel* (Lexington: 2003), 127–8. In this sense, for Rice, the rhetorical failures and frustrations that reappear throughout *Invisible Man* are echoed in Hickman's failure to ultimately convert his own adopted son. In my view, Thomas S. Engeman seems correct when he comments that Hickman's inability to enlist his son into the liberatory work of the Black church "illustrates man's complex liberty and loves, not the untruth of [Hickman's] word" (102). Morrison did not, of course, have access to *Juneteenth* prior to the publication of *The Bluest Eye*. However, she could

Thomas S. Engeman puts it, "religion in [*Invisible Man*] is an ideological support of oppression and alienation" (99). In contrast, Morrison's preachers, who are often women, frequently see as clearly as they speak, and their skill at giving poetic voice to their visions offers a liberatory resource to their communities.

For Baldwin, the matter is a bit different. In *Go Tell It on the Mountain*, *The Amen Corner*, and *Just Above My Head*, Baldwin's fictive preachers, whether men or women, deliver effective, rhetorically powerful sermons that enjoin their congregants to repress their bodily desires and transcend their basic human needs. At the same time, throughout Baldwin's works, "ministers offer a substitute for physical experience through religious ecstasy" (Byerman 188). Thus, Baldwin often stages scenes of preaching to show that the outpouring of emotion and bodily energy witnessed at religious gatherings should be understood as a communal act of sublimation: the anti-somatic sermon and the exuberant physicality of Pentecostal worship are two sides of the same coin. Baldwin clearly understands the African American sermon's thematic range and verbal artistry; nevertheless, the revival sermon that launches Gabriel Grimes's career in *Go Tell It on the Mountain* might be read as expressive of Baldwin's sense of the form's essentially disciplinary function.[3] Grimes masterfully uses anaphora, a central rhetorical device in African American preaching, to catalogue the parts of the body and define each as inherently sinful: "Sin reigns in all our members, sin is the foul heart's natural liquid, sin looks out of the eye, amen, and leads to lust,

---

have accessed the Hickman-Bliss sermon (though disconnected from the broader arc of the novel) because Ellison published this sermon, which appears as Chapter 7 of *Juneteenth*, as a short story, titled "Juneteenth," in the *Quarterly Review of Literature* in 1965. Additionally, in 1966, Ellison offered the American public a reading of this literary sermon on a nationally televised special titled "U.S.A. The Novel." Years later, at a celebration of the long-awaited publication of *Juneteenth* (1999), Morrison read an extended sermonic passage of the novel. In the passage, Hickman, speaking to Bliss, frames white children's transition into adolescence as a fall into a confusing, loveless culture because it requires them to despise the African American women who nursed, raised, and loved them. "The first step in their growing up," Hickman observes, "is to learn how to *spurn* love" (162). This act, the preacher continues, "bores reckless excursions between the brain and the heart," leaving whites with an enduring psychological wound that "snarls the mind" and makes them alienated from their own love and the love of others. Morrison's powerful performance ends with Hickman's devastating closing remarks: "Oh, Bliss, *Bliss*, boy. I get carried away with words. Forgive me ... But one thing I do know: God, Bliss boy, is Love" (166).

[3] Though I agree largely with Byerman's argument that Baldwin's preachers embody the negation of "moral, social, and humanistic values" (187), one must avoid oversimplifying the complexity of Baldwin's preachers. Baldwin's preachers, on rare occasion, seek penitence and offer sermons that confess their moral failures. In *The Amen Corner*, for example, Sister Margaret Alexander presides as an authoritarian religious leader throughout the play. In her final sermon, however, she confesses that she ignored Jesus's injunction to "love all of His children—all of them, everyone!" and seems aware that she transformed her church into a legalistic, self-aggrandizing cult (545). The play's irony is that Margaret utters these words as she descends from the pulpit for the last time: the preacher's proclamation of a humanistic strain of Christianity, Baldwin suggests, necessitates a descent from the place of authority in the African American church.

sin is in the hearing of the ear, and leads to folly, sin sits on the tongue, and leads to murder. Yes!" (117). Though no simple, singular pattern describes Morrison's literary preaching, her preachers often contrast sharply with Baldwin's because they offer sermons that underscore the theological centrality of immanent human needs. Indeed, Grimes's "Sin Is the Foul Heart's Natural Liquid" sermon can be understood as the antithesis of Baby Suggs's "Love Your Heart" sermon. Suggs's sermon—which proclaims the sacredness of the Black body through an extended, celebratory catalogue of its constituent parts—exemplifies Morrison's revision of and departure from Baldwin's literary preaching, as she frequently reimagines the preacher as an artist capable of bringing truth, beauty, and self-love to her people.[4]

Across her many novels, Morrison's fictional sermons engage this important trope in male-authored African American literature; however, her inaugural engagement with literary preaching in *The Bluest Eye* adapts the work of another central patriarch in the US literary canon and a figure of special importance to Morrison, the subject of her Master's thesis—William Faulkner. Through the figures of Church and Claudia MacTeer, Morrison revises the central preachers of William Faulkner's *Light in August*, the Rev. Gail Hightower and the anti-preacher Joe Christmas. Thus, with her initial foray into literary preaching, which reveals a dialectic of repulsion and desire, Morrison narrativizes the sermon, signifies on Faulkner's engagements with literary preaching, and initiates a problematic relationship to a form that deeply shapes her oeuvre.

(Re)performing the Sermon in *The Bluest Eye*: Repulsion, Desire, and Sermonic Doubling

At the end of *The Bluest Eye*, Claudia MacTeer reviews the circumstances that led to Pecola's madness and, like many prophets before her, employs an agricultural

---

[4] The scope of this study precludes an expanded discussion of the relationship between Baldwin and Morrison vis-a-via literary preaching, a topic that could sustain a much longer project because the flow of influence, as Lovalerie King puts it, "was certainly not a one-way street" ("Introduction" 3). Clearly, Morrison's invocation of the sermon in *The Bluest Eye* marks her responsiveness to this pervasive trope in Baldwin's novels. But Baldwin's *Just Above My Head* (1979)—published nine years after Morrison's first novel and featuring a girl preacher who is serially raped by her father—indicates Baldwin's responsiveness to the multifaceted cultural analyses that Morrison performs in *The Bluest Eye*. See Hubbard, *Sermon*; Keith L. Byerman, "Secular Word: Sacred Flesh: Preachers in the Fiction of Baldwin and Morrison," in *James Baldwin and Toni Morrison: Comparative Critical and Theoretical Essays*, edited by Lovalerie King and Lynn Orilla Scott (Palgrave: 2006); and Carol E. Henderson, "Refiguring the Flesh: The Word, the Body, and the Rituals of Being in Beloved and Go Tell It on the Mountain," in *James Baldwin and Toni Morrison: Comparative Critical and Theoretical Essays*, edited by Lovalerie King and Lynn Orilla Scott (Palgrave: 2006) for discussions of Morrison's and Baldwin's engagements with preachers and preaching.

metaphor to describe the nation's moral failure: "This soil is bad for certain kinds of flowers" (Morrison 205). Claudia's closing statement compels readers to cast a retrospective look at the novel and realize that *The Bluest Eye* performs a narrative soil sample, a detailed analysis of a polluted social environment. Throughout the novel, Morrison attempts to identify the ideologies, events, and forces that make the land inhospitable. The novel suggests three primary toxins that combine to create a lethal environment for African American girls: racialized notions of physical attractiveness, the generational legacies of Jim Crow-era violations of the integrity of the African American male body, and family dysfunction amid abject poverty.

Though the novel focuses on these three primary toxins, Christianity also emerges as a cultural formation that poisons the social environment. Throughout most of the narrative diegesis, however, Morrison does not make the connections between religion and this pollution explicit. On multiple occasions, conspicuous religious images and rituals appear after scenes of violence against African American girls. These brief indices of Christianity appear as bubbles that seem to float to the surface of the narrative, momentarily register in the narrative's texture, rapidly burst, and then leave the reader asking what conclusions should be drawn. For example, when the self-loathing, "sugar-brown" (82) woman, Geraldine, casts Pecola out of her house and calls her a "nasty little black bitch" (92), the narrator notes that a portrait of Jesus hangs on the wall with "gay paper flowers twisted around his face" (93). Similarly, the narrator observes that Geraldine uses a "large Bible" to decorate her front room, but this detail passes quickly, and the stately Bible appears as one token of middle-class respectability among many others (83). Another minimalist indication of religiosity occurs when Mr. Henry, the MacTeer's boarder who sexually molests young Frieda, begins singing "Nearer My God to Thee" as Mr. MacTeer drives him away from the family. Finally, Pauline Breedlove also deploys religious rhetoric in her desperate attempt to paper over the pain of a marriage that no longer offers either emotional intimacy or the embodied, this-worldly "power" that she felt during sexual intercourse (131). After recounting the pleasures of her early relationship to Cholly, she states, "It don't make no difference about this old earth. There is sure to be a glory" (131). Her orthodox answer fools no one. Rather, it echoes precisely the hackneyed sermons that James Weldon Johnson describes as serving an anesthetic function in the African American imagination: "It was [the preacher] who instilled into the Negro the narcotic doctrine epitomized in the Spiritual, 'You May Have All Dis World, But Give Me Jesus'" (6). These irruptions of Christian art, hymnody, and rhetoric suggest that Christianity functions in the novel as either a thin religious veneer beneath which people recklessly pursue their various material or sexual desires or as a form of ideological mystification. Indeed, in these scenes, Morrison indicates that Christianity's significance rests in its ability to obscure, at least partially, the forces that determine human action by providing vague metaphysical comfort for both the perpetrators and victims of oppression. Throughout most of the narrative, the novel suggests that religion occupies an ultimately insignificant role in shaping the various characters' behavior and that attention should be directed to the material facts of the media, white oppression, and economic deprivation.

At the conclusion of the novel, however, theological reflection on local and historical crises takes center stage as Morrison engages in her first of many subsequent acts of literary preaching. Morrison's innovative and remarkably complex engagement with the sermon occurs in the climactic scene in which a former preacher named Elihue Micah Whitcomb, who the community has renamed Soaphead Church (due to his penchant for grooming his hair with soap lather and his erstwhile status as a guest preacher), writes a furious letter to God after convincing Pecola that her eyes have miraculously turned blue. Church's letter, as William Dahill-Baue observes, functions as a sermon, a sermon ironically addressed to God and designed to critique God's failure to protect the innocent.[5] Addressing God directly, Soaphead writes that the letter's purpose is to "familiarize you with facts which either have escaped your notice, or which you have chosen to ignore" (176). Throughout his performance, an extended sermonic soliloquy, he revels in a spiritual leader's power to replace God, for the "instrument through which [God] works" to become God himself (174). Church also uses this sermon to defend his serial child molestation, but this defense appears as a rhetorical detour in an address that focuses much more consistently on the apostate preacher's sense of propinquity to the divine and God's failure to protect the weak. Ultimately, Church rejects the responsibility of speaking on behalf of God and asserts the brilliance of his own verbal "miracle," a miracle accomplished by speaking Pecola's eyes into being. "I played You," Church taunts God in the language of the theater, "And it was a very good show!" (182). Church's sermon underscores Morrison's acute awareness of the communal danger represented by hierarchical models of authority associated

---

[5] William Dahill-Baue also regards Soaphead Church's letter as a textualized sermon, a form of preaching that "focuses attention on his literacy and literariness" (571). See William Dahill-Baue, "Insignificant Monkeys: Preaching Black English in Faulkner's *The Sound and the Fury* and Morrison's *Beloved*," *Mississippi Quarterly* 49, no. 3 (1996).

with the clerisy. It underscores the manner in which validating an individual's claims to act as a uniquely empowered spokesperson for God shatters communal responsibility, generates situations that foster abuses of power, and, ultimately, leads to the preacher's megalomania.

Any reading of this performance, however, remains inadequate if it attempts to resolve the multiple and conflicting ways that both Soaphead Church and his sermon function in the novel. The ambivalence that marks this scene easily goes undetected because at first glance Church's disturbing sermon appears as a burning satire, a sermon that underscores a singular message: the hypocrisy of a preacher who aims to assert his equality with God and the innocence of his sexual predation. Soaphead's attempt to blame God for his pedophilia appears so shocking, so perverse, that it threatens to drown out the other features of his sermon. This scene of literary preaching, however, does much more than merely critique, via satire, Soaphead or the cultural formations that he metonymically represents. In reading this scene as a dense, ambiguous, and anxious exploration of the risks and rewards of literary preaching, I take my clue from Morrison's metafictional comment that "all in all, [Church's] personality was an arabesque: intricate, symmetrical, balanced, and tightly constructed" (166). This metafictional comment functions, in fact, as a metafictional compliment, a self-congratulatory gesture. Here, at the close of her first novel, an as-of-yet undiscovered genius marvels at the intricate, tightly constructed, and balanced character she has created in Soaphead. Like any excavation, the following treatment of the "arabesque" Soaphead Church and his sermon demands patience and a circular interpretive praxis.

First, as she often does, Morrison provides her character with a Biblical name that invites criticism because a gap exists between the biblical figure and the namesake. In *The Bluest Eye* this gap underscores this preacher's anger at God. Indeed, Church's commentary on his own names constitutes an important but neglected part of his sermon.[6] Church's given name—Elihue Whitcomb—points us toward a man named Elihu in the biblical Book of Job, a text of established importance in Morrison's work due to its discomfiting meditation on theodicy.[7]

---

[6] For a trenchant discussion of Church's self-given name in relationship to Morrison's use of a *nom de plumb*, see John N. Duvall, *The Identifying Fictions of Toni Morrison: Modernist Authenticity and Postmodern Blackness* (Palgrave: 2000), 35–43. Karen Carmean also provides a valuable discussion of Soaphead's act of self-naming, see *Toni Morrison's World of Fiction* (Whitson: 1993), 25–6.

[7] Long considered the central Biblical text that engages questions of theodicy, the Book of Job tells the story of a man, Job, who suffers tremendous personal loss despite his upright living. Though Morrison's fiction frequently treats the Bible as an intertext, the Book of Job appears to be one of the scriptural narratives that most fascinates her. In a 1981 interview with Charles Ruas, Morrison identifies the Book of Job as a crucial text for African American Christianity: "And of course there

The conspicuous name alone suggests the intentionality of this allusion. However, Morrison's intention with this allusion seems beyond doubt when, at a key juncture in his sermon, Soaphead himself refers to Job prior to asking God a rhetorical question about the meaning of names and whether they indicate something essential about a person's character. After informing God that Pecola asked him for blue eyes, Soaphead writes, "She must have asked you for them for a very long time, and you hadn't replied. (A habit, I could have told her, a long-ago habit broken for Job—but no more.) She came to *me* for them. She had one of my cards. By the way, I added the Micah—Elihue Micah Whitcomb … What makes one name more a person than another?" (180).[8] The odd telegraphic shift signaled by Church's "by the way," a shift that suggests a free association, indicates this submerged linkage between this minor character from the Book of Job and the significance of Soaphead's proper name.

The preaching of the biblical Elihu sharply contrasts that of his fictional namesake. Throughout this scene, Morrison draws attention to Soaphead Church's fury at God, his conviction that God had done a poor job creating the world, and that "it was in fact a pity that the Maker had not sought his counsel" (173). By contrast, Elihu emerges as a preacher incensed that God's character seems to be called into question by Job and his three closest friends. Job's friends respond to Job's suffering by insisting that his misfortune indicates God's displeasure. They deny the possibility of a righteous man suffering and, to protect a vision of God's justice and benevolence, tell Job that his suffering should be understood as punishment for impiety. Though Job rejects their arguments, he insists on his own righteousness. Elihu responds strongly to both Job and his counselors: "Against Job was his wrath kindled, because he justified himself rather than God. Also against his three friends was his wrath kindled, because they had found no answer, and yet had condemned Job" (Job 32:2-3). Elihu offers an extended counter-sermon that denounces the superficial answers to suffering offered by Job and his friends. Elihu calls on Job to trust God in the face of suffering, but, at the same time, refuses to offer systematic answers to the questions the book poses about human suffering. Elihu's sermon

---

was that wonderful, very strange Job, not his original wealth, but his steady, sustained 'I will not do that, I will not do that' all the way through, and then finally, the recompense. That's your test of inner faith" ("Toni Morrison," 117). For a helpful discussion of Job as a crucial biblical intertext for *Sula*, see Beverly Foulks's "Trial by Fire: The Theodicy of Toni Morrison in *Sula*."

[8] In the first part of this passage, Church refers to a moment in the biblical narrative when God directly speaks to Job in the wake of Job's intense suffering (Job 38–40:2). Though God's response hardly satisfies Job's questions and, indeed, dodges the theodical questions that Job raises, Church emphasizes that at least in that moment God seemed to respond to human suffering.

concludes with an affirmation of divine otherness and calls for humility before a God who consistently unsettles humanity's expectations (Job 37:23-24). It would be difficult to identify a message more opposed to Soaphead Church's because Church categorically rejects notions of divine otherness, insisting not only that he can discern the ways of God but also God's failures. Unlike the biblical Elihu, his namesake, Elihue Whitcomb affirms the existence of a God but believes that "God had done a poor job" in creating the world and attempts to correct human suffering through speaking a lie (Morrison, *Bluest*: 173). He insists that "evil existed because God had created it," (172) and one of his sermon's central claims is that God "forgot how and when to be God" (181).

Morrison indicates that Elihue Whitcomb understands the irony of being named after a passionate defender of God's otherness and justice and, thus, he adds a second Biblical name, Micah, to his given name to reflect how he understands his relationship to God. He, like Morrison, knows that names matter. This act of self-naming, which he tells God about in his sermon, highlights his antidemocratic ethos and reveals his "disdain for other people, his arrogance illustrated by his adding 'Micah' ('he who is like God') to his name" (Carmean 26). Church's act of self-naming also suggests his ambition to displace God. Of course, the biblical name does not suggest equality with God, but rather "godliness," a personality that reflects divine virtue. Church, however, rejects godliness in favor of being God-like. Thus, Morrison's engagement with the Book of Job opens a window into Church's character, spotlights the egomaniacal pulses of his sermon, and registers Morrison's anxiety about engaging a form that reifies antidemocratic hierarchies. He rejects a name he associates with defending God and calls himself by another biblical name that suggests his status as God's equal, a status he celebrates when he preaches to God saying, "I did what You did not, could not, would not do: I looked at that ugly little black girl, and I loved her" (Morrison, *Bluest*: 182).

With her palimpsestic construction of Church's sermon, Morrison signifies not only on biblical sources, but also on William Faulkner's *Light in August*. Morrison's revision of Faulkner's preachers (Gail Hightower and Joe Christmas) and their sermons adapts the literary preaching that structures *Light in August* in order to both identify violent pulpit rhetoric as the legacy of colonial conquest and explore the form's affordance of extralegal moral authority. Numerous and striking parallels exist between Soaphead Church and Gail Hightower, the heretical preacher of *Light in August*. Both are formerly married bachelors who enjoy their isolation from their surrounding communities. Hightower resides in an "unpainted and unobtrusive bungalow," which remains "almost hidden" from his neighbors' view (Faulkner, *Light*: 57). Church, a man who briefly lived in a monastery, rents an obscure "back-room apartment from a deeply religious lady" (Morrison, *Bluest*: 171). Both men leave the ministry to take up new professions, and they announce their odd second careers with bizarre signs that they display on their properties. Hightower's sign reads "Rev. Gail Hightower, D.D. / Art Lessons / Handpainted Xmas & Anniversary Cards / Photographs Developed" (Faulkner, *Light*: 58). Church's sign, which hangs from his kitchen window (Morrison, *Bluest*: 167), advertises his services as a "Reader, Adviser, and Interpreter of Dreams" (165). Both men were made infamous through reports published in the newspaper (Faulkner, *Light*: 68–9; Morrison, *Bluest*: 181), and gossip about sexual misconduct surrounds both of the former preachers. The townspeople of Jefferson tell a story of Hightower asking his African American cook to engage in an act that she describes as "against God and nature" (Faulkner, *Light*: 71), and the townspeople of Lorain whisper about Church's horrific acts of pedophilia (Morrison, *Bluest*: 181). Striking as these similarities may be, we should regard them as secondary aspects of their characterization. While both Faulkner and Morrison underscore how racist narratives of national history structure these preachers' psyches and their sermons, Morrison drives further into the past to identify the roots of Church's warped psychology.

Faulkner's portrayal of Hightower's sermon (he seems to preach only one sermon over and over again) describes and parodies a Southern Jeremiad that interpreted the defeat of the Confederacy as a sign of God's special favor (Faulkner, *Light*: 61–3; Noll 78). Morrison offers a similar exploration of how historical forces shape her preacher's theological imagination, but in *The Bluest Eye* she traces this destructive narrative not to the antebellum South but to the colonial Caribbean. Morrison provides this intellectual genealogy by tracing the source of Elihue "Micah" Whitcomb's surname to "a Sir Whitcomb, some decaying British nobleman, who chose to disintegrate under a sun more easeful than England's ... [he] introduced the white strain into the family in the early 1800s" (*Bluest* 167). This surname directs us away from the realm of myth and toward the violent history of the circum-Atlantic world. The subsequent generations of Whitcomb's line become a "family proud of its academic accomplishments and its mixed blood—in fact, they believed the former was based on the latter" (167). Like Hightower, who obsesses over his grandfather's dubious heroism as a confederate soldier, an obsession with a paternal legacy deeply structures Church's preaching, but the "heroism" of Church's progenitor relates only to his racial identity, which in a colonial context has been coded as a priceless inheritance to be "hoard[ed]" (167).

Like his name, Church's body exists as a site of ideological contest, and the legacies of colonialism manifest themselves in his attempts to suppress any visible evidence of his African heritage and his violent hostility for flesh, and, especially, Black flesh. In a 1976 interview with Robert Stepto, Morrison states that she realized the narrative needed someone "who would also believe that [Pecola] was right, that it was preferable for her to have blue eyes" (Morrison, "Intimate": 22). To accomplish this she created a character who thinks "in terms of his own Western Indian background—a kind of English, colonial, Victorian thing drilled into his head which he could not escape. I needed someone to distill all of that, to say, 'Yeah you're right you need them. Here, I'll give them to you,' and really believe that he had done her a favor" (Morrison, "Intimate": 22). According to Morrison, Church, like Hightower, remains trapped in history and unable to think outside of the terms of a narrative that simultaneously destroys him and makes him a threat to the surrounding community. Indeed, one of the sermon's tragic, unintentional messages is that even his awareness of how he's been interpellated as a colonial subject cannot empower Church to break colonial ideology's grip on his imagination.

Given these similarities, it is not surprising that Church's self-aggrandizing sermon demonstrates precisely Gail Hightower's belated recognition that clerics usurp the place of God and use religion as a means of domineering their communities and entertaining their own psychological fantasies (Faulkner, *Light*: 487). For Morrison, however, Hightower's indictment of American clergy fails to acknowledge the material impact of violent pulpit rhetoric—that such preaching, in fact, leads to material damage. Faulkner's Hightower claims that churches align themselves "against truth and against that peace in which to sin and be forgiven which is the life of man" (487). For Hightower, this represents a failure in the realm of abstraction with no discernable material consequences. Morrison politicizes this claim by arguing that Church's perverse sermon celebrates a lie that destroys Pecola. The heretical sermon *matters*, theology matters, Morrison suggests, because it impacts the bodies of society's most vulnerable members. At least within the narrative world of *Light in August*, Hightower's blasphemous sermons do little material damage. One cannot overstate, however, the damage wrought and registered by Soaphead's speech on behalf of God. Soaphead expresses nothing like Hightower's sorrow when he realizes that he'd been a "charlatan preaching worse than heresy" (488). Indeed, Soaphead mocks and challenges God, making the sermon a tool of theological dissent.

Morrison's rewriting of Faulkner's literary preaching in *Light in August*, therefore, goes beyond her revision of Hightower: with Soaphead Church she also rewrites Faulkner's unsettling anti-preacher, Joe Christmas. Thus, in this revision of Faulkner's literary preaching, Morrison embraces the form's affordance of extralegal moral authority. For in Soaphead Church's sermon, dominant ideological messaging exists alongside a subversive, powerful Jeremiad against America's violence toward African American children and God's failure to protect them. Put differently, Church's repellent celebrations of whiteness and his own godlike power coexist with his admirable expressions of prophetic rage against a culture that destroys the Black body and his deeply human anguish that God seems unconcerned about this destruction. Though the most obvious similarity between Christmas and Church relates to their struggles with concerns about their racial ancestry, they both "preach" against the God that they identify as implicated in their oppression. In *Light in August*, Christmas memorably bursts into an African American folk church, attacks an elder, and climbs "into the pulpit … with his hands raised like a preacher" and begins "to curse, hollering it out, at the folks, and he cursed God louder than the women screeching" (Faulkner, *Light*: 323). Morrison adapts Faulkner's anti-preacher, who "preaches" with terrifying screams and oaths against God, by supplying him with articulate grievances against a deity who fails to protect Black children from undeserved suffering:

> You said, "Suffer little children to come unto me, and harm them not." Did you forget? Did you forget about the children? Yes. You forgot. You let them go wanting, sit on road shoulders, crying next to their dead mothers. I've seen them charred, lame, halt. You forgot, Lord. You forgot how and when to be God. (Morrison, *Bluest*: 181)

Ironically, though Soaphead "despise[s]" Dostoevsky's novels (169), he launches an indictment of God that, like Ivan Karamazov's "Grand Inquisitor" speech, focuses on the suffering of innocent children.

By bringing this suffering into focus, Church's sermon gives voice to the novel's central theme. Here, in a moment that produces affective vertigo, the sermon no longer operates as satire or as a dramatization of the dangers associated with clerical authority; rather, it gives anguished expression to Morrison's abiding concerns about the vulnerability of children and the vulnerability of the mother-child bond.[9] In this scene of literary preaching, Church's notation of children

---

[9] Linda Wagner-Martin offers an insightful discussion of Morrison's consistent thematic focus on the mother-child relation in her "Introduction" to *Toni Morrison and the Maternal: From The Bluest Eye to Home* (Peter Lang: 2014).

crying next to their "dead mothers" clearly represents Morrison's abiding concern with the precarity of this primary human relationship. Tessa Roynon is surely right to point out that high-profile acts of terrorism against African American children—including Emmett Till, participants in student sit-ins, and, especially, the four schoolgirls killed in the bombing of a Birmingham church in 1963—shaped Morrison's own political and literary imagination (103–4). In Church's odd reference to the "charred" bodies of children, we should read Morrison's allusion to the four girls murdered by the Ku Klux Klan's infamous bombing of the 16th Street Baptist Church. Moreover, in a moment in which he admits to his own flaws, Soaphead asks God a theodical question that seems to be drawn from the Book of Job, "Tell me, Lord, how could you leave a lass so long so lone that she could find her way to me? How could you?" (180). Church's attempt to shift blame for Pecola's destruction away from himself and the broader community might be read as an index of his inability to accept the serious consequence of human inaction. But, at the same time, his anger and confusion voice a deeply human question about the seemingly "cosmic proportion of Pecola's injury" (Furman 192). In *The Bluest Eye*, the perpetrators are victims, and perhaps more unsettlingly, the most dangerous liars also pose, in sermonic form, the most profound questions.

The status of Church's address as an epistle and literary sermon stands in sharp contrast to the typical pattern of literary preaching in which authors attempt to capture the variable power of the human voice. Church's letter clearly engages the sermonic voice—a literary mode that depends on self-conscious engagement with ministerial language, commentary on sacred texts, and authoritative claims to truth. However, the sermon's status as *text* (as opposed to oral performance) underscores this as a politically significant scene of writing, a fact that Morrison highlights by documenting the care with which the mock-genteel Soaphead crafts the letter. After Pecola leaves his yard, Morrison describes how Soaphead "went to a tiny night table with a drawer, from which he took paper and a fountain pen. A bottle of ink was on the same shelf that held the poison. With these things he sat again at the table. Slowly, carefully, relishing his penmanship, he wrote the following letter" (Morrison, *Bluest*: 176). Morrison's notions of the ink (curiously juxtaposed to a bottle of poison), the writing paper, the fountain pen, and the desk all function to highlight this scene as an intensely meta-textual moment that represents both "Soaphead's entry into authorship" and Morrison's meditation on "the eccentricity, marginality, and even misanthropy of those who pursue their art" (Duvall 28, 30). Indeed, Soaphead calls attention to his own prose in a parenthetical remark near the beginning of the letter: "(while the precision of my prose may be, at times, laborious, it is necessary that I identify myself to you clearly)" (Morrison, *Bluest*: 177). These scenes of prewriting and self-awareness suggest Morrison's own concern with the politics of form.

As other US authors often do with scenes of literary preaching, Morrison devotes a large portion of the narrative to Church's sermon and sets this letter off through intentionally stylized formatting. Unlike other literary preachers in US literature, however, Church's voice "finds expression in writing rather than in the spoken word, a reversal of the oral preaching tradition whereby Soaphead can relate to God only through paper, his business card enclosed" (Baillie 66). His written sermon measures his distance from the dialogic oral art that often defines African American preaching in Morrison's subsequent novels, and this distancing act accords with his patterned avoidance of any activity that suggests his African heritage or that addresses seriously the pressing needs of the African American community. The sermon's status as a text demonstrates the colonization of Church's imagination and his internalization of the Enlightenment's claims that literacy operates as the privileged mark of rationality, and, therefore, humanity.[10]

Yet Church possesses enough self-awareness to understand that the legacies of European colonialism shape his imagination of himself and others. In this sense, Soaphead gives voice to a legitimate and socially explosive complaint that, again, dovetails precisely with Morrison's cultural work. If his writing signals his implication in colonial ideology and formation in theological traditions that have often failed African American communities, it is also the weapon through which he attempts to express his genuine questions about history, theology, and culture. Put differently, though Soaphead problematically embraces literacy as a sign of his superior humanity, he also expresses righteous fury at the epistemic and physical violence he accurately identifies as intrinsic to colonialism. For this reason, he begins his letter to God by reminding God that "once upon a time I lived greenly and youngish on one of your islands" (Morrison, *Bluest*: 176). Soaphead's "once upon a time" suggests a world of myth, a world prior to the incursions of modern "history," in which he lives "greenly" on one of God's islands in the Greater Antilles. He speaks, in other words, not out of his own subjectivity but as representative of the precolonial Caribbean. The arrival of European colonizers who claim this island as theirs by divine right, however,

---

[10] For an extended analysis of the entanglements of "The Age of Reason" and what Morrison refers to as "The Age of Scientific Racism," see Justine Tally, *Toni Morrison's Beloved: Origins* (Routledge: 2009), 1–29. Tally reads Morrison's 1987 essay "Sites of Memory" alongside Foucault's theorization of "knowledge" as an interested mode of discourse that reveals and sustains power relations. For Morrison, literacy functions as a mark of exclusion through which humanity could be denied to populations that have been blocked from attaining it.

occasions a total rupture. Soaphead registers the transition from the prelapsarian Edenic ideal to the nightmare colony with a single one-word paragraph—"Now" (177)—that variously suggests a specific historical moment, the emergence of a new era, and the interruption of a childish dream. Anticipating Claudia MacTeer's lament that "this soil is bad for certain kinds of flowers," Church images forth no technological "machine" disrupting the bucolic "garden," but instead a menacing force that transforms the "garden" to "colony." Still speaking as a representative, he admits to God, "We in this colony took as our own the most dramatic, and the most obvious, of our white masters' characteristics, which were of course their worst" (177).

While never minimizing Soaphead's contemptible sexual predation, Morrison's first engagement with literary preaching places the ideological violence that drives the narratives of Pecola, Cholly, Geraldine, and Pauline within a world-historical horizon. Gurleen Grewal argues persuasively that Church's condensed autobiography, "the last of the novel's studies in alienated consciousness," dramatically "places the other accounts into perspective, for he brings from the West Indies an anglophilia and a consciousness both informed and deformed by a history of colonization" (*Circles* 27). In his epistle-sermon, Soaphead preaches that the social violence that one sees among a postcolonial population is a result of living under colonial oppression:

> Consequently we were not royal but snobbish, not aristocratic but class-conscious; we believed authority was cruelty to our inferiors, and education was being at school. We mistook violence for passion, indolence for leisure, and thought recklessness was freedom ... Our manhood was defined by acquisitions. Our womanhood by acquiescence. (Morrison, *Bluest*: 177)

Soaphead creates the cadence of this especially sermonic passage by using antithesis, juxtaposing virtues with vices, and revealing a pattern of misplaced value. He describes, quite lyrically, Morrison's own assessment of the postcolonial conscious that appears in a variety of domestic forms throughout the novel, all the while remaining a clear figure of authorial contempt whose sermon strangely abjures the material power of the voice. With this scene of literary preaching, Morrison explores an anxiety-producing similarity between the writer and the preacher; however, she upsets the typical unidirectional flow of this identification in US letters, wherein authors play the preacher through their engagements with this performance genre. In *The Bluest Eye*, the fictional preacher becomes a writer every bit as much as the writer becomes the preacher. As a result of this fraught exchange, both immensely powerful vocations are called into question.

The key sign of this vocational questioning occurs in Morrison's provocative notation that Soaphead keeps his bottle of ink next to his bottle of poison. Commenting on this detail, Shelley Wong points out that this

> juxtaposition of the ink and the poison is far from gratuitous. The literal poison on the shelf here merely underscores the novel's repeated concern with a metaphorical poisoning that works through the American culture industry's projection—from the movie screen, from Mary Jane candy wrappers, and from Shirley Temple mugs—of a single image of ideal beauty. (63–4)

What does it mean for a writer to imagine that the ink an authorial surrogate (who is also a target of authorial contempt) uses to write a sermon is a liquid dangerously close to poison? In *The Bluest Eye*, Morrison theorizes writing and preaching as inextricably intertwined and potentially poisonous modes of authoritative cultural engagement. Clearly, she construes both forms as immensely powerful. The *Dick and Jane* primer represents the most clearly poisonous text in the novel, but Church's poisonous letter-sermon confounds any easy designation. His lethal letter-sermon contains insights that might lead to cultural healing; however, Morrison seems to suggest that this mode of engagement always functions as both poison and remedy—the literary sermon as pharmakon.

At the conclusion of the novel, the results of Morrison's examination of the form remain inconclusive, but Claudia MacTeer's concluding sermon, which revises Church's sermon, suggests that Morrison senses that literary preaching's contradictory affordances provide her with a productively troubling form, a form that's very contradictions enable powerful art and authoritative speech about pressing cultural concerns. Claudia begins her sermon by symbolically associating Pecola with flowers that cannot grow, admitting her patterned avoidance of Pecola, and describing Pecola as "all the waste and beauty of the world" (205). After these opening moves, Claudia's soliloquy shifts into the sermonic voice and gathers energy from the repetitious parallelism that both Iain Ellis (135) and Richard Lischer (104) identify as a key sonic effect of African American preaching:

> All of us—all who knew her—felt so wholesome after we cleaned ourselves on her. We were so beautiful when we stood astride her ugliness. Her simplicity decorated us, her guilt sanctified us, her pain made us glow in health, her awkwardness made us think we had a sense of humor … We honed our egos on her, padded our characters with her frailty, and yawned in the fantasy of our strength. (Morrison, *Bluest*: 205)

Claudia's language not only mirrors the syntactical parallelism of Black preaching and trades in religious language (e.g., "guilt" and "sanctification") but also signifies on the language and themes of Isaiah 53, a text of Hebrew scripture wherein the prophet proleptically describes a physically unattractive Messiah's suffering at the hands of the community:

> For he shall grow up before him as a tender plant, and as a root out of a dry ground: he hath no form nor comeliness; and when we shall see him, there is no beauty that we should desire him. He is despised and rejected of men; a man of sorrows, and acquainted with grief: and we hid as it were our faces from him; he was despised, and we esteemed him not. Surely he hath borne our griefs, and carried our sorrows: yet we did esteem him stricken, smitten of God, and afflicted. But he was wounded for our transgressions, he was bruised for our iniquities: the chastisement of our peace was upon him; and with his stripes we are healed. (Isa. 53:2-5)

The key themes of Claudia's opening sermonic salvo—scapegoating, shunning, and psychological projection—all appear in this well-known passage. Yet the key opening image blocks any conflation of Pecola with a Christ figure. Unlike the Messiah that grows "like a root out of dry ground," Claudia images Pecola, like her unborn child, as a flower that will not flourish in polluted soil. Moreover, in Hebrew and Christian theology, the Messiah's self-sacrifice serves a larger redemptive purpose in God's economy and occurs as a result of God's will. Though aspects of her suffering recalls Christ's, Pecola's suffering is not redemptive, self-chosen, authorized by God, or ultimately vindicated by a resurrection. Claudia, thus, simultaneously evokes and frustrates the identification of Pecola as a Messianic figure in order to underscore the tragic superfluity of her suffering and the human cruelty that engenders it.

As Claudia's sermon continues, it echoes precisely Church's sermon, producing within the text an uncanny doubling. Grewal rightly suggests that this textual duplication underscores the novel's key concern with diagnosing "various characters' miseducation" (*Circles* 25); but this reiteration also offers valuable insight into Morrison's nascent strategy of engaging the tradition of literary preaching. Speaking of the community's "fantasy of ... strength," Claudia confesses

> And fantasy it was, for we were not strong, only aggressive; we were not free, merely licensed; we were not compassionate, we were polite; not good, but well behaved. We courted death in order to call ourselves brave, and hid like thieves from life. We substituted good grammar for intellect; we switched habits

to simulate maturity; we rearranged lies and called it truth, seeing in the new pattern of an old idea the Revelation and the Word. (Morrison, *Bluest*: 205-6)

Claudia's final assessment—which represents Morrison's own—validates the human core of Soaphead's sermon and extends its postcolonial critique. Duvall calls Claudia's recapitulation of Church's lines an "act of rhetorical doubling" (30), but it would be more precise to describe this as a scene of *sermonic* doubling. The more precise adjective highlights the ways that Claudia's sermon echoes and adapts Church's sermon. As she does later in both *Song of Solomon* and *Beloved*, Morrison moves an original sermonic utterance from one speaker to another, and the proclamation receives important revisions as it does so. No longer does the male preacher blame a distant God for Pecola's plight, while simultaneously gathering power to himself; instead, the new preacher identifies herself and her community as morally responsible for Pecola's tragedy.

Moreover, in Claudia's reformulation, within the realm of the novel, the sermon now becomes a spoken word and not written text; it becomes an embodied, intimate performance wherein, as Claudia says of her mother's friends' spoken language, "sound meets sound, curtsies, shimmies, and retires" (Morrison, *Bluest*: 15). In Claudia's revision, Morrison capitalizes on the form's ability to afford the author with a performative language that seizes on and can be seized by the body. Morrison begins the novel by confronting readers with the famously speakerly lines, "Quiet as it's kept" (6)—lines that carry, as Morrison puts it, a "'back fence' connotation," the suggestion of a bit of gossip (21). She closes the novel with the equally speakerly cadences of the sermon, the confession not of an embarrassing bit of gossip about another person but of a communal failure. And, as readers, we move with the novel from the back fence to the pew, from listening in on gossip to joining Claudia in an act of bearing witness and confessing wrongdoing. The MacTeer sermon salvages the valuable aspects of Soaphead Church's sermon and adapts them to a new form, siphoning off the sermon's cultural insight and poetry from a figure typified by his arrogance, will to power, and predation. No longer is the sermon the private letter of an isolated monomaniac but the public confession of a prophetic woman who attempts to speak out of and into a community, with the interlocking aims of honoring her friend and urging a community to repentance. Thus, in its adaptation of Church's sermon, the MacTeer sermon becomes emblematic of Morrison's twin strategies of adapting both the sermon as a central performance genre in African American Christianity *and* the tradition of literary preaching in male-authored American literature.

Claudia's authoritative performance concludes with a theologically loaded critique that in "clean[ing] [them]selves on her," Pecola's community wrongly sees "the Revelation and the Word" in "a new pattern of an old idea" (206). In other words, Claudia suggests that the ritualized, communal sacrifice of a twentieth-century African American girl repeats the scapegoating ritual that Trudier Harris describes as "as old as society" (42–3). For the adult Claudia, however, this contemporary performance of a lethal cleansing ritual represents only one aspect of the community's moral failure. More importantly, she laments the way the citizens of Lorain narrate their cruelty as commensurate with their commitments to Christianity, the religion of "the Revelation and the Word" (Morrison, *Bluest*: 206).

The text does not provide any detail about Claudia's religious convictions as an adult, and we cannot discern whether this closing sermonic performance operates as a prophetic critique of dominant theology from within the community's own religious tradition, as is the case with Baby Suggs's critique of an anti-somatic Christianity that deals in abstractions, or as a critique from someone who has seen its hypocrisy and rejected it outright. The text simply will not tell us. Nevertheless, Claudia's piercing juxtaposition of scapegoating rituals and Christian hypocrisy transports us back to Geraldine's living room and summons us to attend more closely to the religious artifacts that pervade the middle-class living room, for Geraldine's perverse purification ritual, which depends on her willingness to symbolically sacrifice a child upon whom she projects the community's alleged failures, confirms Claudia's prophetic denouncement of a middle-class religious formation that "sees in a new pattern of an old idea the Revelation and the Word" (206). We see once again, and more clearly, an adult woman swearing at young Pecola, cleaning herself on Pecola's "ugliness," and expelling the needy girl out of her home. More important, we see once again, and in a new light, Pecola retreating out of Geraldine's door beneath a portrait of Jesus which "look[s] down at [Pecola] with sad and unsurprised eyes, his long brown hair parted in the middle, the gay paper flowers twisted around his face" (92–3). With the victorious wreath of "artificial flowers" and Jesus's neatly parted hair, this image betokens a colonial strain of Christianity that prizes whiteness, victory, and optimism and that legitimizes violence against the Black body.

Yet even as the final page should transport us back to Geraldine's portrait of Jesus, Claudia's closing sermon invites an alternative reading of this image because it draws attention to a disruptive detail that haunts the gaudy painting itself. On ten separate occasions in her sermon, Claudia refers to "see[ing]" or "look[ing]" or "eye[s]" (204–6). Ellison highlights Rev. Homer Barbee's blindness; Morrison incessantly underscores Claudia's perceptiveness and the vision she wishes the community to glimpse. The novel closes by compelling us to *see* Pecola rightly, to see the child that Claudia suggests reminds the nation of our communal failure. And just as Pecola's eyes "were everything," so too the eyes in this portrait carry the interpretive burden. Jesus's "sad and unsurprised eyes" (92) recall Pecola's own eyes that "held the pictures, and knew the sights" (46) of her painful childhood. Moreover, Jesus's eyes contrast strongly with the eyes of both the blue-eyed Mr. Yacobowski, the candy-store clerk, who "does not see her, because for him there is nothing to see" (48) and Soaphead Church who boasts that, by telling her a poisonous lie, he did what God "would not do: I looked at that ugly little black girl, and I loved her" (182). Certainly, Geraldine's portrait of Jesus persists as an index of middle-class religiosity. But Claudia MacTeer—who offers a Black feminist alternative to the patriarchal traditions that dominate the tradition of literary preaching in US letters and voices a critique of Christianity in the thrall of racist, middle-class ideology—enables us to see that Jesus's knowing, mournful glance simultaneously serves as a unique moment of recognition, a moment in which violence against the Black child does not go unnoticed or unmourned. It is this vision of the holiness of the Black body and the horror of its senseless violation that launches Morrison's engagement with literary preaching in *Beloved*. And an analysis of the literary preaching in *The Bluest Eye* allows us to see the prophetic Claudia as a prototype for Baby Suggs, the character through whom Morrison performs one of US literature's most famous and innovative literary sermons.

The Unchurched Preacher and the Circulated Sermon: Literary Preaching in *Beloved*

Long before it became "spiteful" and "full of a baby's venom," Bluestone 124 was a preacher's home (Morrison, *Beloved*: 3). As Woodruff drives the recently freed Baby Suggs through the outskirts of Cincinnati, he tells her that she is being moved into a "nice house" that was originally the home of a preacher who had been reassigned by "Bishop Allen" (172). This is no incidental name to drop at the moment of Baby Suggs's arrival. It would be hard for Woodruff to mention a more significant figure in African American religious history than Bishop Richard Allen. As well as being the founder of the African Methodist Episcopal

Church, Allen tirelessly served in abolitionist causes, gained wide respect as an intellectual, and wrote political pamphlets that became models of the genre (Newman 1). Woodruff's story about Allen's decision to send the preacher away from the community highlights a model of ministry that requires circulation. A preacher might, at any minute, leave the community and create a vacuum in leadership. Thus, when she arrives, Baby Suggs rushes into a ministerial vacuum, and Bluestone 124 transforms into "a cheerful buzzing house where Baby Suggs, holy, loved, cautioned, fed, chastised and soothed" (102). Like her "great heart," the house pulses with healing energy (102). The former leader's mantle has been passed on to Baby Suggs, who promptly establishes herself as a gifted preacher whose powerful "calls" heal the community. This subtle transfer of ministerial power from one spiritual leader to another anticipates the novel's sustained meditation on the circulation of the sermon. The spiritual authority that Baby Suggs inherits and reconfigures will also be "passed on" and adapted yet again.

The following analysis of Morrison's most celebrated instance of literary preaching—Baby Suggs's "Love Your Heart" sermon in *Beloved*—pays special attention to the oft-neglected fact that Baby Suggs disavows the message that she preaches. Yet within the novel's diegesis, a surprising phenomenon emerges after Baby Suggs's bitter renunciation: her crisis of faith and subsequent retreat from a position of spiritual authority enables the multiplication of her sermon's power. Throughout the novel, Morrison traces the circulation of the sermon, a process through which an original sermonic or ministerial energy enlivens the community, departs from it, and returns with amplified, reconfigured, and redistributed force. Morrison's emplotment of the circulated sermon represents an innovative engagement with the tradition of literary preaching in US literature. Through this innovation, Morrison sets out to accomplish two related goals. First, she aims to overcome literary preaching's troublesome affordance of reifying hierarchal, antidemocratic models of authority. Second, through this inventive deployment of the sermon, Morrison seeks to recruit the reader as a copartner in her cultural work. In this sense, Morrison's engagement with literary preaching not only meditates on her identity as an author but also aims to construct the identities of her readers.

To support these claims, I open with an examination of Baby Suggs's characterization and ministry among her congregants, before turning toward the sermon itself and examining how it circulates through the text, how it "passes on" from character to character *despite* Baby Suggs's bitter renunciation. Put in the terms of the novel, Baby Suggs's rejected sermon is "remembered" throughout the text, and her "call" generates multiple communal responses. In

Beloved, the emergence and subsequent disappearance of a particular, poetic, and well-known preacher—a figure for the author herself—enables a radically democratized and disruptive sermonic power to reemerge and heal the community.

In *Beloved*, Morrison aims centrally to resolve literary preaching's tendency to reify antidemocratic, hierarchical models of authority. But Morrison's complex engagement with literary preaching in *Beloved* also counteracts an additional undesirable ideological function of the sermon: the traditional Protestant sermon's tendency to privilege a disembodied, patriarchal Word.[11] Throughout the novel, Morrison suggests a link between this theological construct and the violently antimaternal institution of slavery, an institution in which the all-important "power of naming remains with the white master" (Lawrence 234). *Beloved* repeatedly shows Christian slaveholders, devotees and practitioners of a logocentric patriarchy, using language as their primary tool for disciplining, categorizing, and commodifying African Americans. Schoolteacher—a perverse father figure who "know[s] Jesus by His first name" (Morrison, *Beloved*: 44)—instructs his nephews to write dehumanizing catalogues of Sethe's "animal" and "human" characteristics, devotes himself to authoring a text steeped in scientific racism, and beats Sixo to teach him that "definitions [belong] to the definers—not the defined" (225). Thus, the uniqueness of Morrison's literary preaching in *Beloved* lies, in part, in her effort to unleash the sermon's prophetic and semiotic power while also dismantling the logocentrism of the Protestant sermon. Morrison leverages the hybrid African American Christian tradition of the call-and-response sermon to imagine the sermon as a communal and maternal utterance that affirms the sanctity of the Black body, the strength of the mother-child bond, and the necessity of self-love. Moreover, as the sermon circulates throughout the novel, taking leave of a particular orator, it becomes less an authoritative Word than a healing sound.

---

[11] Morrison's desire to revise this logocentric Protestant doctrine informs the novel's central event: the miraculous incarnation of the lost daughter, Beloved. As Gurleen Grewal observes, "The transmutation from the word 'Beloved' inscribed on the tombstone to the living Beloved reinterprets the Gospel According to St. John: 'And the Word was made flesh, and dwelt among us'" (106). Sethe's deceased daughter, not the eternally begotten Son of the Father, the Word of God, takes on flesh. For discussions of *Beloved*'s revision of patriarchal, logocentric codes, see John Duvall, *The Identifying Fictions of Toni Morrison: Modernist Authenticity and Postmodern Blackness* (Palgrave: 2000), 124–6; Doreen Fowler, "'Reading for the Other Side': *Beloved* and *Requiem for a Nun*," in *Unflinching Gaze: Morrison and Faulkner Re-Envisioned*, edited by Carol A Kolmerten et al. (Mississippi UP: 1997) 144–7; and David Lawrence, "Fleshly Ghosts and Ghostly Flesh: The Word and the Body in *Beloved*," in *Toni Morrison's Fiction: Contemporary Criticism*, edited by David L. Middleton (Garland: 1997), 231–46.

My emphasis on the circulation of the sermon emerges out of a close examination of the narrative's conspicuous focus on Baby Suggs's "great heart" (102). Her "beat and beating" heart receives special attention throughout the diegesis because, in its function as a pump that distributes nutrients to the other organs of the body, it serves as an especially apt and earthy figure for Baby Suggs's ministry, a ministry that highlights the significance of transfer, circulation, and exchange. Valerie Smith notes that readers may be tempted to read "heart" as a metaphor for "compassion or capacity for empathetic identification" but cautions against such simplistic readings by insisting that, especially in Baby Suggs's sermon, the heart refers to a physical organ (*Toni* 70). Smith is correct in cautioning against such banal metaphorical readings, but, at the same time, Baby Suggs refers specifically to the heart as the "prize" that should be loved more than any of the other parts of the body, including the liver and lungs (Morrison, *Beloved*: 104). Obviously, Baby Suggs's prioritization of the heart cannot be explained by reference to physiology alone. What good is a healthy heart without a functional liver or lungs? To make sense of the high value both Baby Suggs and Morrison place on the heart, we must turn toward figurative language. If we emphasize the heart's function as an organ that constantly circulates blood through the body, we can see that the heart serves as a resonant image for Baby Suggs's ministry, which pumps life into the social body.

Throughout the novel, Morrison's describes Baby Suggs's sermonic practice and emphasizes the power and permeability of Baby Suggs's heart. A victim of numerous atrocities at the hands of Christian slaveholders, Baby Suggs rejects the submissive, sentimental piety typified in American literature by Harriet Beecher Stowe's *Uncle Tom's Cabin* (1852) and, more broadly, in Jesus's Sermon on the Mount.[12] She does not tell her followers to "clean up their lives or to go and sin no more" nor does she "tell them the they were the blessed of the earth, its inheriting meek or its glorybound pure" (103). "Accepting no title of honor before her name, but allowing a small caress after it," Baby Suggs, holy, becomes "an unchurched preacher, one who visited pulpits and opened her great heart to those who could use it" (102). Morrison suggests a scene of public oratory that is both intimate and disturbing as she images Baby Suggs's preaching as "open[ing]" her great heart" for the "use" of others. The familiar idiomatic expression suggests the revelation of a long-hidden secret. Morrison's description, however, also suggests a surreal

[12] For a rich discussion of *Uncle Tom's Cabin* as an intertext for *Beloved*, see Duvall (120–31). Duvall draws persuasive parallels between the two novels and argues that Baby Suggs's sermon, which articulates her "religion of the maternal body," should be read as a response to the literary preaching of Uncle Tom. While I generally agree with Duvall's insightful reading of the novel, his assessment of the sentimental theology of Stowe's novel overlooks the intensely prophetic, "unsentimental" preaching that Coleman identifies as inextricably bound up with the novel's cultural work (156–73).

surgical procedure similar to either organ donation or a blood transfusion. Engaging in one of the novel's most provocative instances of magical realism, Morrison suggests that Baby Suggs's open-heart sermons promote the healing and nourishment of other hearts, and this, above all, defines her religious practice.

Baby Suggs's unique approach to preaching derives from her visceral experience of liberation. Shortly after she crosses over the Ohio River, she begins to take an index of her own body: "But suddenly she saw her hands and thought with a clarity as simple as it was dazzling, 'These hands belong to me. These my hands.'" This personal inventory moves inward as Baby Suggs begins to feel heart palpitations that produce euphoria instead of anxiety. She feels a "knocking in her chest" and asks, "Had it been there all along? This pounding thing?" (166). This sensation leads her to begin laughing uncontrollably and inspires her to develop "her own brand of preaching, having made up her mind about what to do with the heart that started beating the minute she crossed the Ohio River" (173).

Baby Suggs focuses on extending her experience of self-ownership to the broader community, and to do so she develops not only a new, embodied "brand of preaching" but also a new vision of the worship space. Although Baby Suggs successfully serves as a visiting preacher for traditional denominations (102), her own ministry involves relocation beyond churches' physical structures. In the Clearing, a woodland space symbolically beyond the confines of traditional dogma and ritual, Baby Suggs leads the congregants through a communal healing ceremony and delivers a sermon that proclaims "the godliness of physicality rather than spirituality" (Tally, *Origins*: 3). Roxanne Reed suggests that this relocation enables Baby Suggs to gain authority because the Clearing represents a distance from "the structured hierarchical spaces of traditional pulpits" (67). The novel, however, makes clear that Baby Suggs does not struggle to establish her authority in traditional pulpits (Morrison, *Beloved*: 102). In fact, in his recollections of Baby Suggs's ministry, Stamp Paid recalls her "authority in the pulpit" (208), a line that confirms Baby Suggs ability to appropriate the traditional site of male authority when she served as a guest preacher at many local churches. Her movement to the Clearing, motivated by her love for the traumatized community, indicates her keen sense of spatial politics. Like the "strong poets" that Richard Rorty describes in *Philosophy and the Mirror of Nature* (1979), Baby Suggs's tactical move creates "new logical spaces wherein fresh thoughts can be thought and familiar things redescribed" (qtd. in Tally, *Origins*: 51). Baby Suggs becomes an "unchurched preacher" in order to draw her followers into a new, hospitable space where they can "let go," emote freely, and begin reclaiming and loving their bodies (Morrison, *Beloved*: 111).

Prior to delivering her sermon proper, Baby Suggs begins the service with a call to worship that identifies her as a unique type of preacher. In her analysis of Baby Suggs's sermon, Cynthia Dobbs notes: "Curiously, this sermon does not begin with words. To begin her 'fixing ceremony,' Baby Suggs asks the children to laugh, the men to dance, and the women to cry. Thus, instead of an authoritative orator beginning to speak 'the Word' *to* the people, we have a kind of prologue acted out *by* the people" (565). Here, Dobbs overstates her otherwise important observation. While Baby Suggs certainly resists many of the authoritarian and logocentric structures of Protestant leadership, the "fixing ceremony" does not suggest as wholly a democratic practice as Dobbs implies. The fixing ceremony does not begin with a gentle invitation to organic action but with a series of intensely loaded ritual acts. Like many of Nathaniel Hawthorne's fictional preachers, Baby Suggs sits atop a "huge flat-sided rock," installing herself in a natural pulpit and assuming the posture of a Rabbi (Morrison, *Beloved*: 102). Moreover, prior to the ceremony's beginning, Baby Suggs bows her head and prays before the silent congregation. They do not join her in prayer but silently watch her "from the trees," where they remain until the moment she beckons them (103). Finally, before she speaks the words that will begin the sermon, she dramatically puts down her walking stick, an act that signals to the gathered community that "she was ready" to begin (104). This act signifies a willing surrender of phallic power, and, more importantly, it functions as an embodied quotation of Aaron's first miracle before Pharaoh—the casting down and transforming of his staff into a serpent. Aaron's miracle signals the beginning of God's liberation of the Hebrew slaves (Exod. 7:17). Baby Suggs's repetition of this militant gesture signals the inauguration of a second Exodus.

Additionally, Baby Suggs's liturgy begins with an explosive command drawn from scripture. She does not "ask" the people to laugh, dance, and cry; she demands it. She shouts out, "Let the children come!" and the narrative records an immediate rush of children into the Clearing (Morrison, *Beloved*: 103). The men and women respond in a similarly energetic manner. Before turning to the dynamics of this revival and the content of Baby Suggs's innovative sermon, I want to point out that she draws the opening line of her ceremony from the Gospel of Mark. Thus, the fixing ceremony *does* begin with words drawn from Christian scripture. In the Biblical passage, Jesus criticizes some of his followers for blocking children from approaching him and says, "Suffer the little children to come unto me, and forbid them not" (Mk 10:14). If the line sounds familiar to Morrison scholars, it should. Soaphead Church refers to this same passage in his angry letter to God. In *The Bluest Eye*, Morrison places this line in the mouth of Soaphead Church—a perverse but occasionally perceptive preacher—and leverages it as a Jeremiad against God's failure to protect African American children from the effects of racism (181). In *Beloved*, however, Morrison fashions this same passage as a joyous command for the children to participate in a communal worship event. While Baby Suggs does not advocate the subservient morality associated with Jesus's Sermon on the Mount, she embraces his words of radical inclusion for society's most despised members.[13]

Above all, Baby Suggs aims for her sermon to heal the body by reclaiming its sanctity. Linda Wagner-Martin describes her as "the genesis of mother love for all the parishioners in the clearing" (71). Like a mother speaking to her newborn child about their beautiful body, Baby Suggs lovingly catalogues the congregants' body parts. Her maternal catalogues establish her as a rival to Schoolteacher, whose racist, pseudoscientific catalogues traumatize Sethe. At the same time, this maternal catalogue includes instructions for enacting a gospel of self-love:

> Here ... in this place, we flesh; flesh that weeps, laughs; flesh that dances on bare feet in grass. Love it. Love it hard. Yonder they do not love your flesh. They despise it. They don't love your eyes; they'd just as soon pick em out. No more do they love the skin on your back. Yonder they flay it. And O my people [here Morrison/Baby Suggs delivers on the epigraph's promise of calling the neglected community "my people"] they do not love your hands. Those they use, tie, bind, chop off and leave empty. Love your hands! Love them. Raise them up and kiss them. Touch others with them, pat them together, stroke them on your face 'cause they don't love that either. *You* got to love it, *you*! ... *You* got to love it. This is flesh I'm talking about here. Flesh that needs to be loved ... And all your inside parts that they'd just as soon slop for hogs, you got to love them. The dark, dark liver—love it, love it, and the beat and beating heart, love that too. More than eyes or feet. More than lungs that have yet to draw free air. More than your life-holding womb and your life-giving private parts, hear me now, love your heart. For this is the prize. (Morrison, *Beloved*: 104)

---

[13] The corporeal, communal practices that occur in the Clearing receive considerable focus in extant criticism of Baby Suggs's ministry—and they should. However, we should also note that Baby Suggs's proclamation of "the Word," represented in this section, matters tremendously to Stamp Paid, undoubtedly a voice of wisdom in the novel. Significantly, in his pleas for Baby Suggs to return after her retirement, Stamp asks her to preach 'the Word" five times (see Toni Morrison, *Beloved* [Vintage International, 2004], 209–11). It is possible to argue that Stamp's pleas reflect a male perspective at odds with Suggs's (and Morrison's) attempt to "break the back of words" (308), but I would argue that his pleas highlight the value of her articulate preaching as an effective, although perhaps limited, means of "re-calling" individual and social bodies. Understandably, Stamp cannot imagine a more powerful, therapeutic form of preaching than Baby Suggs's; he cannot anticipate that her sermon will circulate and receive important revisions in her absence.

Baby Suggs's sermon counters any religious tradition that celebrates dependency on the divine or any other for self-worth. Here, flesh becomes vested with religious significance typically reserved only for the soul. Dobbs astutely notes that "while such an intertwining of body and spirit may be integral to many African religions, we need to go back to Whitman for such strong linkages in American literature" (565–6). Clearly Whitman's celebration of the body carried tremendous political potential, which he occasionally used to critique American slavery. Whitman's writing, however, responds immediately to Victorian attitudes toward embodiment and sexuality. Baby Suggs's calling of her people, as Dobbs points out, specifically addresses "the horrors of slavery" (556). Thus, we must note that Baby Suggs's authoritative sermon does not merely take aim at an antimaterial religious formation. More importantly, she targets a violent form of global capitalism that transforms the Black body into a marketable commodity.

Smith accurately identifies the aim of Baby Suggs's sermon as the aim of the novel, describing both as aimed toward the project of "reclaiming bodies" from the vicious codes of slavery ("Circling" 348) and "encouraging the former slaves and the reader to linger over the free black body ... and to love it as flesh" (*Writing* 70–1). Similarly, John Duvall reads Baby Suggs as an authorial figure: "Having healed herself through the writing of her first four novels, Morrison now figures as an artist who can truly heal the community ... In the female preacher of *Beloved*, one might say, Morrison reveals her aspirations for her art and communal role" (126–7). In this sense, Morrison participates in the tendency of US writers to engage in literary preaching at moments of intense cultural dialogue. To fully comprehend this sermon's cultural work, Baby Suggs's sermon must be read not only within the context of the fictive world but also in relation to the broader cultural-ethical problems suggested by the novel's opening pages.

On the title page of *Beloved*, a haunting dedication confronts the reader: "Sixty Million and more." The dedication gestures toward the unaccountable damage wrought by slavery and its lingering effects in the national psyche. For Morrison, remembering the suffering wrought by slavery must be done in a manner that enables the act of remembrance to be something other than wholly destructive. In a 1988 interview about her aim in writing *Beloved*, she asserted that there "is a necessity for remembering ... in a manner in which the memory is not destructive. The act of writing a book, in a way, is a way of confronting it and making it possible to remember" ("In" 247–8). The page that follows the dedication presents the reader with an epigraph, drawn from the Book of

Romans, that comments on the previous page: "I will call them my people, which were not my people; and her beloved, which was not beloved." The epigraph suggests both Morrison's method in the novel *and* the central message of Baby Suggs's sermon: to call and rename the traumatized and forgotten. Given this study's interest in Morrison's telescoping of her project through Baby Suggs's career, we should note that the verb *call* in this scriptural verse explicitly suggests Baby Suggs's sermonic performance, which she insists her followers describe as only a "call" (Morrison, *Beloved*: 208).

Baby Suggs's designation of her preaching as a "call" also indicates the novel's crucial engagement with the dialogic call-and-response format of African American preaching and worship, a sermon form marked by its "circularity" (Zauditu-Selassie 124). By engaging this form of African American preaching, Morrison imagines the sermon as a communal performance. In distinction to more linear, hierarchical modes of preaching, a sermon in the call–and-response tradition accumulates rhetorical force by engaging congregants and summoning them to respond verbally to the preacher. Through this exchange, the congregants make meaningful contributions to the sermon—compelling the preacher to repeat certain phrases, establishing the speaker's rhythm, affirming specific insights that they find especially valuable, or supporting the preacher by expressing encouragement. Historians trace this dialogic rhetorical form to the West African ring shout and note its presence in the earliest records of African American worship through the present day (Lischer 135). Although Baby Suggs's worship services are less straightforwardly democratic than other critics have suggested, she clearly engages the congregants in a manner that values their responses.

Morrison reveals Baby Suggs's embrace of the call-and-response aesthetic and the communal ethic it implies in a scene during which Baby Suggs demonstrates to her congregants what it might mean to enact an ethic of embodied self-love. Crucially, this moment suggests that Baby Suggs practices what she preaches and that to enact this self-love she requires the community's assistance. After she finishes speaking, she begins dancing "with her twisted hip," and the dance communicates "the rest of what her heart had to say while the others opened their mouths and gave her the music" (Morrison, *Beloved*: 104). Baby Suggs's dance conveys the insufficiency of words alone, even words as powerful as her sermon and Jesus's command to welcome the vulnerable. Morrison suggests a sermonic event that blurs the boundaries between congregant and preacher and begins to accomplish what language cannot. Baby Suggs's heart infuses the hearts of the congregants, and their communal performance of music and dance suggests a self-propagating sermonic energy that circulates through the population. As Baby Suggs's dance gives the congregants the "rest of what her heart had to say," the part that cannot be put in human language, the congregants respond with a "four-part harmony" that perfectly expresses their now "deeply loved flesh" (104). Their four-part harmony coalesces with her dance. Her dance, in turn, represents the wordless expression of her four-chambered heart.

This moment of intense circulation, intersubjective exchange, and healing, however, disappears from the novel as rapidly as it appears. Indeed, in an unsettling juxtaposition, the paragraph that immediately follows Baby Suggs's sermon describes her "dismiss[ing] her great heart" and proving herself "a liar" (104). She abruptly stops performing the rituals, refuses to return to the Clearing, and retires to her bed to contemplate colors. In the aftermath of Sethe's act of infanticide, Baby Suggs comes to believe she has lied to the community: "There was no grace—imaginary or real—and no sunlit dance in the Clearing could change that" (105). Her "heartstrings" break and her "big old heart [begins] to collapse." While she refuses to speak "the Word" that heals the community anymore, she does continue to speak authoritatively on questions of theology and race. These pessimistic counter-sermons refuse to offer any affirmation and, instead, speak of a world of foreclosed futures. "Those white things have taken all I had or dreamed," Baby Suggs testifies, "There is no bad luck in the world but whitefolks" (105). Her partner in supporting the newly freed slaves, Stamp Paid, urges her to return to the Clearing: "Listen here, girl ... you can't quit the Word. It's given to you to speak. You can't quit the Word, I don't care what all happened to you" (209). She responds to his impassioned pleas by repeating, three times, the phrase "I'm saying they came in my yard," a denial that expresses the vulnerability of African Americans in the era of the Fugitive Slave Law. Stamp Paid suggests that she is trying to punish God by refusing to preach, and she replies, Job-like, "Not like He punish me" (211). If, as many critics suggest, Baby Suggs's sermon in the Clearing voices the central aim of the novel, what should we make of her dramatic rejection of her moving and urgent religious vision?

Baby Suggs's crisis of faith, a crisis often overlooked in criticism of the novel, is *the* crucial move in Morrison's attempt to engage literary preaching in a manner that does not reify conservative and hierarchical forms of authority. The vacuum created by Baby Suggs's retirement strongly recalls the ministerial vacuum created by the relocation of the original preacher who lived in 124 Bluestone, but after Baby Suggs's retirement no individual preacher rushes into this vacuum. In *The Bluest Eye* and *Paradise*, Morrison critiques the preacher's authority in the US cultural imaginary by dramatizing preachers' tendencies to use the sermon to manipulate their congregations or to justify their own aggressive acts. Baby Suggs's sudden retirement reveals that Morrison remains concerned about literary preaching's tendency to affirm hierarchical models of authority even when her engagement with literary preaching involves an identification with a preacher as communally oriented and self-giving as Baby Suggs. By imagining a genuinely communal sermon, Morrison aims to nullify this nettlesome affordance and the ambivalence it generates. Before a collective response can begin to flourish, however, the individual preacher must renounce her gospel of self-love, go into seclusion, and eventually die. Considered meta-textually, this fictional examination of the afterlife of the sermon opens a window into Morrison's meditation on how a politically and ethically motivated artist might measure her legacy and cultural impact. Has the celebrity artist's heart sufficiently enlivened the hearts of her readers and enabled them to extend her work? Can the sermon remain effective in a community if the preacher subsequently rejects her radical faith? Can the healing power of "a great heart," a therapeutic "Word," or, perhaps, an award-winning novel survive if the original heart breaks, the preacher recants, or the novelist loses hope?

In no uncertain terms, Morrison shows the community's sorrow at the loss of Baby Suggs's leadership. Moreover, Baby Suggs dies in renunciation of her own sermon. Despite her disavowal, however, the community's rememory of her allows the liberatory themes of her sermon to continue to shape their social world. The concept of *rememory*, Sethe's evocative term for her relationship to the past, denotes the manner in which subjective memories make the past palpable and forceful in the present. The prefix "re-" makes clear Morrison's sense of "memory as always already re-created: that memory is never a stable, singular calling up of the past, but rather a partially invented, subjectively selected narrative of the past" (Dobbs 568). Although rememory leads to the ultimately destructive presence of Beloved, it also enables Baby Suggs's sermon to provide a healing, although ghostly, presence in the community. Her sermon, in other words, haunts the community. Through this remembrance of Baby Suggs and her sermon, Morrison suggests that the sermon continues to circulate though the memories of those who originally heard it. In the terms of Morrison's key figure for Baby Suggs's ministry, although Baby Suggs's heart stops pumping, it does not stop the circulation of the sermon because her parishioners became participants in a system strong enough to carry forward her work despite her absence. The cultural work of Baby Suggs's "call" does not end with her bitter retirement. The community's response indicates the sermon's enduring impact. Indeed, the sermon itself becomes stronger precisely because it becomes the joint effort of many additional preachers. In this way, the preacher becomes secondary to the communally shared message that affirms the sanctity of the Black body and the urgency of positive self-regard.

The circulation and rememory of Baby Suggs occurs in several key scenes. In the initial scene of Baby Suggs's remembrance, Sethe returns to the Clearing in order to seek assistance. She enters the Clearing and "remember[s] the smell of leaves simmering in the sun, thunderous feet and the shouts that ripped pods off the limbs of the chestnuts. With Baby Suggs' heart in charge, the people let go" (Morrison, *Beloved*: 111). Clearly, she longs to again "let go" and open her heart to Baby Suggs, to surrender to a spiritual authority who takes "charge" in a specific space. We should also note that this scene of remembrance involves tremendous forgetting. It is a scene of selective memory because Sethe aims to reconnect with Baby Suggs as she was before she gives up her office. After sitting on Baby Suggs's rock, Sethe begins to feel her fingers caressing her neck. In this attempt at remembrance, Sethe's subjective rememory of Baby Suggs conjures her tender care for the body, a "long-distance love … equal to any skin-close love she had known" (112). Beloved—also a remembered object of Sethe's trauma and the tangible spirit of all those brutalized by US slavery—interrupts Baby Suggs's intimate touch and begins to strangle Sethe. Beloved's attack blocks Sethe's ability to fully remember Baby Suggs; it chokes the circulation that Sethe hopes to open up. The contest between Baby Suggs's caress and Beloved's choking grip reveals one of the central struggles of rememory in the novel. In the detail that Beloved's breath, at this moment, smells "exactly like new milk" (115), Morrison suggests not only Beloved's identity but also indicates that this moment is a struggle between the rememory of Baby Suggs and the rememory of another "baby."

Denver's first steps toward reengaging the community represent the second crucial scene in which we observe the circulation and reemergence of Baby Suggs's sermon. This scene reveals that her sermon takes on new complexity and power because of her absence. As Denver realizes that Beloved's presence poses a threat to both her life and Sethe's, she determines that she must engage the broader community for help. However, she resists taking her first steps off the porch because the community shuns her family, and she remains terrified by the unpredictability of white people. While Mrs. Jones, Denver's former teacher, paves the way for Denver's escape (Schapiro 168), Denver's rememory of Baby Suggs catalyzes her movement off the porch. At this crisis moment, the rememory of Baby Suggs provides Denver with a word that allows her to begin to counter the harm being done by Beloved. In part, Denver's remembrance of her grandmother draws on her knowledge of Baby Suggs's message of self-love and the holiness of the Black body. Denver was an infant during the years that Baby Suggs preached in the Clearing, but in what seems to have been a momentary re-embrace of her faith in the body's essential integrity, Denver recalls Baby Suggs telling her "that I should always listen to my body and love it" (Morrison, *Beloved*: 247).[14]

As Denver stands on the porch, her memory of these affirming words collides with the memory of Baby Suggs's constant expressions of ubiquitous danger. As these narratives compete, we read Denver's rememory at work and see, through this process, the sermon circulate, invigorate a new parishioner's heart, and emerge with greater force. Initially, Denver recalls Baby Suggs's critiques of white people who refused to behave as "real humans did" and her announcement of defeat: "There's more of us they drowned than there is all of them ever lived from the start of time. Lay down your sword. This ain't a battle; it's a rout" (287). Confronted by these defeatist words, Denver remains frozen and cannot leave the yard. However, suddenly, as if by miracle, this ambivalent act of remembrance seems to literally revive Denver's failing heart. This healing registers both in Denver's imagined dialogue and, unsurprisingly, in her chest:

> Her throat itched; *her heart kicked*—and then *Baby Suggs laughed*, clear as anything. "You mean I never told you nothing about Carolina? About your daddy? You don't remember nothing about how come I walk the way I do and about your mother's feet, not to speak of her back? I never told you all that? Is that why you can't walk down the steps? My Jesus my."
>
> But you said there was no defense.
>
> "There ain't."
>
> Then what do I do?
>
> "Know it, and go on out the yard. Go on." (287–8; emphasis added)

In this key moment of circulation, the remembered message once tied to the Clearing now appears to be fully operational on Denver's porch. Additionally, this scene recalls Baby Suggs's uncontrolled laughter at feeling the beating of her own heart (166). By coupling the sudden "kicking" of Denver's heart with Baby Suggs's laughter "clear as anything," Morrison suggests the expansion of the Clearing and the circulation of Baby Suggs's life-affirming sermon.

---

[14] I am indebted to Nancy Berkowitz Bate for pointing out this passage in which Baby Suggs's rearticulates the central theme of her sermon from her deathbed. Although I do not agree with Bate that this suggests that Baby Suggs "never relinquishes faith in her gospel of the body" (27), it does help make sense of Denver's desire to remember her Grandmother during this crisis moment in 124.

Baby Suggs's initial sermon receives important revisions in this moment. Through its circulation among other bodies, the submerged sermon reemerges with a difference. The imagined dialogue resolves the tension between Baby Suggs's dire warnings and her earlier paeans to the sanctity of the body. In the initial sermon, preached in the security of the Clearing, Baby Suggs draws a sharp distinction between the Clearing and the "yonder" world that suggests an incommensurability between these two spaces. Here, her sermon, *as filtered through Denver's own crisis*, suggests the necessity of loving one's own flesh not only in consecrated time-space of the Clearing but also—and perhaps especially—in the "yonder" and at moments when such an act entails danger. Kathleen Marks points out that Baby's remembered words "connect Denver to the absent grandmother, mother, and, most importantly, father. Halle, who worked to pay off a nearly $124 debt, is brought before the mind of his daughter, who is now called to save 124 Bluestone Road from its debt of pain" (107). The circulated sermon provides Denver with an inhabitable legacy and enables her to reconnect with others from whom she can learn to practice self-love. Barbara Schapiro identifies this as the central lesson of Baby Suggs's original sermon and points out that this lesson "cannot be learned in isolation; self-love needs a relational foundation and a social context" (169). Denver reengages the world beyond 124 because Baby Suggs's sermon continues to circulate through rememory, and, ultimately, the circulation of her sermon galvanizes the community to confront the painful memories that Beloved metonymically represents.

Most dramatically, the circulation of Baby Suggs's sermon among the community empowers the women's exorcism of Beloved. After reemerging from 124, Denver describes Beloved's violence toward Sethe to the women in the community. Ella, who in former years participated in Baby Suggs's "fixing ceremonies," leads these women to fill the vacuum created by Baby Suggs's long absence. Ella's connection to Baby Suggs, although stronger than other members of the community, is not unique. The other women whom Denver approaches "knew her grandmother and some had even danced with her in the Clearing" (Morrison, *Beloved*: 293). Ella's uniqueness derives from her similarity to Sethe; Ella, too, has committed an act of infanticide as a response to a crisis created by slavery (Powell 152). A victim of serial rape at the hands of her masters, Ella refuses to nurse her son, "a hairy white thing," and the boy dies shortly after his birth (Morrison, *Beloved*: 305). She identifies strongly with Sethe and sees in Beloved a threat that her son might terrorize her in a similar manner. Thus, her desire to intervene arises from her identification with Sethe and her rememory of Baby Suggs, her spiritual mother.

The women's rememory of Baby Suggs's sermon occurs in two parts. First, when the women discuss what should be done about Beloved, we see the circulation of the sermon in their dialogue. Crucially, the women's affirmation of Baby Suggs's sermon defies her rejection of her own religious vision. In this climatic scene, the sermon's positive effects appear to be distinct from the personality of the preacher. Indeed, in the terms of the novel's conclusion, the passing on of the preacher allows the sermon to be passed on. As the women discuss Beloved's terrorization of Sethe, they piece the story together. Ella speaks first:

"It's sitting there. Sleeps, eats and raises hell. Whipping Sethe every day."

"I'll be. A baby?"

"No. Grown. The age it would have been had it lived."

"You talking about flesh?"

"I'm talking about flesh."

"Whipping her?"

"Like she was batter."

"Guess she had it coming."

"Nobody got that coming." (301; emphasis added)

Commenting on the two lines about "flesh," Duvall astutely observes that these "two lines, suggesting the call-response form of an African-American church service, particularly echo one of Baby Suggs's lines from the Clearing—'This is flesh I'm talking about here'" (130). Additionally, we should note that the content of Ella's address mirrors Baby Suggs's own. She refuses to cede Sethe's body to physical violation: "Nobody got that coming" (Morrison, *Beloved*: 301). Finally, Ella's initial response strongly mirrors Baby Suggs's own ministry in that she begins her healing work with a short prayer but refuses to substitute prayer for direct human action. One woman asks her: "Shall we pray?" Ella responds humorously: "Uh huh … First. Then we got to get down to business" (302). It would be difficult to find a more apt disciple of Baby Suggs's theology than Ella. She remains committed to practicing what Baby Suggs preached, despite Baby Suggs's renunciation.

The ambiguous rescue scene—an exorcism accomplished through corporate hollering, singing, and chanting—serves as the final scene of the sermon's circulation. Here, the circulation of the sermon merges explicitly with the novel's focus on haunting and rememory. As the thirty women gird themselves to attempt to rescue Sethe, they draw on resources of African folk religion and Christianity: "Some brought what they could and what they believed would work. Stuffed in apron pockets, strung round their necks, lying in the space between their breasts. Others brought Christian faith—as shield and sword. Most brought a little of both" (303). When they arrive at Bluestone 124, they begin their communal rememory of Baby Suggs. They recall her feeding them at her home:

> The first thing they saw was not Denver sitting on the steps, but themselves. Younger, stronger, even as little girls lying in the grass asleep. Catfish was popping grease in the pan and they saw themselves scoop German potato salad onto the plate. Cobbler oozing purple syrup colored their teeth. They sat on the porch, ran down to the creek, teased the men, hoisted children on their hips or, if they were the children, straddled the ankles of old men who held their little hands while giving them a horsey ride. Baby Suggs laughed and skipped among them, urging more. Mothers, dead now, moved their shoulders to mouth harps ... [T]here they were, young and happy, playing in Baby Suggs' yard, not feeling the envy that surfaced the next day. (304)

This rememory pulses with excess, bodily joy, and parental-daughter union. The sensual appeal of foods, the ecstasies of play and athleticism, and the soothing pleasures of dance coalesce to remember a time in which Baby Suggs's ministry transformed them. Baby Suggs's laughter and the pounding of newly freed hearts recurs throughout the novel, and this moment of intensified circulation represents the final appearance of her coded laughter. In this collective remembrance, the women return to the event that initiated the community's abandonment of Baby Suggs and Sethe—the feast that Baby Suggs throws to honor Sethe. The community initially sees Baby Suggs's "reckless generosity" as an arrogant appropriation of Jesus's ability to multiply food in order to feed a multitude: "Loaves and fishes were His powers—they didn't belong to an ex-slave" (161–2). Their resentment prevents them from warning Baby Suggs and Sethe of Schoolteacher's approach, and it contributes significantly to both Sethe's killing of Beloved and the community's subsequent dissolution. Within this lush rememory of bodily pleasure, however, the women acknowledge the essential goodness of Baby Suggs's generosity and see it as a logical extension of her ministry. By doing so, they mend their relationship with Baby Suggs, forgive themselves, and reclaim their agency.

In this rememory, the women identify themselves as Baby Suggs's spiritual daughters, and their subsequent actions reveal the intensity of their sustained, although dormant, connection to their ancestor. As Doreen Fowler rightly notes, "Slavery, as Morrison realizes it in *Beloved*, institutionalizes the repression of mother-power" ("Reading" 141). At the novel's conclusion, this repressed mother-power returns as a political force. Some of the women—both daughters and mothers—begin to pray, and Denver can hear them chanting words of agreement. "Yes, yes, yes, oh yes," the praying women chant, "Hear me. Hear me" (Morrison, *Beloved*: 305). Yet, just as Baby Suggs's prayers play a minor role in her ministry, so, too, do the prayers of these women play a minor role in this final scene of sermonic circulation.

The return of Baby Suggs's healing sermon appears most powerfully as a communal utterance that transcends language and, thus, attacks conventional, oppressive linguistic codes. As Ella stares at 124, her rememory of Baby Suggs's ministry collides with the memory of her own act of infanticide. The idea that her un-nursed son might, like Beloved, come to torment her "set[s] her jaw to working" and she begins to "holler" (305). Ella's primal scream mirrors Baby Suggs's dance in the Clearing because both acts viscerally express a fierce and culturally denied maternal love that transcends language. Ella's cry, engendered by the juxtaposition of the joyous memory of her spiritual mother and the unspeakable memory of her act of infanticide, gives voice, but not words, to an ineffable maternal bond.

Spontaneously, the other women join their voices to Ella's, and, together, they search for "the right combination, the key, the code, the sound that broke the back of words" (308). As the women join their voices, Baby Suggs's maternal sermon reemerges as a radically democratized force. The chorus of women transform Baby Suggs's sermon, which involves words and quotations from scripture, the Word of God, into a prelinguistic sound. Additionally, as the women each contribute to this primal cry, the text suggests a multiplication of "preachers." Previously, the community rejected Baby Suggs's love when she demonstrated it by, perhaps miraculously, multiplying her food. Eighteen years later, again standing in the yard of Bluestone 124, the community re-embraces Baby Suggs's vision and participates in a more miraculous multiplication: the individual preacher becomes a chorus of thirty.

Numerous critics identify this eruption of a collective maternal utterance as emblematic of "the pre-symbolic communication with the Mother" that Julia Kristeva describes as *chora* and Hélène Cixous suggests is recovered through the development of écriture féminine (Tally, "Trilogy": 88). As Toril Moi puts it, Cixous theorizes that

> the voice in each woman ... is not only her own, but springs from the deepest layers of her psyche: her own speech becomes the echo of the primeval song she

once heard, the voice, the incarnation of the 'first voice of love' which all women preserve alive ... the Voice of the Mother, that omnipotent figure that dominates the fantasies of the pre-Oedipal baby. (Moi 112)

Moreover, this often-suppressed pre-symbolic mode of communication holds the resource for profound cultural transformation because it challenges stale narratives of order. Kristeva argues that irruptions of the pre-symbolic semiotic or *chora* "tap into a well of as yet unordered language processes and unarticulated sounds to generate new possibilities for thought and for society" (Rivkin and Ryan 454). *Beloved* validates this theorization of a powerful but submerged "primeval song" that generates "new possibilities" as the women improvise a song that enables both Sethe's and the community's liberation.

Morrison's novel, however, does not merely recycle French feminist theory in fictional form. One of the problems with reading the exorcism as a simple victory of the pre-symbolic over the symbolic register of patriarchal language and culture is that, in Kristeva's narrative of subjectivity, ego formation depends on the alienation of the infant from the mother. Put simply, a return to the abundance of undifferentiated maternal union seems, above all, to suggest the loss of the subject, not her salvation. Yet Morrison's novel does not so much dramatize Kristevan psychoanalytic theory as it riffs on this theory from the historical vantage point of slavery, an intensely antimaternal cultural formation that destroyed the mother-child bond for profit. To submit to culture, for the slave community, was often an act of "social death," not, as it is typically narrated in Lacanian and Kristevan theory, an ultimately paradoxical act of ego formation. For Morrison, the emergence of a community of mothers and daughters who voice a non-patriarchal language enables Sethe and the broader community to begin anew. This rescue scene does not result in an immediate healing. It is a flood after which a diseased social order can, perhaps, begin again.

Morrison figures this moment as one of both communal and religious significance. The women "took a step back to the beginning. In the beginning there were no words. In the beginning was the sound, and they all knew what that sound sounded like" (Morrison, *Beloved*: 305). The cry, thus, suggests a countermyth to the myth of origins recounted in the scriptural Book of Genesis wherein "the Word" precedes all matter—a collective maternal wail replaces the divine Word. Both Sethe and Beloved respond strongly to this maternal sound because, as Stave notes, "[Sethe] and Beloved share their inconsolable longing for mother love" ("From" 111). Thus, both women need desperately to hear the women's cry, a communal response to the violations of the mother-child bond that pervade the novel and an angry expression of a desire for the maternal union that slavery repeatedly denied them.

This maternal cry—a circulation *and* evolution of Baby Suggs's sermons—frees both women. For Beloved, the sound speaks of her mother's intense feeling for her and enables her to see Sethe's actions as a particular manifestation of a more general maternal-child desire that Barbara Christian calls "mother-love/mother-pain, daughter-love/daughter-pain" (qtd. in Grewal 97). Beloved sees her mother's love-pain for her enacted differently when Sethe attempts to attack a white man who she believes is coming, once again, to take her daughters from her. This does not suggest that Beloved's insatiable need becomes fully satisfied; the ending of the novel will not allow such a reading. However, the women's rememory of Baby Suggs's sermon addresses her longing to the extent that she leaves 124 when she sees Sethe decide to attack the white rider instead of her or Denver. Crucially, Sethe's act of maternal protection causes Beloved to begin smiling (309). These conjoined events—the women's collective screaming/singing and Sethe's attack of the supposed oppressor—compel Beloved, and by extension "the past," to retreat, "at least to a point that will allow healing" (Powell 153).

For Sethe, this wordless sermon reconnects her with Baby Suggs and her followers, drawing her back within a community that provides the fluid social context in which self-love might flourish. Her pain over her lost mother and children no longer appears as hers alone, nor does it mark her as wholly distinct in her community. Their cry indicates that they might share her story because each of the women understands Sethe's desire to, as Andrea O'Reilly puts it, "be a daughter to her mother, and a mother to her daughter" (89). More importantly, they share a sense of the violation of this crucial matrilineal heritage under slavery's antimaternal regime. The eruption of a shared maternal language enables Sethe to break from the calcified narrative of individual guilt that defines her life. As she stands at the door holding Beloved's hand, she hears the voices of these women shift from a scream into a song:

> It was as though *the Clearing had come to her* with all its heat and simmering leaves, where the voices of the women searched for the right combination, the key, the code, the sound that broke the back of words. Building voice upon voice until they found it, and when they did it was a wave of sound wide enough to sound deep water and knock the pods off chestnut trees. It broke over Sethe and she trembled like the baptized in its wash. (Morrison, *Beloved*: 308; emphasis added)

Two features of this scene, suffused with images of both spiritual and physical rebirth, appear especially significant for Morrison's engagement with literary preaching in *Beloved*. First, Sethe's sense that the Clearing comes to her confirms Morrison's effort to free the sermon from the individual authority of the preacher by showing the manner in which the sermon circulates through the work of the community. Sethe does not say, as one might expect, that she senses that *she is* once again back in the Clearing. The sermon's healing force does not stay in the Clearing but now, through the women's agency, becomes active at the site of Sethe's trauma.

Secondly, as Sethe constructs her rememory of the Clearing, she observes a sound that she describes as "wide enough to sound deep water," a sound that "broke the back of words" (308). These observations provide crucial insight into Morrison's own attempt to write in a manner that somehow transcends the medium of words. Water and ink seem to be sworn enemies. On the one hand, then, we should read this primal sound wave as a counterattack to the linguistic violence represented by Schoolteacher's meticulous documentation of Sethe's rape and her "animal" characteristics (226, 228–9). This primal scene, a scene of weaponized writing, inaugurates Sethe's deepest trauma and ultimately motivates her to kill her infant daughter: "And no one, nobody on this earth, would list her daughter's characteristics on the animal side of the paper. No. Oh no" (296). Here, Morrison deploys a maternal sound that threatens the careful orderings of an oppressive patriarchal culture and reveals the inadequacy of oppressive language systems that Sethe and Morrison alike identify with patriarchy and racism.

On the other hand, the sound serves less as a sword than a shield in a scene that enacts a homecoming. The scene dramatizes the reunion of an exile with her community and images forth a sense of solidarity that cannot be expressed in language. In the "sound wide enough to sound deep water" that breaks over and heals Sethe, Morrison engages the language of Psalm 42, a Hebrew poem of exile that deals centrally with water imagery and recounts the healing powers of memory and sound. The Psalmist describes his exile in language that recalls Sethe's longing for the excess and community symbolized by the Clearing: "My tears have been my meat day and night, while they continually say unto me, Where is thy God? When I remember these things, I pour out my soul in me: for I had gone with the multitude, I went with them to the house of God, with the voice of joy and praise, with a multitude that kept holyday" (Ps. 42:3-4). The Psalmist, like Sethe and the chorus of thirty singers, eventually finds a unifying resource in an ill-defined, water-like sound through which the exile communicates beyond language: "Deep calleth unto deep at the noise of thy waterspouts: all thy waves and thy billows are gone over me … [H]is song shall be with me" (Ps. 42:7-8). Morrison exploits the ambiguity of this Psalm, which expresses a theory of pre-linguistic communication surprisingly similar to Kristeva's, as she constructs a scene in which memory, sound, and song unite to usher Sethe into a new mode of communal being. Additionally, the imagery of waves washing over the Psalmist parallels Morrison's description of the women's song that "broke over Sethe" and left her "trembl[ing] like the baptized in its wash" (Morrison, *Beloved*: 308). The women's healing song validates and amplifies Baby Suggs's spiritual vision and shows that, ultimately, her sermon—like Morrison's novel—succeeds only when it is received, revised, and expressed in the acts of a community.

Like the preachers she admires, Morrison constructs this multivalent scene less as a conclusion than as a provocation—"something is supposed to happen so the listener participates" (Morrison, "Toni": 101). Throughout *Beloved*, Morrison embraces the sermon, one of her central "moorings," only to unmoor it from the preacher and the specific time-space of the sermon's initial utterance. The ambiguous exorcism scene, which completes the novel's emplotment of the circulated sermon, continues to generate scholarly engagement and informed discussion. Again and again, Morrison encourages her readers to contribute to the novel's meaning and message, just as the chorus of women's "response" amplifies Baby Suggs's "call" (Morrison, "An Interview with Toni Morrison," by McKay 147). At the same time, Morrison clearly aims for the novel to do more than catalyze scholarship and discussion. The denouement promotes an engaged communal ethics centered on, as Ella puts it, "get[ting] down to business" (Morrison, *Beloved*: 302). Through her uniquely democratic engagement with literary preaching, Morrison suggests that the social responsibilities of the writer—which Morrison describes elsewhere as "bear[ing] witness" and "effect[ing] change"—become the readers' responsibilities as well (Morrison, "An Interview with Toni Morrison," by Jones and Vinson 183). Thus, in her most famous novel, Morrison's ingenious literary preaching discloses not only one of the most significant and variable anchors of her fiction but also her longing for a readership that remains haunted by her novels, responsive to their core messages, and empowered to contribute to the cultural healing they aim to effect.

Coda

"That's the Pulpit Speaking"

This project began with a markedly different conception of literary preaching than the one to which it eventually led. Initially, I intended to explore the form's ubiquity and portability across eras by recourse to a concept that theorists of design call a skeuomorph. According to Katherine Hayles, a skeuomorph is a "design feature that is no longer functional in itself but that refers back to a feature that was functional at an earlier time" (17). For example, when one takes a photograph with a smartphone, the phone often emits a sound effect that replicates the noise made by the rapid opening and closing of a camera shutter, the familiar "click" that signals that the photo has been taken. The smartphone's sound effect, of course, serves a purpose. It is helpful to know when the picture has been captured. But what is skeuomorphic about this noise is its reproduction of a sound that arose from a necessary design feature in the past. The smartphone need not "click." Any noise would serve the purpose. The familiar "click" provides users with a comforting transition from one technology to another. As Hayles puts it, "Skeuomorphs visibly testify to the social or psychological necessity for innovation to be tempered by replication" (17). The skeuomorph often limits creativity and innovation; it is a sign of necessary conformity to a former way of doing things.

In the early stages of this project, it seemed to me that literary preaching functioned as a something like a skeuomorph, an entrenched cultural form in US letters that was relevant during the heyday of religious revivalism but now remains a part of our books, films, and music primarily because readers, moviegoers, and listeners expect it to be there when artists begin to inveigh against their culture's besetting sins. As such, instances of literary preaching in twentieth- and twenty-first-century texts seemed like failures of creativity, acts of conformity to a literary tradition established in the mid-nineteenth century but no longer necessary to engage contemporary readers. Though we should be careful not to overlook the continued influence of preaching (or religion, more generally) in US culture, we seem to be on safe ground when we assert that the sermon does not resonate with a contemporary audience in precisely the manner it did in Emerson's and Whitman's era. This is not the golden age of oratory, and the most famous preachers in America are targets of ridicule by both religious and secular groups. Though I was surprised to read Whitman's description of being moved to tears by Father Taylor's prayers and sermons, I could not imagine him responding with anything other than rage to the celebrity preachers of our cultural moment. Given the changed status of the sermon in US culture, I wondered why modern and contemporary US authors did not just depart from the form, adapt to a new cultural scene, and end the longstanding engagement with the preacher?

It still seems to me that one might aptly characterize some late-twentieth- and twenty-first-century scenes of literary preaching as skeuomorphic; however, Toni Morrison's literary preaching in *Beloved* resisted being read in this manner and clearly represents a virtuosic creative achievement, not an act of aesthetic conformity to a moribund tradition. Morrison's ingenious literary preaching in *Beloved*—wherein, counterintuitively, the preacher's renunciation enables the sermon's flourishing—demanded a more nuanced critical frame because Morrison refuses to allow the sermon to offer the authoritative word and reimagines it as a cultural form that operates most effectively when it circulates in a community's acts and utterances. As I demonstrate in the Chapter 4, Baby Suggs's sermon haunts the community, takes on new meaning as it circulates, and empowers creative acts of communal healing. And, in precisely this manner, Morrison's emplotment of the circulated sermon images forth Morrison's vision of the novel itself. It is not a transcendent, self-contained, morally authoritative statement but a provocative, material call that haunts its readers and requires readerly participation to achieve its meaning.

In this sense, Morrison's aesthetic vision bears a striking affinity to Whitman's. In a way that anticipates Morrison, Whitman, throughout *Leaves of Grass*, images his departure as a way of opening space for readerly participation in his democratic project. As I argue in Chapter 1, however, Whitman remains conflicted about his own poetic efforts at self-containment, often undoing these efforts even as he continues to worry about the ideological function of his literary preaching and the messianic aura he constructs. More thoroughly than Whitman, Morrison refuses any efforts at closing or concluding her novels. Informed by an African American sermonic aesthetic, she glories in staking her novels' meaning on readers' responses to her calls. Though Morrison abjures the traditional hierarchical power distributions associated with the preacher, she does so in a way that paradoxically multiplies the literary sermon's potency and unsettles traditional notions of what it means to properly read a novel. Thus, I quickly realized that with her literary sermons, Morrison *was* adapting to a new cultural scene, introducing new terms of engagement between author and audience, and complexly refashioning the tradition of literary preaching. At the same time, Morrison also seized on the sermon's semiotic cadences and deployed the form to comment on her literary predecessor's engagements with the sermon.

As Morrison's engagements with the sermon became simultaneously more vivid and more complex, instances of literary preaching from the mid-nineteenth century onward appeared newly strange, compelling, and, most importantly, interlinked. Literary preaching began to seem less like an artifact of a specific historical era and more like a sonnet—an evergreen literary form that continues to be adapted, repurposed, explored, and deployed to a variety of effects. Literary preaching, once identified as a form that offers authors a constellation of enabling and productively troubling affordances, emerges as a significant, transhistorical tradition in US literature. Numerous US authors can be understood as fervid practitioners of the form, each fashioning the form to their purposes and negotiating its paradoxical affordances. Historical, biographical, and regional particularities surely shape authors' various uses of literary preaching, and these particularities deserve careful historical contextualization. But the form's pervasive influence on US literature cannot be understood fully without untethering critical analysis from the historicist frameworks that dominate contemporary literary criticism.

Throughout the foregoing pages, we've seen that an awareness of literary preaching's various affordances enables us to offer new readings of familiar texts and allows us to discern engaging lines of literary influence and reception. Puzzling elements of familiar narratives, such as Hawthorne's weird penchant for too-quickly dismissing his radical women preachers, become readily comprehensible. Odd incidents in literary history, such as James T. Fields's decision to excise the scene of literary preaching that contains Davis's critical theological statement in *Life in the Iron-Mills*, can be understood in a new light. We see how Whitman's reception of Emerson's vision of the poet-as-preacher resembles Hurston's and Faulkner's reception of James Weldon Johnson's vision of the preacher-as-poet in *God's Trombones*. And we see, too, how Morrison's literary preaching responds to the literary preaching of Ellison, Baldwin, and Faulkner in a way that, in turn, recalls Davis's and Faulkner's adaptations of Hawthorne's pulpit exchanges. Additionally, US authors' seemingly obsessive tendency to take up the form in successive works—variously embracing, rejecting, and modifying their own literary sermons—makes sense if we can see these attempts as symptomatic of a sustained effort to grapple with a uniquely perplexing form. Because the form's dialectical tensions refuse to resolve, it summons artists even after they have attempted to offer their final statements regarding the form's utility. It is worth noting, for example, that in *The Mansion* (1955), Faulkner once again embraces literary preaching even after his seemingly definitive denunciation of the form in *Light in August*. Similarly, Morrison returns to the form in *Paradise* (1997), even though *Beloved* seems to provide a conclusive statement of her vision of the relationship between her novels and the sermon. As we watch the unfolding of the American literary tradition, we should not be surprised to see new attempts to harness this variously attractive and repulsive form. When future writers engage in literary preaching, they will be participating in a well-established tradition in US letters, one that's simultaneously fueled and frustrated America's most recognizable authors.

Much remains to be said about the shaping influence of literary preaching on US literature, in part, because many more authors' works invite new scholarship along the lines suggested in this study. Studies of these authors will undoubtedly bring welcome breadth, nuance, and texture to the story that I've begun to tell in these pages. I am particularly interested, too, in considering the portability of the form across other creative outlets, particularly film and music. Such scholarship would, no doubt, provide valuable insight into the significant impact of the sermon on US cultural production.

At the outset of this project, I often asked myself why American writers could not just reject or ignore the preacher and be done with literary preaching. Why did they fixate on embracing a sermonic form that they often seemed to distain? Now I answer that question with another one: why would any artist reject such a sustainable, established, and productively troubling form? Why would any artist, in other words, reject a form that consistently nourishes powerful art, connects one's work to an established tradition in major works, suggests the alluring possibility of breaking through linguistic representation, and enables authoritative speech about pressing cultural concerns?

One of the most significant engagements with the form in twenty-first century US literature occurs in Marilynne Robinson's Pulitzer-Prize winning *Gilead* (2004). In the epistolary novel, ailing minister John Ames writes a long, free-form letter for his seven-year-old son to read when he reaches the appropriate age. Considered within the tradition of literary preaching, Ames might fruitfully be understood as a figure for many American authors. He admits his distaste for "pulpitish" talk, but he cannot dismiss it entirely and admits that "the way [he] think[s]" seems to be inflected by his long propinquity to pulpit (29). Throughout the novel, Ames and his friend, George Boughton, also a minister, share a private joke about moments when their everyday speech patterns become indistinguishable from preaching. At moments when Ames attempts to ascribe ultimate meaning to the complexity of the human experience, Boughton cautions, "That's the pulpit speaking" (43). Both of Robinson's ministers express suspicion of pulpit rhetoric—even their own. Yet in a charged moment in his letter, the dying Ames tries to communicate his guiding vision to his young son. And as he does so his speech veers inexorably toward the sermonic: "Whenever I take a child into my arms to be baptized, I am, so to speak, comprehended in the experience more fully, having seen more of life, knowing better what it means to affirm the sacredness of the human creature" (91). The vision of the holiness of the human creature articulated here resonates with the visions of both Whitman and the fictional Baby Suggs. Ames, Whitman, and Suggs share a strikingly similar belief in humanity's inherent sacredness, and they understand that belief to carry profound ethical ramifications. Moreover, all three want to preach this affirming vision to convert their auditors' or readers' imaginations about what it means to be a human among other humans. As soon as he pens this line, however, Ames realizes that he's ascended into the pulpit, despite his previously stated desire to "resist that inflection" (29). His response to this realization registers his uneasiness with the form, but it simultaneously underscores the irresistible draw of literary preaching: "That's the pulpit speaking," he admits to his son, "but it's telling the truth" (91). Each of the authors examined in *Resistance and the Sermon in American Literature* understands precisely what he's trying to say.

Works Cited

Apess, William. "A Looking-Glass for the White Man." In *On Our Ground: The Complete Writings of William Apess, a Pequot*, edited by Barry O'Connell. Massachusetts UP, [1833] 1992, 55–161.

Arsić, Branka. *On Leaving: A Reading in Emerson*. Harvard UP, 2010.

Aspiz, Harold. "Science and Pseudoscience." In *A Companion to Walt Whitman*, edited by David D. Kummings. Blackwell, 2006, 216–32.

Awkward, Michael. "'The Evil of Fulfillment': Scapegoating and Narration in *The Bluest Eye*." In *Toni Morrison's The Bluest Eye: Modern Critical Interpretations*, edited by Harold Bloom. Chelsea House, 1999, 65–104.

Baillie, Justine. *Toni Morrison and the Literary Tradition: The Invention of an Aesthetic*. Bloomsbury, 2013.

Baldwin, James. *The Amen Corner*. In *Black Theater, U.S.A.: Forty-Five Plays by Black Americans, 1847–1974*, edited by James V. Hatch. Free Press, [1954] 1974, 516–46.

Baldwin, James. *Go Tell It on the Mountain*. Vintage International, [1953] 2013.

Baldwin, James. *Just Above My Head*. Delta, [1979] 2000.

Bate, Nancy Berkowitz. "Toni Morrison's *Beloved*: Psalm and Sacrament." In *Toni Morrison and the Bible: Contested Intertextualities*, edited by Shirley A. Stave. Peter Lang, 2006, 26–70.

Baym, Nina. *The Shape of Hawthorne's Career*. Cornell UP, 1976.

Becker-Leckrone, Megan. *Julia Kristeva and Literary Theory*. Palgrave Macmillan, 2005.

Berlant, Lauren. "History's Burial in *The Blithedale Romance*: Rethinking Hollingsworth." In *The Blithedale Romance*, edited by Richard H. Millington. Norton Critical Edition, Norton, [1852] 2011, 350–9.

Besse, Joseph. *A Collection of the Sufferings of the People Called Quakers*, vol. 2, London, 1753. *HathiTrust Digital Library*, hdl.handle.net/2027/uc1.31175034931157 (accessed May 27, 2022).

Bleikasten, André. *The Ink of Melancholy: Faulkner's Novels, from The Sound and the Fury to Light in August*. Indiana UP, 1990.

Bleikasten, André. *The Most Splendid Failure: Faulkner's The Sound and the Fury*. Indiana UP, 1976.

Blotner, Joseph. *Faulkner: A Biography*. Random House, 1984.

Bouldin, Elizabeth. *Women Prophets and Radical Protestantism in the British Atlantic World, 1640–1730*. Cambridge UP, 2015.

Buell, Lawrence. *Emerson*. Belknap Press of Harvard UP, 2003.

Buell, Lawrence. *Literary Transcendentalism: Style and Vision in the American Renaissance*. Cornell UP, 1973.

Byerman, Keith L. "Secular Word: Sacred Flesh: Preachers in the Fiction of Baldwin and Morrison." In *James Baldwin and Toni Morrison: Comparative Critical and Theoretical Essays*, edited by Lovalerie King and Lynn Orilla Scott. Palgrave, 2006, 187–204.

Carmean, Karen. *Toni Morrison's World of Fiction*. Whitston Publishing, 1993.

Castille, Philip Dubuisson. "Dilsey's Easter Conversion in Faulkner's *The Sound and the Fury*." *Studies in the Novel* 24, no. 4 (1991): 423–33.

Chamberlain, John. "Books of the Times." *New York Times*, May 3, 1934, 17. https://archive.nytimes.com (accessed February 2, 2023).

Colacurcio, Michael J. *The Province of Piety: Moral History in Hawthorne's Early Tales*. Duke UP, 1995.

Coleman, Dawn. *Preaching and the Rise of the American Novel*. Ohio State UP, 2013.

Collier-Thomas, Bettye. *Daughters of Thunder: Black Women Preachers and Their Sermons, 1850–1979*. Jossey-Bass, 1998.

Connely, Marc. *The Green Pastures*, edited by Thomas Cripps. U of Wisconsin P, [1930] 1979.

Cowley, Malcolm. *The Faulkner-Cowley File: Letters and Memories, 1944–1962*. Penguin Books, 1978.

Dahill-Baue, William. "Insignificant Monkeys: Preaching Black English in Faulkner's *The Sound and the Fury* and Morrison's *Beloved*." *Mississippi Quarterly* 49, no. 3 (1996): 457–73.

Danticat, Edwidge. Foreword. In *Their Eyes Were Watching God*, edited by Zora Neale Hurston. HarperPerennial, [1937)] 2006, ix–xvii.

Davis, Rebecca Harding. *Bits of Gossip*. In *Rebecca Harding Davis: Writing Cultural Autobiography*, edited by Janice Milner Lasseter and Sharon M. Harris. Vanderbilt UP, [1904] 2001, 23–113.

Davis, Rebecca Harding. *Life in the Iron Mills*, edited by Cecelia Tichi. Bedford Cultural Edition, Bedford/St. Martins, [1861] 1998.

Davis, Rebecca Harding. "One Week an Editor." In *The Galaxy*, vol. 16. Sheldon, 1873, 652–61. *HathiTrust Digital Library*, hdl.handle.net/2027/hvd.32044019301779 (accessed March 27, 2023).

Davis, Rebecca Harding. "Women in Literature." In *A Rebecca Harding Davis Reader*, edited by Jean Pfaelzer. U of Pittsburgh P, [1891] 1995, 402–4.

Davis, Thadious M. *Faulkner's "Negro": Art and the Southern Context*. Louisiana State UP, 1983.

Deloria, Philip J. *Playing Indian*. Yale UP, 1998.

Dobbs, Cynthia. "Toni Morrison's *Beloved*: Bodies Returned, Modernism Revisited." *African American Review* 32, no. 4 (1998): 563–78.

Douglas, Ann. *The Feminization of American Culture*. Anchor Press, [1977] 1988.

Du Bois, W. E. B. "Criteria of Negro Art." In *The Portable Harlem Renaissance Reader*, edited by David Levering Lewis. Penguin, [1926] 1995, 100–5.

Duncan, David James. *The Brothers K.* Doubleday, 1992.

Duvall, John. *The Identifying Fictions of Toni Morrison: Modernist Authenticity and Postmodern Blackness.* Palgrave, 2000.

Easton, Alison. "Hawthorne and the Question of Women." In *The Cambridge Companion to Nathaniel Hawthorne*, edited by Richard H. Millington. Cambridge UP, 2004, 79–97.

Eckard, Paula Gallant. *Maternal Body and Voice in Toni Morrison, Bobbie Ann Mason, and Lee Smith.* Missouri UP, 2002.

Edmundson, Mark. *Song of Ourselves: Walt Whitman and the Fight for Democracy.* Harvard UP, 2021.

Edwards, Jonathan. "Sinners in the Hands of an Angry God." *A Jonathan Edwards Reader*, edited by John E. Smith, Harry S. Stout, and Kenneth P. Minkema. Yale Nota Bene, [1741] 2003, 89–105.

Ellis, Iain. *Rebels Wit Attitude: Subversive Rock Humorists.* Skull Soft, 2008.

Ellison, Ralph. *Juneteenth.* Vintage International, 1999.

Ellison, Ralph. *Invisible Man.* Vintage International, [1952] 1995.

Emerson, Ralph Waldo. "An Address Delivered before the Senior Class in Divinity College." In *Ralph Waldo Emerson and Margaret Fuller: Selected Works*, edited by John Carlos Rowe. Houghton Mifflin, [1838] 2002, 78–93.

Emerson, Ralph Waldo. "An Address . . . on . . . the Emancipation of the Negroes in the West Indies." In *Ralph Waldo Emerson and Margaret Fuller: Selected Works*, edited by John Carlos Rowe. Houghton Mifflin, [1844] 2002, 207–29.

Emerson, Ralph Waldo. "Eloquence." In *The Collected Works of Ralph Waldo Emerson, Vol VII: Society and Solitude*, edited by Ronald A. Bosco and Douglas Emory Wilson. Belknap, [1870] 2007, 30–51.

Emerson, Ralph Waldo. *The Complete Sermons of Ralph Waldo Emerson*, vol. 4, edited by Wesley Mott. U Missouri P, 1993.

Emerson, Ralph Waldo. *The Correspondence of Thomas Carlyle and Ralph Waldo Emerson, 1834–1872*, vol. 1, edited by Charles Eliot Norton, 3rd ed. James R. Osgood, 1883.

Emerson, Ralph Waldo. "Eloquence." In *The Collected Works of Ralph Waldo Emerson, Vol VII: Society and Solitude*, edited by Ronald A. Bosco and Douglas Emory Wilson. Belknap, [1870] 2007, 30–51.

Emerson, Ralph Waldo. "Father Taylor." *The Atlantic Monthly*, August 1906, 177–81. *The Atlantic Archive*, www.theatlantic.com/archive/ (accessed December 6, 2022).

Emerson, Ralph Waldo. *Journals and Miscellaneous Notebooks of Ralph Waldo Emerson*, 16 vols., edited by William H. Gilman, Alfred R. Ferguson, George P. Clark, Merrell R. Davis, Merton M. Sealts, Ralph H. Orth, A. W. Plumbstead, Harrison Hayford, J. E. Parsons, Ruth H. Bennett, Linda Allardt, Susan Sutton Smith, Ronald A. Bosco, and Glen M. Johnson. Harvard UP, 1960–82; Cited parenthetically as *JMN*, with volume and page number.

Emerson, Ralph Waldo. *Journals of Ralph Waldo Emerson: With Annotations*, 10 vols., edited by Edward Waldo Emerson and Waldo Emerson Forbes. Houghton Mifflin, 1910.

Emerson, Ralph Waldo. *Nature*. In *Ralph Waldo Emerson and Margaret Fuller: Selected Works*, edited by John Carlos Rowe. Houghton Mifflin, [1836] 2002, 23–58.

Emerson, Ralph Waldo. "The Poet." In *Ralph Waldo Emerson and Margaret Fuller: Selected Works*, edited by John Carlos Rowe. Houghton Mifflin, [1844] 2002, 186–206.

Emerson, Ralph Waldo. "Self-Reliance." In *Ralph Waldo Emerson and Margaret Fuller: Selected Works*, edited by John Carlos Rowe. Houghton Mifflin, [1841] 2002, 93–114.

Engeman, Thomas S. "*Invisible Man* and *Juneteenth*: Ralph Ellison's Literary Pursuit of Racial Justice." In *Ralph Ellison and the Raft of Hope*, edited by Lucas E. Morel. U of Kentucky P, 2004, 91–104.

Faulkner, William. *Absalom, Absalom*. Vintage International, [1936] 1990.

Faulkner, William. *As I Lay Dying*. Vintage International, [1930] 1990.

Faulkner, William. *Essays, Speeches, and Public Letters*, edited by James B. Meriwether. The Modern Library, 2004.

Faulkner, William. "Frederick Gwynn's Literature Class—15 February 1957." MSS 6187 Readings by William Faulkner, Small Special Collections Library, University of Virginia, Charlottesville, Virginia.

Faulkner, William. *Go Down, Moses*. Vintage International, [1942] 1990.

Faulkner, William. "Interview with Jean Stein: William Faulkner, the Art of Fiction No. 12." *The Paris Review, Interviews, vol. 2*, edited by Philip Gourevitch. Picador, 2007, 34–57.

Faulkner, William. *Light in August*. 1932. Vintage International, 1990.

Faulkner, William. *The Mansion*. Vintage, [1955] 1965.

Faulkner, William. *The Sound and the Fury*. Vintage International, [1929] 1990.

Faulkner, William. "1699–1945. Appendix: The Compsons." In *The Portable Faulkner*, edited by Malcolm Cowley. Penguin Books, [1945] 2003.

Fleming, Robert E. "James Weldon Johnson's *God's Trombones* as a Source for Faulkner's Rev'un Shegog." *CLA Journal* 36 (1992): 24–30.

Folsom, Ed. "Foreword to Section 31," *WhitmanWeb*, https://iwp.uiowa.edu/whitman web/en /writings/song-of-myself/section-31 (accessed July 17, 2015).

Foulks, Beverly. "Trial by Fire: The Theodicy of Toni Morrison in *Sula*." In *Toni Morrison and the Bible: Contested Intertextualities*, edited by Shirley A. Stave. Peter Lang, 2006, 8–25.

Fowler, Doreen. "Beyond Oedipus: Lucas Beauchamp, Ned Barnett, and Faulkner's *Intruder in the Dust*." *MFS Modern Fiction Studies* 53, no. 4 (2007): 788–820.

Fowler, Doreen. "'Reading for the Other Side': *Beloved* and *Requiem for a Nun*." In *Unflinching Gaze: Morrison and Faulkner Re-Envisioned*, edited by Carol A. Kolmerten, Stephen M. Ross, and Judith Bryant Wittenberg. Mississippi UP, 1997, 139–51.

Furman, Jan. *Toni Morrison's Fiction: Revised and Expanded*, U of South Carolina P, 2014.

Garner, Thurmon. "Playing the Dozes: Folklore as Strategies of Living." In *African American Communication and Identities: Essential Readings*, edited by Ronald Jackson. Sage, 2004, 80–8.

Gates, Henry Louis, Jr. "Their Eyes Were Watching God: Hurston and the Speakerly Text." In *Zora Neale Hurston: Critical Perspectives Past and Present*, edited by Henry Louis Gates and Anthony Appiah. Amistad, 1993, 154–203.

Gates, Henry Louis, Jr. "Zora Neale Hurston: 'A Negro Way of Saying.'" Afterword. In *Their Eyes Were Watching God*, by Zora Neale Hurston. HarperPerennial, [1937] 2006, 197–205.

Goodman, Susan. *Republic of Words the Atlantic Monthly and Its Writers, 1857–1925*. UP of New England, 2011.

Gougeon, Len. *Virtue's Hero: Emerson, Antislavery, and Reform*. U of Georgia P, 1990.

Grewal, Gurleen. "Beholding 'A Great Tree of Life': Eros, Nature and the Visionary in *Their Eyes Were Watching God*." In *"The Inside Light": New Critical Essays on Zora Neale Hurston*, edited by Deborah Plant. Praeger, 2010, 103–12.

Grewal, Gurleen. *Circles of Sorrow, Lines of Struggle: The Novels of Toni Morrison*. Louisiana State UP, 1998.

Gura, Philip F. *American Transcendentalism: A History*. Hill and Wang, 2007.

Gura, Philip F. *Truth's Ragged Edge: The Rise of the American Novel*. Farrar, Straus and Giroux, 2013.

Hankins, Barry. *The Second Great Awakening and the Transcendentalists*. Greenwood Press, 2004.

Harris, Sharon M. *Rebecca Harding Davis and American Realism*. U of Pennsylvania P, 1991.

Harris, Trudier. *Fictions and Folklore: The Novels of Toni Morrison*, U of Tennessee P, 1991.

Harris, W. C. *E Pluribus Unum Nineteenth-Century American Literature & the Constitutional Paradox*. U of Iowa P, 2005.

Harriss, M. Cooper. "Preacherly Texts: Zora Neale Hurston and the Homiletics of Literature." *Journal of Africana Religions* 4, no. 2 (2016): 278–90.

Hatch, Nathan O. *The Democratization of American Christianity*. Yale UP, 1989.

Hawthorne, Nathaniel. "Endicott and the Cross." In *Young Goodman Brown and Other Tales*, edited by Brian Harding. Oxford UP, [1838] 2008, 168–74.

Hawthorne, Julian. *Nathaniel Hawthorne and His Wife: A Biography*, vol. I. Houghton Mifflin, 1884. *HathiTrust Digital Library*, https://hdl.handle.net/2027/uiug.30112071857616 (accessed April 20, 2023).

Hawthorne, Nathaniel. *The Blithedale Romance*, edited by Richard H. Millington. Norton Critical Edition, Norton, [1852] 2011.

Hawthorne, Nathaniel. "The Gentle Boy." In *Young Goodman Brown and Other Tales*, edited by Brian Harding. Oxford UP, [1832] 2008, 3–37.

Hawthorne, Nathaniel. *The House of the Seven Gables*, edited by Robert S. Levine. Norton Critical Edition, Norton, [1851] 2006.

Hawthorne, Nathaniel. *The Scarlet Letter*, edited by Leland S. Parson. Norton Critical Edition, Norton, [1850] 2005.

Hawthorne, Nathaniel. *The Whole History of Grandfather's Chair*. In *The Century Edition of the Works of Nathaniel Hawthorne*, vol. 6, edited by William Charvat, Roy Harvey Pearce, and Claude M. Simpson. Ohio State UP, [1840] 1972, 5–212.

Hayles, N. Katherine. *How We Became Posthuman: Virtual Bodies in Cybernetics, Literature, and Informatics*. U of Chicago P, 1999.

Hein, David. "The Reverend Mr. Shegog's Easter Sermon: Preaching as Communion in Faulkner's *The Sound and the Fury*." *The Mississippi Quarterly* 58, nos. 3–4 (2005): 559–80.

Hemenway, Robert E. *Zora Neale Hurston: A Literary Biography*. U of Illinois P, 1977.

Henderson, Carol E. "Refiguring the Flesh: The Word, the Body, and the Rituals of Being in *Beloved* and *Go Tell It on the Mountain*." In *James Baldwin and Toni Morrison: Comparative Critical and Theoretical Essays*, edited by Lovalerie King and Lynn Orilla Scott. Palgrave, 2006, 149–65.

Herrero-Brasas, Juan A. *Walt Whitman's Mystical Ethics of Comradeship: Homosexuality and the Marginality of Friendship at the Crossroads of Modernity*. State U of New York P, 2010.

Higgins, Therese E. *Religiosity, Cosmology, and Folklore: The African Influence in the Novels of Toni Morrison*. Routledge, 2001.

Holifield, E. Brooks. *Theology in America: Christian Thought from the Age of the Puritans to the Civil War*. Yale UP, 2003.

The Holy Bible. King James Version. Zondervan Publishing House, 1983.

Hubbard, Dolan. *The Sermon and the African American Literary Imagination*. U of Missouri P, 1994.

Humphrey, Richard Alan. "Foot Washing." In *Encyclopedia of Religion in the South*, 2nd ed., edited by Samuel S. Hill and Charles H. Lippy. Mercer UP, 2005, 323–4.

Hurston, Zora Neale. *Jonah's Gourd Vine*. HarperPerennial, [1934] 1990.

Hurston, Zora Neale. *A Life in Letters*, edited by Carla Kaplan. Doubleday, 2002.

Hurston, Zora Neale. "Race Cannot Be Great Until It Recognizes Its Talent." *Washington Tribune*, December 29, 1934.

Hurston, Zora Neale. *The Sanctified Church*. Turtle Island, 1981.

Hurston, Zora Neale. *Their Eyes Were Watching God*. HarperPerennial, [1937] 2006.

Janson, Drude Krog. *A Saloonkeeper's Daughter*, translated by Gerald Thorson, edited by Ørm Overland. Johns Hopkins UP, [1887] 2002.

Johnson, James Weldon. *Complete Poems*, edited by Sondra Kathryn Wilson. Penguin Books, 2000.

Johnson, James Weldon. *God's Trombones: Seven Negro Sermons in Verse. Complete Poems*, edited by Sondra Kathryn Wilson. Penguin Books, [1927] 2000, 5–48.

Kaplan, Carla. "The Erotics of Talk: 'That Oldest Human Longing' in *Their Eyes Were Watching God*." In *Zora Neale Hurston's Their Eyes Were Watching God: A Case Book*, edited by Cheryl A. Wall. Oxford UP, 2000, 137–64.

Kevorkian, Martin. *Writing beyond Prophecy: Emerson, Hawthorne, and Melville after the American Renaissance*. Louisiana State UP, 2013.

Killingsworth, M. Jimmie. *The Cambridge Introduction to Walt Whitman*. Cambridge UP, 2007.

King, Lovalerie. *The Cambridge Introduction to Zora Neale Hurston*. Cambridge UP, 2008.

King, Lovalerie. "Introduction: Baldwin and Morrison in Dialogue." In *James Baldwin and Toni Morrison: Comparative Critical and Theoretical Essays*, edited by Lovalerie King and Lynn Orilla Scott. Palgrave, 2006, 1–9.

Kuebrich, David. *Minor Prophecy: Walt Whitman's New American Religion*. Indiana UP, 1989.

Kuebrich, David. "Religion and the Poet-Prophet." In *A Companion to Walt Whitman*, edited by David D. Kummings. Blackwell, 2006, 197–215.

Kuebrich, David. "Soul, The." In *Walt Whitman: An Encyclopedia*, edited by David D. Kummings and J. R. Lemaster. Garland, 1998, 669–70.

Larson, Rebecca. *Daughters of Light: Quaker Women Preaching and Prophesying in the Colonies and Abroad, 1700–1775*. Knopf, 1999.

Lasseter, Janice Milner. "The Censored and Uncensored Literary Lives of *Life in the Iron-Mills*." *Legacy* 20, nos. 1–2 (2003): 175–90.

Lawrence, David. "Fleshly Ghosts and Ghostly Flesh: The Word and the Body in *Beloved*." In *Toni Morrison's Fiction: Contemporary Criticism*, edited by David L. Middleton. Garland, 1997, 231–46.

Levine, Caroline. *Forms: Whole, Rhythm, Hierarchy, Network*. Princeton UP, 2015.

Lischer, Richard. *The Preacher King: Martin Luther King, Jr. and the Word that Moved America*. Oxford UP, 1995.

Locke, Alain. "The New Negro." In *The Portable Harlem Renaissance Reader*, edited by David Levering Lewis. Penguin, [1925] 1995, 46–51.

Magee, Rosemary. "Preacher, White." In *The New Encyclopedia of Sothern Culture: Religion*, edited by Samuel S. Hill, vol. 1. UP of North Carolina, 2006, 118–21.

Marks, Kathleen. *Toni Morrison's Beloved and the Apotropaic Imagination*. Missouri UP, 2002.

Marsh, John. *In Walt We Trust: How a Queer Socialist Poet Can Save America from Itself*. Monthly Review Press, 2015.

McInnis, Maurie Dee. *Slaves Waiting for Sale: Abolitionist Art and the American Slave Trade*. Chicago UP, 2011.

McLoughlin, William G. *Revivals, Awakenings, and Reform: An Essay on Religion and Social Change in America, 1607–1977*. U of Chicago P, 1978.

Melville, Herman. "Bartleby, the Scrivener." *Melville's Short Novels*, edited by Dan McCall. Norton Critical Edition, Norton, [1853] 2002, 3–34.

Melville, Herman. *Benito Cereno*. *Melville's Short Novels*, edited by Dan McCall. Norton Critical Edition, Norton, [1855] 2002, 34–102.

Melville, Herman. *The Confidence Man: His Masquerade*, edited by Hershel Parker and Mark Niemeyer. Norton Critical Edition, 2nd ed., Norton, [1857] 2006.

Melville, Herman. *Moby-Dick; or, The Whale*, edited by Hershel Parker and Harrison Hayford. Norton Critical Edition, 2nd ed., Norton, [1851] 2002.

Melville, Herman. "The Paradise of Bachelors and the Tartarus of Maids." *Herman Melville: Pierre, Israel Potter, The Piazza Tales, The Confidence Man, Uncollected Prose, Billy Budd*, edited by Harrison Hayford. Library of America, [1855] 1984, 1257–79.

Miles, Diana. *Women, Violence & Testimony in the Works of Zora Neale Hurston*. Peter Lang, 2003.

Moi, Toril. *Sexual/Textual Politics*. Routledge, 2002.

Morone, James A. *Hellfire Nation the Politics of Sin in American History*. Yale UP, 2003.

Morris, Saundra. "Poetry and Poetics." In *Emerson in Context*, edited by Wesley T. Mott. Cambridge UP, 2014, 75–84.

Morrison, Toni. *Beloved*. Vintage International, [1987] 2004.

Morrison, Toni. *The Bluest Eye*. Plume, [1970] 1994.

Morrison, Toni. "In the Realm of Responsibility: A Conversation with Toni Morrison," by Marsha Darling. In *Conversations with Toni Morrison*, edited by Danille Taylor-Guthrie. Mississippi UP, [1988] 2007, 246–54.

Morrison, Toni. "An Interview with Toni Morrison," by Bessie W. Jones and Audrey Vinson. In *Conversations with Toni Morrison*, edited by Danille Taylor-Guthrie. Mississippi UP, [1985] 2007, 171–87.

Morrison, Toni. "An Interview with Toni Morrison," by Nellie McKay. In *Conversations with Toni Morrison*, edited by Danille Taylor-Guthrie. Mississippi UP, [1983] 2007, 138–55.

Morrison, Toni. "'Intimate Things in Place': A Conversation with Toni Morrison," by Robert Stepto. In *Conversations with Toni Morrison*, edited by Danille Taylor-Guthrie. Mississippi UP, [1976] 2007, 10–29.

Morrison, Toni. "The Language Must Not Sweat: A Conversation with Toni Morrison," by Thomas LeClair. In *Conversations with Toni Morrison*, edited by Danille Taylor-Guthrie. Mississippi UP, [1981] 2007, 119–28.

Morrison, Toni. *Paradise*. Knoph, 1998.

Morrison, Toni. *Song of Solomon*. Vintage, [1977] 1996.

Morrison, Toni. "Toni Morrison," by Charles Ruas. In *Conversations with Toni Morrison*, edited by Danille Taylor-Guthrie. Mississippi UP, [1981] 2007, 93–118.

Morrison, Toni. "Unspeakable Things Unspoken: The Afro-American Presence in American Literature." *Michigan Quarterly Review* 28, no. 1 (1989): 1–34.

New Revised Standard Version Bible. Oxford UP, 2009.

Newman, Richard S. *Freedom's Prophet: Bishop Richard Allen, the AME Church, and the Black Founding Fathers*. New York University UP, 2009.

Noll, Mark. *The Civil War as a Theological Crisis*. UP of North Carolina, 2006.

On the Waterfront. Directed by Elia Kazan, Columbia Pictures, 1954.

O'Reilly, Andrea. *Toni Morrison and Motherhood: A Politics of the Heart*. State U of New York P, 2004.

Outka, Paul. "Poems, Eyelashes, and other Nonhuman Objects." *J19: The Journal of Nineteenth-Century Americanists* 1, no. 2 (2013): 411–16.

Packer, Barbara L. "The Transcendentalists." In *The Cambridge History of American Literature* vol. 2, edited by Sacvan Bercovitch and Cyrus R. K. Patell. Cambridge UP, 1994, 331–604.

Parini, Jay. *One Matchless Time: A Life of William Faulkner*. HarperCollins, 2004.

Pattison, Dale. "Sites of Resistance: The Subversive Space of *Their Eyes Were Watching God*." *MELUS* 38, no. 4 (2013): 9–31.

Peters, Pearlie Mae Fisher. *The Assertive Woman in Zora Neale Hurston's Fiction, Folklore, and Drama*. Routledge, 2016.

Pfaelzer, Jean. *Parlor Radical: Rebecca Harding Davis and the Origins of American Social Realism*. U of Pittsburgh P, 1996.

Pfister, Joel. "Plotting Womanhood: Feminine Evolution and Narrative Feminization in *Blithedale*." In *The Blithedale Romance*, edited by Richard H. Millington. Norton Critical Edition, Norton, [1852] 2011, 317–30.

Placher, William C. *A History of Christian Theology: An Introduction*. Westminster John Knox Press, 1983.

Plant, Deborah G. *Zora Neale Hurston: A Biography of the Spirit*. Praeger, 2007.

Polk, Noel. *Children of the Dark House: Text and Context in Faulkner*. UP of Mississippi, 1998.

Pollack, Vivian. "'Bringing Help for the Sick': Whitman and Prophetic Biography." In *Leaves of Grass the Sesquicentennial Essays*, edited by Susan Belasco, Ed Folsom, and Kenneth M. Price. U of Nebraska P, 2007, 244–65.

Powell, Betty Jane. "'Will the Parts Hold?': The Journey Toward a Coherent Self in *Beloved*." *Understanding Toni Morrison's Beloved and Sula*, edited by Solomon Iyasere and Marla W. Iyasere. Whitston, 2000, 143–54.

Pulp Fiction. Directed by Quentin Tarantino, Miramax, 1994.

Reed, Roxanne. "The Restorative Power of Sound: A Case for Communal Catharsis in Toni Morrison's *Beloved*." *Journal of Feminist Studies in Religion* 23, no. 1 (2007): 55–71.

Reynolds, David S. *Beneath the American Renaissance: The Subversive Imagination in the Age of Emerson and Melville.* Knopf, 1988.

Reynolds, David S. *Walt Whitman's America: A Cultural Biography.* Knopf, 1995.

Reynolds, Larry. *Devils and Rebels: The Making of Hawthorne's Damned Politics.* U of Michigan P, 2008.

Rice, H. William. *Ralph Ellison and the Politics of the Novel.* Lexington Books, 2003.

Richardson, Robert D. *Emerson: The Mind on Fire: A Biography.* U of California P, 1995.

Rivkin, Julie, and Michael Ryan. "Introduction: The Class of 1968—Poststructuralism par lui-même." In *Literary Theory: An Anthology*, edited by Julie Rivkin and Michael Ryan, 3rd ed. Wiley, 2017.

Robinson, David M. *Apostle of Culture: Emerson as Preacher and Lecturer.* U of Pennsylvania P, 1982.

Robinson, David M. "Poetry, Poetic Perception, and Emerson's Spiritual Affirmations." In *Shaping Belief: Culture, Politics and Religion in Nineteenth-Century Writing*, edited by Victoria N. Morgan and Clare Williams. Liverpool UP, 2008, 95–112.

Robinson, Marilynne. *Gilead.* Farrar, Straus, and Giroux, 2004.

Rogin, Michael Paul. *Subversive Genealogy: The Politics and Art of Herman Melville.* Knopf, 1983.

Rosenberg, Bruce A. "The Oral Quality of Rev. Shegog's Sermon in William Faulkner's *The Sound and the Fury*." *Literatur in Wissenschaft und Unterricht* 2, no. 1 (1969): 73–88.

Roynon, Tessa. *The Cambridge Introduction to Toni Morrison.* Cambridge UP, 2013.

Ryan, James Emmett. *Imaginary Friends: Representing Quakers in American Culture, 1650–1950.* U of Wisconsin P, 2009.

"Sally, n.1." In *OED Online*. Oxford UP. www.oed.com/view/Entry/170072 (accessed September 20, 2015).

Saunders, Laura. "Ellison and the Black Church: The Gospel according to Ralph." In *The Cambridge Companion to Ralph Ellison*, edited by Ross Posnock. Cambridge UP, 2005, 35–55.

Schapiro, Barbara. "The Bonds of Love and the Boundaries of Self in Toni Morrison's *Beloved*." In *Understanding Toni Morrison's Beloved and Sula*, edited by Solomon Iyasere and Marla W. Iyasere. Whitston, 2000, 155–72.

Sedgwick, Ellery. *The Atlantic Monthly, 1857–1909: Yankee Humanism at High Tide and Ebb.* U of Massachusetts P, 1994.

Sewall, Samuel. *Diary of Samuel Sewall, 1674–1729*, vol. 1. Massachusetts Historical Society, 1878, *HathiTrust Digital Library*, hdl.handle.net/2027/hvd.hc4w43 (accessed November 17, 2015).

Shakespeare, William. *The Winter's Tale*, edited by Cedric Watts. Wordsworth, 2004.

Sheldon, Charles M. *In His Steps.* Revell, [1896] 1985.

Shurr, William. "Life in the Iron-Mills: A Nineteenth-Century Conversion Narrative." *ATQ* 5, no. 4 (1991): 245–57.

Singal, Daniel Joseph. *William Faulkner: The Making of a Modernist*. North Carolina UP, 1997.

Smith, Caleb. *The Oracle and the Curse: A Poetics of Justice from the Revolution to the Civil War*. Harvard UP, 2013.

Smith, Valerie. "'Circling the Subject': History and Narrative in *Beloved*." In *Toni Morrison: Critical Perspectives Past and Present*, edited by Henry L. Gates, Jr. and Anthony Appiah. Amistad, 1993, 342–55.

Smith, Valerie. *Toni Morrison. Writing the Moral Imagination*. Wiley-Blackwell, 2012.

Sowder, Michael. *Whitman's Ecstatic Union: Conversion and Ideology in* Leaves of Grass. Routledge, 2005.

Stave, Shirley A. "From Eden to Paradise: A Pilgrimage through Toni Morrison's Trilogy." In *Toni Morrison: Memory and Meaning*, edited by Adrienne Lanier and Justine Tally. UP of Mississippi, 2014, 107–18.

Stave, Shirley A. *Toni Morrison and the Bible: Contested Intertextualities*. Peter Lang, 2006.

Stay, Byron. "Hawthorne's Fallen Puritans: Eliot's Pulpit in '*The Blithedale Romance*.'" *Studies in the Novel* 18, no. 3 (1986): 283–90.

Stowe, Harriet Beecher. *Uncle Tom's Cabin*, edited by Elizabeth Ammons. Norton Critical Edition, 3rd ed., Norton, [1852] 2017.

Sundquist, Eric J. "'The Drum with the Man's Skin': Jonah's Gourd Vine." In *Zora Neale Hurston: Critical Perspectives Past and Present*, edited by Henry Louis Gates and Anthony Appiah. Amistad, 1993, 39–66.

Tally, Justine. "The Morrison Trilogy." In *The Cambridge Companion to Toni Morrison*, edited by Justine Tally. Cambridge UP, 2007, 75–91.

Tally, Justine. *Toni Morrison's Beloved: Origins*. Routledge, 2009.

Tebbetts, Terrell. "Postmodern Criticism." In *A Companion to Faulkner Studies*, edited by Charles A. Peek and Robert W. Hamlin. Greenwood Press, 2004, 125–61.

There Will Be Blood. Directed by Paul Thomas Anderson, Paramount Vantage, 2007.

Thomas, Marion A. "Reflections on the Sanctified Church as Portrayed by Zora Neale Hurston." In *Critical Essays on Zora Neale Hurston*, edited by Gloria L. Cronin, G. K. Hall, 1998, 215–24.

Thoreau, Henry David. "Resistance to Civil Government." *Transcendentalism: A Reader*, edited by Joel Myerson. Oxford UP, [1849] 2000, 546–65.

Tompkins, Jane P. *Sensational Designs: The Cultural Work of American Fiction, 1790–1860*. Oxford UP, 1985.

Trowbridge, John Townsend. "Reminiscences of Walt Whitman." *The Atlantic Monthly*, February 1902, 163–75. *The Atlantic Archive*, www.theatlantic.com/archive/

Twain, Mark. "The War Prayer." Perennial, [1923] 2002.

Wagner-Martin, Linda. *Toni Morrison and the Maternal: From the Bluest Eye to Home*. Peter Lang, 2014.

Wall, Cheryl A. "Zora Neale Hurston: Changing Her Own Words." In *Zora Neale Hurston: Critical Perspectives Past and Present*, edited by Henry Louis Gates and Anthony Appiah. Amistad, 1993, 76–97.

Wallace, Robert K. *Douglass and Melville: Anchored Together in Neighborly Style*. Spinner Publications, 2005.

Watson, James G. *William Faulkner: Self-Presentation and Performance*. U of Texas P, 2000.

Weldon, Roberta. *Hawthorne, Gender, and Death: Christianity and Its Discontents*. Palgrave Macmillan, 2008.

Wells Brown, William. *Clotel; or, The President's Daughter*, edited by Robert S. Levine. Bedford-St. Martin's, [1853] 2000.

West, Cornell. *The American Evasion of Philosophy: A Genealogy of Pragmatism*. Macmillan, 1989.

West, Margaret Genevieve. *Zora Neale Hurston & American Literary Culture*. UP of Florida, 2005.

Whitman, Walt. *Leaves of Grass*, edited by Ed Folsom and Kenneth Price, 1855. *The Walt Whitman Archive*, www.whitmanarchive.org (accessed February 27, 2023).

Whitman, Walt. *Leaves of Grass*, edited by Ed Folsom and Kenneth Price, 1856. *The Walt Whitman Archive*, www.whitmanarchive.org (accessed March 25, 2023).

Whitman, Walt. *Leaves of Grass*, edited by Ed Folsom and Kenneth Price, 1860. *The Walt Whitman Archive*, www.whitmanarchive.org (accessed April 10, 2023).

Whitman, Walt. *Leaves of Grass*, edited by Ed Folsom and Kenneth Price, 1891. *The Walt Whitman Archive*, www.whitmanarchive.org (accessed April 18, 2023).

Whitman, Walt. *Notebooks and Unpublished Prose Manuscripts*, 6 vols., edited by Edward F. Grier. New York UP, 1984; Cited parenthetically as *NUPM*, with volume and page number.

Whitman, Walt. *Prose Works 1892*, edited by Floyd Stovall. New York UP, 1963; Cited parenthetically as *PW*, with volume and page number.

Whitman, Walt. *The Uncollected Poetry and Prose of Walt Whitman, Much of Which Has Been but Recently Discovered*, edited by Emory Holloway. Doubleday, Page, 1921; Cited parenthetically as *UPP*, with volume and page number.

Williamson, Joel. *William Faulkner and Southern History*. Oxford UP, 1995.

Wilson, Anthony. "Music of God, Man, and Beast: Spirituality and Modernity in *Jonah's Gourd Vine*." *Southern Literary Journal* 35, no. 2 (2003): 64–78.

Wilson, Charles Reagan. "Faulkner in the Southern Religious Culture." In *Faulkner and Religion*, edited by Doreen Fowler and Ann J. Abadie. UP of Mississippi, 1991, 21–43.

Wineapple, Brenda. *Hawthorne: A Life*. Knopf, 2003.

Winthrop, John. "A Model of Christian Charity." *The Puritans in America: A Narrative Anthology*, edited by Alan Heimert and Andrew Delbanco. Harvard UP, [1630] 1985, 81–92.

Wong, Shelley. "Transgression as Poesis in *The Bluest Eye*." In *Toni Morrison's The Bluest Eye: Updated Edition*, edited by Harold Bloom. Chelsea House, 2007, 53–66.

Zauditu-Selassie, K. *African Spiritual Traditions in the Novels of Toni Morrison*. Florida UP, 2009.

Index

16th Street Baptist Church 163

Adger, John 116
African Methodist Episcopal Church 170
Alcott, Bronson 88–9, 89 n.7
Allen, Richard 170–1
Anderson, P.T. 4
anti-sermon 115–16, 118, 119, 121–2
anti-preacher 118–22, 154, 162
Apess, William 10
Arsić, Branka 31, 31 n.4
Aspiz, Harold 46 n.11, 47
The Atlantic Monthly 34, 87, 98–101
   opposition to religious dogmatism 99
   "Yankee humanism" in 98–9
authorial surrogation 22, 33, 36, 54, 57, 59
authorial doubles 62, 65, 71–2, 109–10, 125, 151, 166, 177

Baldwin, James 4, 152, 153–4, 193
Ballie, Justine 164
Bate, Nancy Berkowitz 182 n.14
Baym, Nina 81
Becker-Leckrone, Megan 15
Beecher, Henry Ward 10, 36 n.10
Beecher, Lyman 61
Bellingham, Richard 66
Bercovitch, Sacvan 68
Berlant, Lauren 74, 76
Besse, Joseph 66
Bleikasten, André 107 n.2, 108, 110, 114
Blotner, Joseph 112 n.5
Bouldin, Elizabeth 66
Brewster, Margaret 66, 69, 71–2
Brook Farm 74
Brown, William Wells 4
Buell, Lawrence 23, 29 n.3, 59
Burns, Robert 26
Byerman, Keith L. 153, 153 n.3, 154 n.4

call-and-response 141–2, 149, 151, 152, 171, 178, 184

Cane Ridge Revival 10, 60
capitalism 7, 35, 87–9, 94, 99–100, 177
Carlyle, Thomas 21
Carmean, Karen 157 n.6, 159
Castille, Philip 113, 114
Chamberlain, John 130–1
Christian, Barbara 188
circuit riding 61
civil rights movement 10
Civil War, American 35, 89, 100 n.14, 116, 120
Cixous, Hélène 186
clerical ideology 1–2, 16–17, 22, 36
Colacurcio, Michael J. 67
Coleman, Dawn 5, 9, 11, 25, 173 n.12
colonialism 75, 160–1, 164–5, 169
Connelley, Marc 124
Cowley, Malcolm 101
cultural work 5

Dahill-Baue, William 156, 156 n.5
Dante 30
Danticat, Edwidge 142
Davis, Rebecca Harding 5, 61, 63, 87, 119, 193
   Bits of Gossip 88–9
   complex vocational identification 63, 86–7, 102 (*see also* authorial doubles)
   counter-sermons 87, 95–6, 97, 99–101
   extralegal moral authority 62, 90–2, 95–7, 100
   Hawthorne's influence on 63, 88–9, 95
   industrial capitalism, critique of 87–8, 94, 99–100
   Life in the Iron-Mills 63, 88, 90–101, 136
   performative sensuality 62, 94 (*see also* semiotic)
   Protestantism, response to 89–90, 93–4
   reification of clerical ideology 63, 87, 100–1
   Transcendentalism, response to 88–90, 89 n.7

"Women in Literature" 101–2
Davis, Thadious M. 107 n.2
Deloria, Philip 17–18, 18 n.5
Demosthenes 26
Dickens, Charles 25
Dobbs, Cynthia 175, 177, 180
domestic ideology 65, 73, 78, 84, 86
Dostoevsky, Fyodor 162
Douglas, Ann 17
Douglass, Frederick 7, 10
Du Bois, W. E. B. 123
Duncan, David James 4, 16
Duvall, John 16, 157 n.6, 163, 168, 173 n.12, 177, 184

Easton, Allison 71
Eckard, Paula Gallant 15 n.4
Edmundson, Mark 56
Edwards, Jonathan 10
Eliot, John 74–8, 83
Ellis, Iain 166
Ellison, Ralph 4, 152, 170, 193
  Invisible Man 152–3
  Juneteenth 152 n.2
Emerson, Edward 25
Emerson, Ralph Waldo 34–6, 39, 40, 45 n.8, 48, 50, 56, 60 n.2, 88, 98, 99, 119, 146, 192, 193
  complex vocational identification 26
  diagnoses of failed sermons 23–4
  Divinity School Address 21, 23, 27 n.2, 29 n.3, 27–30, 31, 33, 34, 57
  on Edward Taylor 24–6
  extralegal moral authority 27, 30–3
  Journals 22, 23–7, 40, 45 n.8
  Nature 31
  performative sensuality 26 (*see also* semiotic)
  "The Poet" 23, 25, 27, 27 n.2, 30–3, 34
  poet as preacher (*see also* authorial surrogation) 22, 30, 57
  reification of clerical authority 26
  remedy for failed Christianity 29–30
  self-reliance, definition of 22–3
  "Self-Reliance" 28
Engemen, Thomas S. 152 n.2, 153
Epictetus 40

Faulkner, William 4, 16, 154, 159–62, 193, 194
  Absalom, Absalom! 116
  and access to literary heritage 107, 115, 118
  As I Lay Dying 14, 16, 108
  anti-sermons 115–16, 118–19, 121–2
  childhood exposure to preaching 107
  and complex vocational identification 109–10, 114, 123 (*see also* authorial doubles)
  and extralegal moral authority 110–15
  Go Down, Moses 116
  Light in August 106, 115–23, 159–62
  and performative sensuality 108–9 (*see also* semiotic)
  and reification of clerical ideology 114–15, 122–3
  The Sound and the Fury 106, 107–15
Fields, James T. 63, 87, 95, 97–101, 193
Finney, Charles Grandison 36 n.10
Fleming, Robert 107
Folsom, Ed 48
Foulks, Beverly 158 n.7
Fourier, Charles 74
Fowler, Doreen 112 n.5, 172 n.11, 185
Furman, Jan 163

Gannett, Lewis 131
Garner, Thurmon 141
Gates, Henry Louis, Jr. 135, 135 n.15, 145
Goodman, Susan 98, 99 n.13
Grewal, Gurleen 144, 165, 167, 172 n.11, 188
Gura, Philip 74, 87, 90 n.7

Hankins, Barry 60 n.1, 61
Harriss, M. Cooper 135 n.15
Harris, Sharon M. 89 n.7, 91
Harris, Trudier 169
Harris, W. C. 44, 45 n.9
Harvard Divinity School 21
Hatch, Nathan O. 52 n.12
Hathorne, William 64
Hawthorne, Nathaniel 5, 16, 59, 61, 87, 88–9, 93, 95, 100, 101, 115, 118–20, 175, 193
  The Blithedale Romance 74–86, 93, 95, 117

complex vocational identification 62,
63–5, 70–2, 84–5, 101 (*see also*
authorial doubles)
counter-sermons in 16, 69–70, 77
extralegal moral authority 62–5, 72,
73–4, 77–8, 80–2
"The Gentle Boy" 16, 65–74, 80, 81, 85,
86, 93, 95, 117
idealisms, dangers of 64–5, 67, 80–81
performative sensuality 13–14, 62, 76
(*see also* semiotic)
reassertions of narrative control (*see
also* literary pulpit exchange) 62–3,
72–4, 84–6
reification of clerical ideology 62, 72,
84, 101
The Scarlet Letter 13–14, 64, 66,
74, 76, 93
*The Whole History of Grandfather's
Chair* 75, 77
women preachers in 65, 71–4, 77–8, 80–6
Hayes, Will 56–7
Hayles, Katherine 191
Hein, David 111 n.4
Hemenway, Robert 123, 130 n.10
Henderson, Carol E. 154 n.4
Herrero-Brasas, Juan A. 56
Hibbard, Billy 61 n.3
Hicks, Elias 38–9, 39 n.6
Holifield, E. Brooks 59, 60, 60 n.1
Holmes, Oliver Wendell 98, 99
Homer 30, 131
Hubbard, Dolan 142, 142 n.17, 143, 145,
152, 154 n.4
Humphrey, Richard Alan 143
Hurston, Zora Neale 4, 5, 193
and access to literary heritage 126–7
call-and-response 141–2
and complex vocational identification
124–5, 128, 131, 134 (*see also*
authorial doubles)
and extralegal moral authority 141, 143
and folk preachers 123–34
and James Weldon Johnson 124, 125, 130
Jonah's Gourd Vine 106, 123–34
performative sensuality 124–7, 129 (*see
also* semiotic)
Their Eyes Were Watching God
106, 134–47

and women preachers 134–7, 141–7

Janson, Drude Krog 4
Jesus 24, 28, 29, 44, 49, 55, 95–7, 99–100,
111, 112, 146, 155, 169–70, 173,
175–6, 178, 185
Johnson, James Weldon 13, 14, 107, 109,
114, 120, 123–5, 127, 130–1,
155, 193
and folk preachers 13, 103–5
God's Trombones 103–5, 107, 108
Jones, Abner 59
Jones, Bessie W. and Audrey Vinson 190

Kaplan, Carla 144
Kazan, Elia 4
Kevorkian, Martin 17, 18 n.6, 64
Killingsworth, M. Jimmie 46 n.10
King, Lovalerie 132, 135, 136, 153 n.4
Kristeva, Julia 14–15, 186–7, 190
Kuebrich, David 34, 46 n.10, 47, 57

Larson, Rebecca 66
Lasseter, Janice Milner 87, 90, 95, 96, 97,
97 n.12, 101
Lawrence, David 172, 172 n.11
LeClair, Thomas 149
Levine, Caroline 2–3, 6, 7
Lind, Jenny 25
Lischer, Richard 127, 129 n.9, 166, 178
literary preaching
affordances of 3, 6, 12–19
access to literary heritage 12, 15–16,
193–4
complex vocational identification (*see
also* authorial double) 12, 17–19
extralegal moral authority 5, 9, 12
performative sensuality (*see also*
semiotic) 12–15
reification of clerical ideology
12, 16–17
as dialectical form 1–2
form and historical criticism 3–4,
10–12
texts and films involving 4
types of, 4–5
literary pulpit exchange 61–3, 65, 71–4,
77–9, 84–6, 87, 95, 101, 120
"The Lost Cause" 117

Locke, Alain 123
Lowell, James Russell 98, 99

Magee, Rosemary 116
Marks, Kathleen 183
Marsh, John 35
Martineau, Harriet 25
McCarthy, Cormac 4
McInnis, Maurice Dee 8
McKay, Nellie 149, 190
McLoughlin, William 61, 61 n.3
Medusa 69, 78
Melville, Herman 4, 6–10, 19, 25
Methodist and Methodism 24–5, 37, 42, 61, 107
Miles, Diana 140
Milton, John 30
Moi, Toril 15, 186
Morone, James 71
Morris, Saundra 24
Morrison, Toni 4, 7, 16, 149–54, 192–4
  access to literary heritage 151–4, 159–62, 168
  ambivalence toward literary preaching 150, 157, 166
  Beloved 4, 5, 111, 170–90, 192–3
  The Bluest Eye 151, 154–70, 175, 179
  Book of Job, The 157–9, 157 n.7, 158 n.8, 163
  circulated sermon 170–90
  complex vocational identification 150, 165, 171–2 (*see also* authorial doubles)
  extralegal moral authority 150, 159, 162, 166, 169–70, 172
  performative sensuality 168, 179, 186–90 (*see also* semiotic)
  on preaching and church 149–50
  reification of clerical ideology 171, 179–80
  "Unspeakable Things Unspoken" 7
Mott, Wesley T. 23 n.1

National Association of Colored People (NAACP) 103
Newman, Richard S. 171
Noll, Mark 116, 160

O'Connor, Flannery 4
O'Reilly, Andrea 188

Oliphant, Margaret 85
Outka, Paul 43

Packer, Barbara 60 n.2
Parini, Jay 21
Parker, Theodore 60 n.2
Pattison, Dale 140, 142, 145 n.19
Peters, Pearlie Fisher 139
Pfaelzer, Jean 92 n.10
Pfister, Joel 78, 82, 83, 85
Placher, William C. 43 n.7
Plant, Deborah 130 n.10
Pollack, Vivian 52
Polk, Noel 110
Powell, Betty Jane 183, 188
Presbyterian Kentucky Synod 60
prophetic unsettlement 1, 33, 36, 62, 68, 72, 110
pulpit exchange 59–61
Puritans and Puritanism 13, 64, 65–74, 76, 80–1

Quakers and Quakerism 38–9, 46 n.10, 65–74, 91, 91 n.8

Railton, Stephen 106
Reed, Roxanne 174
Reynolds, David S. 5 n.1, 25, 35, 36 n.5, 38, 39, 46 nn.10 and 11
Reynolds, Larry 67 n.5, 70, 75
Rice, H. William 152, 152 n.2
Richardson, Robert D. 22, 25, 27
Ripley, George 74
Rivkin, Julie and Michael Ryan, *Literary Theory: An Anthology* 15
Robinson, David M. 28, 31 n.4, 32, 33
Robinson, Marilynne 4, 194–5
Rogin, Michael 8
Rorty, Richard 174
Rosenberg, Bruce 107 n.2
Roynon, Tessa 163
Ruas, Charles 149, 150 n.1, 157 n.7
Ryan, James Emmett 91 n.8, 97

Saunders, Laura 152 n.2
Schapiro, Barbara 181, 183
Seaman's Bethel 25
Second Church (Boston) 22, 23
Second Great Awakening 5–6, 9, 59–60, 60 n.1, 73, 77

Sedgwick, Ellery 98, 99 n.13
semiotic 12–15, 33, 37, 76, 109, 172, 187–90, 193
Sewall, Samuel 66
Shakespeare, William 26
  Hamlet 82–83
  The Winter's Tale 79, 81
Shaw, Lemuel 7, 8
Sheldon, Charles M. 4
Shurr, William 92 n.9
Singal, David 109, 110
skeumorph 191–2
slavery 7–8, 11, 89
Smith, Caleb 9 n.2, 120
Smith, Valerie 173
Socrates 40
Sowder, Michael 36 n.5
Stave, Shirley A. 150 n.1, 187
Stay, Byron 77, 80
Stepto, Robert 161
Stone, Barton 60, 60 n.1
Stowe, Harriet Beecher 4, 16, 173
Sunquist, Eric 129, 131 n.11, 140

Tally, Justine 164 n.10, 174, 186
Tarantino, Quentin 4
Taylor, Edward 7, 24–6, 39–41, 45 n.8, 52, 192
Tebbetts, Terrell 109
Thomas, Marion A. 142
Thoreau, Henry David 8, 17
Till, Emmett 163
Tomkins, Jane
Transcendentalism 42, 46 n.10, 60 n.2, 88–90, 89 n.7
Trowbridge, John Townsend 34
Truth, Sojourner 10
Turner, Nat 10
Twain, Mark 4, 16

Unitarian and Unitarianism 27, 29, 46 n.10, 60 n.2

Wagner-Martin, Linda 162 n.9, 176
Wall, Cheryl 135, 136
Wallace, Robert 7, 10
Watson, James G. 109 n.3
Weldon, Roberta, 83 n.6
West, Cornell 50
West, M. Genevieve 124, 132 n.12, 140, 145
Whitman, Walt 22, 25, 65, 87, 119, 130, 177, 192, 195
  1837 revivals 37–8
  and access to literary heritage 34–5
  and complex vocational identity 39
    (*see also* authorial double)
  democracy and religious belief 34–5, 43, 50–1
  and extralegal moral authority 42, 45
  and Ecclesiastes 48–9
  influential preachers 38–41
  messianic expectations 35–6
  and nineteenth-century religion 34–5, 46 n.10, 46–7
  and performative sensuality 37–41, 45
    (*see also* semiotic)
  poet as preacher 33, 35–6, 41–57 (*see also* authorial surrogation)
  Preface to 1855 *Leaves of Grass* 34, 41–4, 52
  reification of clerical ideology 22, 39, 42, 52–6
  "Song of Myself" 34, 36, 38, 43–4, 45–56
  and vision of the human 43, 46–51, 50
Whitmanite Cults 56
Wilson, Anthony 133 n.14
Wilson, Charles Reagan 117, 120
Williamson, Joel 145
Wineapple, Brenda 74, 85
Winthrop, John 10
Wong, Shelley 166

Zauditu-Selassie, K. 178

www.ingramcontent.com/pod-product-compliance
Lightning Source LLC
Chambersburg PA
CBHW052109300426
44116CB00010B/1591